The Kid

The Kid

(WHAT HAPPENED AFTER
MY BOYFRIEND AND I DECIDED
TO GO GET PREGNANT)

An Adoption Story

Dan Savage

A DUTTON BOOK

The names and identifying characteristics of some of the individuals depicted
in this book have been changed to protect their privacy.

DUTTON
Published by the Penguin Group
Penguin Putnam Inc., 375 Hudson Street, New York, New York 10014, U.S.A.
Penguin Books Ltd, 27 Wrights Lane, London W8 5TZ, England
Penguin Books Australia Ltd, Ringwood, Victoria, Australia
Penguin Books Canada Ltd, 10 Alcorn Avenue, Toronto, Ontario, Canada M4V 3B2
Penguin Books (N.Z.) Ltd, 182–190 Wairau Road, Auckland 10, New Zealand

Penguin Books Ltd, Registered Offices: Harmondsworth, Middlesex, England

First published by Dutton, a member of Penguin Putnam Inc.

First Printing, September, 1999
1   3   5   7   9   10   8   6   4   2

 REGISTERED TRADEMARK—MARCA REGISTRADA

LIBRARY OF CONGRESS CATALOGING-IN-PUBLICATION DATA
Savage, Dan.
The kid: what happened after my boyfriend and I
decided to go get pregnant / Dan Savage.
p.   cm.
ISBN 0-525-94525-3 (alk. paper)
1. Gay adoption—United States.   2. Gay parents—United States.
I. Title.
HV875.72.U6S28   1999
362.73'4'086'64—dc21   99-32506
CIP
Printed in the United States of America
Set in Bembo
Designed by Julian Hamer

This book is printed on acid-free paper. ∞

for Terry . . .

Acknowledgments

I owe a tremendous debt to my family. Much thanks to my mom and stepdad, Judy and Jerry Sobiesk; my boyfriend's mom and stepdad, Claudia and Dennis Biggs; my father and my stepmom, Bill and Joellen Savage; and my wonderful siblings Billy, Eddie, and Laura. I wouldn't get a thing done if it weren't for my assistant, Kevin Patnik, and my boss, Tim Keck. Bob Fikso and Kate Flack helped every step of the way, as did Mark and Diane Spaur and Emily White and Rich Jensen. Some parts of this book were first heard on public radio's *This American Life*. Much thanks to Ira Glass and the producers at *This American Life*, Nancy Updike, Alix Speigel, and Julie Snyder. At Dutton, I'd like to thank my editor, Brian Tart; Carole DeSanti for her patience; and Kara Howland and Alexandra Babanskyj for their assistance. Much thanks to my literary agent Elizabeth Wales; also to Nancy Shawn, Elise Harris, Lisa Schwartz, Jason Sellards, and Mark Van-S. For their encouragement and advice at different stages of this process, much thanks to Urvashi Vaid, Suzie Bright, Andrew Sullivan, Billy Savage, and especially my very good friend David Schmader. Also thanks to Angeline Acain, the Portland Public Library, and the staff at the Mallory Hotel. And a very special thanks to Suzie Arnold, Ann Lawrence, Marilyn Strong, and Shari Levine.

Fertilization

Younger Brother Dynamics

My boyfriend likes to listen to dance music when he drives. He likes to listen to dance music when he cooks, cleans, wakes, sleeps, reads, picks his nose, and screws. There isn't much he doesn't enjoy doing listening to dance music. I'll listen to dance music when I'm under recreational general anesthesia (that is, if I'm really high), or if I'm in a dance club somewhere, dancing. Since I don't get high or go to clubs often, I don't listen to dance music much. As for listening to dance music out of context— no drugs, no dance club, no *dancing*—well, frankly, I don't see the point.

But Terry was techno before techno was cool, and his attachment to dance music has been a rich source of conflict in our relationship. We've both made sacrifices on the bloody altar of coupledom: I no longer listen to the radio while I go to sleep, to give one piddling example, as he can't sleep with the radio on; he no longer goes clubbing all night long (if I couldn't have a radio in the bedroom, then, by God, his ass had better be in my bed to justify the sacrifice). But he's been having a hard time completely letting go of dance music because much of his pre-me social life revolved around it. After monogamy, dance music has been our single biggest "issue." Monogamy was a quickie fight, over and done with: he didn't want me sleeping around, and I didn't want to fight. Should a day come when I do put someone else's dick in my mouth, he won't dump me because: (a) I'd do all I could to make certain he never found out; and (b) if he did find out, well, he's promised to work through it.

We'd been together two years, so our fights had become highly ritualized ceremonies, and the dance-music-in-the-car fight was one we had down pat. We were in a car, driving to Portland, Oregon, and he was subjecting me to Iceland's pixie lunatic, Björk. I didn't think this was fair, as I don't like dance music, and when we were doing ninety on I-5, I couldn't escape.

The fight didn't begin at the start of the trip. They never do. I'm a conflict-avoidance champ (see monogamy, p. 3), and if we fought at the beginning of every road trip I would, like a dog that associates a ride in the car with a trip to the vet, refuse to get in the car. Had I anticipated this fight, I would have insisted that we fly, or take the train, or ship ourselves UPS, or get to Portland on some form of transport that puts nice, reasonable people in charge of the music. But Terry was tricky, taking advantage of my memory problems. Before we got in the car, and for about the first forty-five minutes of any trip, Terry was on his best behavior. He lulled me into the car with false promises of books on tape, or conversation. Then, when we were too far from home to turn back, and going too fast for me to jump, he put on a CD he knew I'd object to—*chunk-ka tcha, chunk-ka tcha, chunk-ka tcha*—and with fleeing not an option, I had no choice but to turn and fight.

"You know I can't stand dance music, especially in a car, so why do you do this?" I said, typically. "While I'll happily put up with Björk at home, because I can leave, or blow my brains out, or beat you to death with a hammer, I think it is unfair of you to subject me to Björk when I'm trapped in a car."

And we were off! I didn't have a driver's license, Terry pointed out, which forced him to do all the driving. Therefore, he should get to pick the music. Yes, but while he might have a license, he didn't own a car, and I happened to be paying for this rental. Therefore, as the automobile's temporary legal guardian, I should have some say in the music I was subjected to. I was being unreasonable, he said. He was being selfish, I responded. Yi, yi, grrr, icha-yiy, Björk sings.

Thinking it was a compromise, the boyfriend turned the music down. All we could hear now was the beat: boom-boom-boom. Which, as it happens, was the thing about dance music that drove me out of my mind. I was not satisfied. I sulked. He drove. He said something bitchy. I said something bitchy. We fought on for about twenty-five more miles, and finally, unable to enjoy Björk for my bitching and sulking, the boyfriend snapped off the CD player, and we sat in silence.

An hour and fifteen minutes of silence later, we were in Portland.

We'd driven down to Portland from Seattle on a wet spring day because, in our wisdom and maturity, my boyfriend and I had decided to become parents. We were in Portland to get pregnant.

This was my first visit to Portland. During the seven years I'd lived in Seattle, just three hours away, it had never before occurred to me to visit Portland. Seattle's a hilly, damp place with a lot of water and trees. Portland's a hilly, damp place with a lot of water and trees. Portland and Seattle both have Pioneer Squares, Hamburger Marys, homeless street punks, and huge bookstores. Why would anyone who lives in Seattle vacation in Portland?

My boyfriend Terry, however, was very familiar with Portland. His father spent a couple of years dying here in the mid-nineties. Daryl, Terry's father, had non-alcohol-related cirrhosis of the liver. Daryl went to Portland's Oregon Health State University hospital for a liver transplant, but when they opened him up, they found cancer. They cut out the cancer, put in the new liver, and sewed Daryl up. But the cancer returned, and promptly attacked Daryl's new liver. When they opened him up a second time, the doctors decided he was too far gone to "waste" another liver on, his own bad luck for not being Mickey Mantle. It was in Portland that Terry, his mother, and his brother were informed that their husband and father had less than a year to live.

Three months later Daryl Miller was dead.

For Terry, Portland was the city of bad news. The hospital where Terry's father got his liver and a little while later the bad news squatted on a hill overlooking the Willamette River. It looked like a cross between L.A.'s Getty Center and a clump of East German apartment blocks, and there was no escaping the sight of OHSU as you drove into Portland. As we crossed the Steel Bridge over the Willamette on our way to the Mallory Hotel, the hospital where Daryl died came into view. Looking grim, Terry pointed it out to me.

"I hate this place," Terry said. "I hate fucking Portland." The bridge dipped down and we drove into Portland's old downtown as OHSU slipped out of sight.

The adoption agency we were pinning our hopes on was based in Portland. It had offices in Seattle, and with the exception of a required two-day seminar in Portland, all the preparation—the paperwork, the intake interviews, the jumping through hoops—could be accomplished in Seattle. Once the two-day seminar was over, Terry insisted, we were never coming back to Portland. Ever.

Our agency did "open" as opposed to "closed" adoptions. In an open adoption, the pregnant woman, called the birth mother in agency-speak, selects a family for her child, and has a mutually agreeable amount of ongoing contact with her child, usually two or three visits a year, with photos and letters exchanged at set times. In an open adoption, there are no secrets: the kid grows up knowing he was adopted, and knowing who his bio-parents are. Our agency was the first and still is one of the few in the country to do truly open adoptions. Since a lot of people were unfamiliar with the concept, and since some were spooked by it, the agency's managers felt they needed at least two days to explain how it all worked.

It also gave the agency a chance to weed out couples who didn't get it. Since the agency placed more children than any other in the Pacific Northwest, couples who weren't into openness sometimes attempted to adopt a kid through the agency. These couples might come to resent or fear the birth mom after they got their baby, and attempt to interfere with her right to visit, or make her feel unwelcome when she did. The agency felt it was in the best interest of all concerned that the children they placed wound up with couples truly committed to the concept.

So here we were in Portland, checked into the Mallory, this fussy ol' lady of a hotel, ready to demonstrate our commitment. But if we didn't get out of our hotel room in the next fifteen minutes, we weren't going to make it to the seminar on time, which would make a bad impression, which would call into question our commitment. And if we didn't get a kid out of this, the drive and the fight would all have been for nothing.

But we couldn't leave, because my boyfriend had locked himself in the bathroom and wouldn't come out.

Which was my fault. While I'd been right to stand my ground about blasting dance music in the car, I should have dropped it after I'd gotten my way. But I kept right on picking, making snide remarks about Björk when we were getting out of the car and walking into the hotel. Had Terry won, he would've done the same to me. After monogamy and dance music, picking was our biggest issue. We both had older brothers; I was the third of four kids, and he was the second of two. Younger brothers are less powerful than older brothers, so persistence and stamina are our survival/revenge strategies. Older siblings may hit harder, but younger brothers move faster, and we are relentless. And like all younger brothers everywhere, neither of us knew when to stop. We took jokes, wrestling matches, and "playful" fights past the point where they were fun or sexy, right up to the point where someone, usually me, got hurt.

In straight relationships the younger-brother dynamic is sometimes present, but only when a younger brother is present, and most women date only one younger brother at a time. Only in gay relationships can two younger brothers come together. The younger-brother dynamic was why, when the hotel receptionist asked us how our drive down was, I opened my fool mouth and said, "Fine, except for the Icelandic lunatic in the car with us." I'd gone too far and someone—Terry this time—got hurt. But I was not responsible for my actions; my birth order made me do it.

From inside the bathroom, the boyfriend wanted to know why I couldn't let it go. He'd turned Björk off an hour and half ago. We weren't even in the car anymore. Why couldn't I leave it alone?

"It's stressful enough being in Portland at all," Terry said from behind the green bathroom door. He wasn't locked in the bathroom because he was crying, but because we were fighting, and when we fight we prefer to have a door between us. A closed door. "We have to be the presentable, nonthreatening, happy, happy, happy gay couple in a room full of straight people for two days. Why do you have to pick now to be such a prick?"

" 'Cause I'm a brat," I said to the door. "I'm a brat just like you. And what is this locked-in-the-bathroom stuff but your final dig?"

He didn't answer.

"We gotta go be presentable now, Terry."

Silence.

"I'm sorry I called Björk a lunatic. She's a genius."

Nothing.

"Honey, let's go get pregnant. You can name the baby after Björk, teach him Icelandic folk songs, I don't care."

Still nothing. Finally, in desperation, I lied.

"You can listen to whatever music you want in the car all the way back to Seattle."

The door opened. All was forgiven.

We met right after I turned thirty. Terry was twenty-three, but told me he was twenty-four, thinking the extra year made him sound more mature. I was in a gay bar for the first time in three months. The end of a particularly rocky relationship had kept me in my apartment for weeks, wondering why I'd ever wanted to suck cock in the first place. This relationship ended months before our lease expired, so my ex and I continued to live together. He worked through his grief by stuffing as many cocks in his mouth as he could get his hands on, and then coming home and telling me about it. We all grieve in our own ways. I stayed home and moped; he went out and screwed. The totally unfair part was that *I* dumped *him*. Why was he out there having a grand old time while I stayed at home eating bags of cheap cookies and reading *The Rise and Fall of the Third Reich* for the fourth time? Not fair.

I hadn't had sex in four months the night I met Terry. So, in all honesty, I couldn't have cared less how mature he sounded, and there was no need for him to lie about his age. I was primarily concerned with how he looked, and he looked good. We were in a bar, so I knew he had to be at least twenty-one, but he looked like a kid. He had shoulder-length hair, a huge mouth, and beautiful lips. He was wearing a tight T-shirt and dancing with friends. Terry awakened the dormant pederast that lurks in my soul. Like a lot of people, male and female, I have no interest in messing around with actual teenagers, but grown men who could pass for teenagers? Matt Damon? Johnny Depp? Brad Pitt? The male beauty ideal at the end of the twentieth century is distinctly adolescent, and on this issue I march in lockstep with the larger culture. Cute? Boyish? Hairless? Bring 'im in and strap 'im down.

We were at Re-bar, a funky bar on the edge of downtown Seattle, on a Wednesday night. It was Re-bar's fifth anniversary party, and the place was packed. I was gossiping with Ginger, one of Re-bar's drag queens, while she worked coat check.

"Look at that cute boy with the hair and lips," I said to Ginger, nodding at the cute boy with the long hair and pretty mouth on the dance floor.

When the cute boy with the long hair and pretty mouth came over to coat check to get something out of his coat pocket, Ginger seized the opportunity to embarrass and humiliate me.

"Isn't this the boy you were talking about?" Ginger brayed. "Say something to him." I glared at her. "Talk," she commanded.

"You have a pretty mouth."

Oh. My. God. I sounded like the rapists in *Deliverance*.

"The better to eat you with," said the boy with the long hair and pretty mouth as he turned and walked back over to his friends.

A little later, and a whole lot drunker, he was back. It seemed he was serious about that better-to-eat-you-with comment. We chatted for a few minutes, just long enough to establish that we were both single, both of us dug the music (he meant it, I was being polite), and neither of us smoked. Then we made our way to Re-bar's only bathroom with a lock on the door.

Terry and I didn't consummate our relationship in the toilet, although Ginger did shove a handful of condoms under the door. Instead, we headed back to my place for some hi-how-are-ya-wanna-fuck-gay-boy-bar-slut sex. Making out in the bathroom broke the ice and allowed us to verify that neither was lying about being a nonsmoker. And before I take anyone home, I always make sure I like the taste of his spit. Terry's spit tasted a lot like beer, and I like beer, so I invited him back to my place. My ex had just moved out, taking the furniture with him, and I don't remember much of what we did in an empty apartment, but I do remember thinking, *Wow, this guy is a great kisser.*

The next morning, I couldn't remember the name of the cute boy with the long hair and the amazing lips, so I had to peek at his driver's license while he was in the bathroom. That's when I learned his real age and full name. Terry looked like the perfect transitional boyfriend. I had the trajectory of the entire relationship mapped out: I'd enjoy the pleasures of pederasty without any of the legal trouble; Terry would learn how to tie some interesting knots; we'd have a falling out over something stupid, not speak for a couple of months, and then be friends.

But it didn't work out quite that way. Despite my best efforts to find fault with Terry early enough to smother my growing infatuation—he hadn't been to college, he didn't know what he wanted to be when he grew up, I was seven years older, he worked in a *video* store—we kept on seeing each other.

It helped that, right after we spent the night together, he came down with a bad cold, awakening my warm and nurturing side. I saw him every night that first week, bringing him Thai food and renting him videos. Slowly, gradually, over two days, I fell in love.

On paper, you couldn't design a worse match. He was a club kid. Not the murderous drug-pushing New York City variety, but the kinda club kid who follows DJs, reads British music magazines, and works a seventies look. I don't like music, don't dance, and wouldn't follow a DJ to water in a desert. A mutual friend, a DJ as it happens, who knew both of us before we met, said that when he heard the news, he laughed out loud.

"Never in a million years would I have put you two together," Riz said. "Never you two, never, never."

If I'd met Terry a year or two earlier, I wouldn't have put us together, either. I wouldn't have seen him again after that first night. But here's what sealed it for me, here's what made it love: early in our two-day courtship, when he was sick, I bought him a book he'd mentioned. When I gave it to him, he was so excited he got out of his sickbed and jumped up and down. The book? Gore Vidal's *United States*, a twenty-five-pound collection of forty years' worth of Vidal's essays. Most twenty-three-year-old fags don't have a clue who Gore Vidal is, and Terry not only knew who he was but cared enough to jump up and down.

We'd been together ever since, and things had taken on an air of permanence: joint checking accounts, mutual decisionmaking about major purchases, vacation destinations, dinner plans, and so on. Though he spent practically every night at my place after the night we met at Re-bar, Terry kept his own apartment for nearly

two years. My last boyfriend and I had moved in together pretty
quickly, and I didn't want to jinx things with my new boyfriend.

Two years into this relationship, I still called Terry my boyfriend, much to my mother's dismay.

"He's not your boyfriend!" my mother instructed me. "You're
thirty-two years old! He's twenty-six! You're not boys! You live
together! You're talking about having children! He's your partner,
Danny, not your 'boyfriend'!" The older she got, the more my
mother spoke in exclamation points.

Terry might not have been my boyfriend, but I felt silly calling
him anything else. "Partner" made me feel as if we were cowboys
or lawyers or the Clintons. It's just so . . . genderless. Straight people find it comforting, I guess, for its very genderlessness. Not co-
incidentally, the place you most often see "partner" used in the
shacked-up-deviants sense is *The New York Times* obits of high-
profile homos. Straight people and press organs that want to ac-
knowledge gay relationships while at the same time pushing the
two-penises stuff as far out of their minds as possible love "partner." I hate it.

Other alternatives to "boyfriend" had their own problems.
Calling Terry my lover made me feel like Pepe Le Pew, some
skunk with a French accent, and I wouldn't call him my spouse
because he wasn't. Until same-sex marriage was legal, something
I expected to happen around the time my children's children's
children were long dead, I could only call Terry my husband or
spouse if I was willing to say those words with little quotation
marks stuck on each end. This I was unwilling to do. Not that we
hadn't thought of throwing ourselves a faux wedding, inviting
friends and family, and extracting our fair share of gifts, but we
couldn't bring ourselves to do it.

Terry didn't want to get "married" or have a "wedding" or say
"I do" because, he said, he didn't want to act like straight people,
which is an odd thing for a gay man about to adopt a child to say.
Can you act much straighter than having babies? Before we could
think seriously about getting a kid, Terry and I had to make a serious commitment to each other. We wouldn't have a pretend
"wedding" or exchange "rings," and we wouldn't be changing
partners quite so casually as we once did. After the kid came, if I

ever left Terry, or if he ever left me, it'd have to be for some very good reason. But there'd be no wedding, and I'd never have a "husband." For me, my discomfort with gay weddings was articulated by a close friend, who observed that gay people getting married is like retarded people getting together to give each other PhDs. It doesn't make them smarter, and it doesn't make us married.

As we drove from our hotel to the adoption seminar, the "boyfriend" issue came up. We hadn't been together all that long, by gay or straight standards, and Terry didn't want us to emphasize our relationship's relative youth for fear of harming our chances. But when the inevitable go-round-the-table-and-introduce-yourselves moment came, we'd have to say something. We had already agreed to lie about how long we'd been together, tacking on at least one extra year. But stuck in traffic on one of Portland's bridges, we couldn't come to an agreement on an acceptable alternative to "boyfriend." We resolved to avoid the issue by avoiding any relationship-defining terms. We wouldn't say boyfriend or partner or lover or anything, we'd just introduce ourselves as Dan and Terry. If any of the straight people at the seminar weren't savvy enough to figure out that we were homos, well, someone else would have to clue them in.

While we searched for parking, we tried to remind ourselves why we wanted a kid, another question we were sure to be asked during the seminar. There were a lot of reasons, and we'd discussed them at great length with each other, with friends, and with family. But as Terry pulled into a parking space, we were both so nervous that we couldn't recall a single one.

A Kind of Progress

The seminar was held at the other end of Portland from the Mallory, in Lloyd Center, an enormous and unsurprisingly soulless shopping mall. We parked near the Toys "R" Toxic and walked in. Lloyd Center was all plate glass, primary colors, canned music, and the usual-suspect collection of Gaps, Cinnabons, and chain department stores. For a weekday, the mall was crowded. In the food court, clumps of wary seniors eyed packs of surly teens. The only unique thing about Lloyd Center was the ice-skating rink plopped down in the middle of the atrium. At first, the rink seemed absurd, but then what wasn't absurd about this environment? Why not an ice rink?

Lloyd Center, like all malls, was designed to prevent the making of beelines. We were late and in a hurry, but we were forced to wander around looking for the conference rooms. We headed up an escalator, consulted a color-coded map that only added to our confusion, crossed a sky ramp, stopped in the food court for coffee, cut through one of Lloyd Center's two Baby Gaps, doubled back through the J. C. Penney's, and wound up back in front of Toys "R" Toxic. As mall design goes, Lloyd Center's was more devious than most, which was appropriate considering that Tonya Harding—a more devious figure skater than most—sometimes practiced on Lloyd Center's rink.

We looked at another map, and were forced to wander past the temptations of Cinnabon again and again, searching for the conference rooms. It was fitting that we'd come to a shopping mall to begin the "adoption process." Children in the United States being the ultimate consumer item.

As it turned out, Lloyd Center's conference rooms weren't in Lloyd Center proper (very devious), but hidden behind an un-marked glass wall at the back of a cafeteria on the second floor of an attached office tower linked to the mall by yet another sky ramp. The office tower was not on any of the color-coded maps, so the three times we returned to the color-coded map next to the Cinnabon were a waste of time and willpower. The fight at the hotel, coupled with the hard time we had finding Lloyd Center's conference rooms, made us about ten minutes late, and we were the last couple to arrive.

We were also the youngest, the malest, and the gayest.

As we walked in, six couples sitting around the large confer-ence table in the large beige room looked up at us. Tinted win-dows overlooked a parking lot, and with only two empty seats left at the table, it was abundantly clear that everyone was waiting on us. Someone from the agency handed us a notebook and gestured to the open seats. Unless they took advantage of our late arrival to warn the other couples that homos would be taking a place at the table with them today, our arrival must have come as a shock. If Terry and I had arrived first and some other gay couple had shown up at the last minute, I would have been shocked; this wasn't somewhere I would expect to find other gay men, so I couldn't imagine the straight folks weren't surprised when we walked through the door. But it was smiles and nods all around as we took our seats.

The conference room had the tense feel of a classroom before a standardized test. Everyone sat, willing themselves to stay calm and only succeeding in making themselves more nervous. The rest of the couples appeared to be between their late thirties and late forties, except for a couple across the table from us who looked late-twenties-to-early-thirties. Everyone was well dressed, well groomed, and well fed. Everyone was also white. The look was professional, upscale, and suburban, the guys in Dockers and the girls in tasteful blouses with skirts or pants. No one was guilty of too-big jewelry or too-big hair. Terry and I, in our jeans and T-shirts, baseball hats and running shoes, looked about as out of place in this room as we would at a coronation.

Sitting at the table, nervously pretending to review the agenda in our notebook, I found myself wondering who at the table disapproved.

The straight couples in this room had more important things on their minds than our homosexuality, of course. Homos can fall into the bad habit of seeing homophobes under every bed, so attached are we, at times, to our own oppression. Still, we were deep behind enemy lines. Making or adopting babies isn't something "they" expect to see "us" doing. I was willing to give everyone in the room the benefit of the doubt. It could very well have been that no one here disapproved of two gay men adopting a child. All these adoptive-parents-to-be could be as progressive as the agency they hoped to adopt from. Maybe the looks I saw six husbands shoot six wives were in my head.

Then I remembered some info the agency sent us when we first called, which included self-authored profiles of couples in the middle of the adoption process. More than half described themselves as Christian. Not all Christians hate homos, of course, and some Christians are themselves homos. But still, in America in the late nineties, it's safe to assume that most people who go out of their way to let you know they're Christians don't care for homos. So, come to think of it, odds seemed pretty good that someone at the table believed that my boyfriend and I were going to hell, and had no right to take a baby down with us.

As we waited for the seminar to begin, no one talked. No one made eye contact, either, which allowed me to look at each couple sitting around the table. Who hated us? Who could it be? Somebody there must have, but who? The guy sitting next to me who looked a lot like my father? The woman wearing huge glasses in the pink sweater? The couple who looked like they listened to NPR 24/7?

Maybe I was being paranoid—okay, I was definitely being paranoid—but what choice did we have? With overt displays of antigay attitudes frowned on in polite society, it is harder to tell when and where we're not wanted. Folks who don't like homos don't feel they can vent their prejudice as freely as they once did. Even when we're somewhere we are definitely not wanted, like the army, the folks who don't want us there go out of their way to be polite about it.

When Colin Powell, for instance, went on television to voice his support for the military's ban on openly gay soldiers, he began his remarks by saying that gay Americans were just as brave, patriotic, and true-blue as any other Americans. He liked gay people fine, he just wanted us the hell out of his army. We were bad for morale, the general said. Except, of course, when straight people want to go out dancing. Straights crowd into gay bars and dance clubs on Friday and Saturday nights, and no one's morale seems to suffer. Now, I personally have never wanted to join the army. Giving guns to straight boys, sending them far, far away, and ordering them to shoot at each other: why would anyone want to mess that up? That's a perfect system, in my opinion, and if something ain't broke, don't mess with it.

But, of course, I know other gays and lesbians want to be sailors, soldiers, and jar-head bad-asses, and so I recognize the ban on gays in the military as an injustice. And while I hope that someday the ban is overturned, I'm not going to lose sleep in the meantime. What was most interesting about the whole gays-in-the-military fiasco, however, was how Powell and everyone else felt obliged to dress their positions up in hey-I'm-not-a-bigot drag. They felt compelled to pay us compliments (brave! patriotic! true-blue!) even as they strove to perpetuate an injustice against us. Appear to be nice while keeping a foot on our necks. This is progress, I suppose.

Since hatred styles itself as tolerance these days, how are we supposed to tell the difference? What do you do when disapproval, indifference, tolerance, and acceptance all look exactly the same? Social tolerance has become the norm for most straight people, which is nice, but at the same time *appearing* tolerant has become the norm for everyone else. How are we supposed to tell the nice straight people and the bigoted straight people apart if everyone has the same look on their face?

Unfortunately, we can't, at least not until they run for office. And, again, this may be progress, but it's a kind of progress that induces paranoia on the part of the tolerated. When you can't tell the difference between people who hate you and people who don't, it's easy to feel you have no choice but to assume the worst. In some circumstances, the socially intolerant will kill us (R.I.P., Matthew Shepard). It seemed unlikely that we were gonna be murdered here in Lloyd Center's conference rooms (on the ice rink maybe) and, as I lived to type the tale, obviously we weren't murdered. Carrying this "Gee, does anyone in this room want to kill me?" tension around with us wherever we go takes its toll.

I find myself unsettled in this way more and more frequently. A few years after the military thing, I joined the Republican party. I lived in a heavily Democratic gay neighborhood, and thought it would interesting to see what the Republicans in my neighborhood looked like. Also, I didn't want to accidentally sleep with any of them. So I attended the Republican precinct caucuses during the '96 presidential campaign. There were even fewer Republicans in my precinct than I suspected; I was the only one at the caucus. The lonely Republican party official explained that if I cared to sign up, I would automatically be my district's Republican Precinct Committee Officer, and a delegate to the upcoming county and state conventions. When I found out delegates could make motions to amend the party platform, I cared to sign up.

The Republican platform in my county contained all the usual gay-bashing planks, so I went to the convention and made a few motions. A few dozen. I moved to remove the antigay planks, I moved to amend them, I moved to add a pro–gay rights plank, I made a motion to welcome gays and lesbians into the Republican party. Rules allowed for five minutes to make a motion, debate for four minutes, then a minute to respond. I had a captive audience of sixteen hundred Republican activists. All of my motions failed, of course, and my sixteen hundred fellow delegates loudly booed me every time I stood to make another motion. (The daily papers credited me with derailing the convention.) But no one at the convention was actually unpleasant to me personally. Even in the bathroom. And the ladies and gentlemen seated around me in the stands were as nice as could be; some even made suggestions on how better to present my next motion, which they proceeded to vote down.

As homophobes have gotten used to the idea of us, they've become more subtle. Arresting us, electroshocking us, and killing us have gone out of style. Of course, gay-bashing remains a popular coming-of-age ritual for disturbed young straight boys all over the country (R.I.P., Billy Jack Gaither), but it is no longer sanctioned by the state (the men who murdered Matthew Shepard and Billy Jack Gaither will, with any luck, soon be resting in peace themselves).

Even the most recent attacks on gays and lesbians by religious conservatives arrived disguised as compassion. When Christian conservatives began buying ads in newspapers and on television promoting an almost entirely fictional "ex-gay movement," the National Gay and Lesbian Task Force called the campaign a "kinder and gentler homophobia." Men and women who claimed to have "freed themselves" from the gay lifestyle beamed at us from full-page ads in *The New York Times* and other papers. It was hard to take these ads seriously. Many gays and lesbians asked, "What harm could they do?"

A considerable amount, as we quickly discovered. Gays and lesbians were never the true targets of these ads and their "message of compassion." The target was straight people, and the message was not that Jesus loves the little homos, all the little homos of the world. No, the advertisers wanted straight people to believe that the only thing preventing them from living in a world free of homosexuality were those stubborn gays and lesbians ("Why can't they just give themselves to Jesus Christ?"). By arguing that we didn't *have* to exist, these ads implicitly argued that we had no right to exist.

This was an attempt by religious conservatives to introduce a deadly new kind of hatred into American culture: eliminationist homophobia. In his book *Hitler's Willing Executioners: Ordinary Germans and the Holocaust*, Daniel Goldhagen described prewar German anti-Semitism as unique and murderous; he called it eliminationist. German Christian churches inspired visions of Jews as "Christ-killers," and Jews came to be regarded as a poisonous anti-race that had to be eliminated in order to purify German culture. Well, Christian conservatives in America were attempting to inspire visions of gays and lesbians as "Christ-rejectors," and of homosexuality as a "behavior" that must be eliminated to purify American culture. And they were calling it compassion!

The distance is short between some people's arguing that gays and lesbians as a group have no right to exist, and someone else's taking it into his own hands to end the existence of an individual gay or lesbian person; in the wake of these ads came the murders of Matthew Shepard and Billy Jack Gaither. If the religious right is serious about "washing the stain of homosexuality off the face of this great nation," as one fundy web site I read puts it, there will have to be more murders. Few gays and lesbians will subject themselves to "reparative therapy" quacks, and the vast majority of us have no interest in becoming "ex-gay." Homosexual behavior cannot be eliminated without eliminating homosexual people.

Still, these days even the biggest antigay bigots take pride in appearing indifferent to the presence of homos. We can sweep into almost any room, even into Republican conventions, and brows hardly rise. The bigot may grip the facial muscles, locking a casual expression in place, but he doesn't sneer, spit up, or throw things. He plays it cool.

And that's what I thought I saw around the table at Lloyd Center: gripped faces, expressions locked into place. They were playing it cool. One minute I was thinking, *They hate us, they really hate us.* The next minute, I thought: *Don't be so self-involved; they didn't even notice that we're both men.* The next, I hoped that maybe all these nice straight couples were just as nervous as Terry and I. Maybe they couldn't have cared less. Maybe they got lost in the mall too, and they all rushed in a split second before we got there, and everyone was out of breath. Maybe this seminar was a statistical anomaly, and there were no Christian fundies in the room at all. Maybe they were all progressive Democrats, with gay and lesbian friends and neighbors, and they couldn't have been more delighted that Terry and I were there. Maybe they were all bi.

Since we can no longer tell the difference between a bigot and our best friend, we should give everyone the benefit of the doubt and assume folks are tolerant until they prove themselves otherwise. But if we do that, we make it easier for the bigot with a smile on his face to sneak up on us. So I'm inclined to assume the worst.

Early in the gay lib movement, gay politicos wished every closet-case homo in the country would turn blue. If we couldn't hide, the logic went, we'd have to fight. (Then a whole bunch of us did turn blue in the early eighties, and, just as predicted, we came out fighting.) These days, I find myself wishing the bigots would turn blue. If bigots were blue, we'd only have to take a quick look around when we walked into a conference room full of straight people, or wanted to sit at a bar in Wyoming and have a beer. No blue people, no worries. We'd know whom we had to fight, and when we had to fight, and, more important, we'd know when we could finally relax.

Grieving Our Infertility

The director of the agency officially welcomed all of us to the two-day seminar, "Adoption: A Lifelong Process," rousing me from my paranoid fantasies. Ruth had headed the agency for three years, but first she was a client. She showed us a picture of her adopted son and told us she knew what we were going through. Ruth had a look of practiced empathy on her face. We saw this look a lot over the next two days, from the counselors, lawyers, and adoptive parents who came to share their experiences and answer our questions. Doubtless, Ruth's concern was genuine, but she'd probably given this speech thirty-six times already. She'd probably heard a similar speech herself before she adopted her son through the agency. Empathy had become a mark she hit.

Ruth was in her early thirties, attractive, with curly brown hair; she had that contradictory mix of concern and distance that sets social workers apart from mere mortals. The parent-wannabes sitting around the table were not quite abstractions to her, but we were pretty close—we were clients. As she spoke, Ruth made it clear that she and the agency cared very deeply about each and every one of us. But her tone communicated that she wouldn't be getting involved in our private dramas. She had too much work to do. Her overt message was compassion, but her covert message was "You're here, you're adopting, get used to it."

Apparently it took some getting over for the straight couples, who in agency-speak had "come to" or "arrived at" adoption, as if it were a physical destination. I was unprepared for the funereal tone of the seminar's first day. And as Ruth's opening comments picked up steam, Terry and I began to feel more out of place, and even more conspicuous than we had when we first walked through the door.

I opened my ten-pound notebook and peeked at the agenda: "Grieving Your Infertility." "Coping with Infertility." "Infertility and Its Impact on Adoption." "Losses Inherent in Adoption." I nudged Terry and slid the notebook over. His eyebrows shot up. Infertility was never an issue for us, just a fact, so we hadn't spent much time thinking about it, let alone learning to cope with it. And there were no "losses inherent in adoption" for us, but only victory. When I came out in 1980, it didn't occur to me that one day I would be able to adopt a child. I assumed, incorrectly, that it was illegal for gay men to adopt children. After all, gay men didn't have families—we were a threat to families.

My boyfriend passed me a note: "Maybe they should have let us skip the first day."

Ruth walked the group through our infertility issues. "Infertility can sabotage the adoption process," Ruth explained. "You felt you had no control over your fertility, so you may attempt to impose control over this process. Or you may come to resent the child you adopt because it isn't your dream biological child. You're successful people, with successful lives and successful relationships—having a child is probably the first thing you have not succeeded at, your first failure as individuals."

At this point, we were positive we should have skipped the first day. The boyfriend and I had accepted our infertility a long time ago, and sitting with the straight couples, we felt our very presence was mocking their "loss."

"If you need to feel sad or angry about not having your 'own' biological children—that's fine," Ruth continued. "But do not let those feelings dominate your life. Enter parenting from a place of abundance, not a place of need. . . ."

In high school and college, my straight friends would point out the many disadvantages of being gay; it was supposed to be a joke, but they sounded serious. Their understanding of sexuality was pretty limited, and so was mine at the time, and they were trying to talk me out of being gay. They didn't want to lose my friendship, and they assumed they would if I "turned" gay. In 1980, being gay still meant going off and joining a secret society, moving away and becoming someone else. They would spot me on a street corner years later, wearing leather pants and a teal T-shirt, waiting for a bus. To prevent this fate, my friends would warn me that gays couldn't get married, or hold certain jobs, or live where we wanted to. And we couldn't have kids.

I would respond by pointing out the many advantages of being gay, as I saw them at the time. Before he got the boot, Jimmy Carter showed Iran he meant business by making high school–age boys register for the draft. When Ronald Reagan became president, it looked like he'd be declaring war on the Sandinistas any day and calling us up. Advantage, gay: they didn't take my kind in the army, so I wouldn't get shot up in Central America. But the ultimate advantage of being gay in 1980 was that it freed me from having to worry about birth control. For my straight friends, birth control was a major headache; first they had to worry about getting it, then they had to worry about hiding it from their parents. Advantage, gay: I didn't have to worry about the pill, or condoms, or missed periods, or babies, or abortions. On this one point they agreed that being gay was better than being straight. Then the tables turned, of course, and I was spending more time worrying about death control than my straight friends ever spent worrying about birth control. And if their birth control failed and they got pregnant, they could always have abortions; if my death control failed, and I got infected, there was no way to abort the virus. I would die. Advantage, straight.

After years of careful birth control it must have come as a shock to the straight couples around the table to learn that they needn't have bothered. Unable to have "their own" kids, they'd had to reconcile themselves to having someone else's before they could walk into this conference room. As we went around the table and introduced ourselves, everyone put on brave faces, trying to get to Ruth's "place of abundance," but it was clear from some watery eyes and thrust-out chins that having to sit in this room represented a painfully humiliating defeat. Each told or hinted at horror stories: tens of thousands of dollars spent on unsuccessful fertility treatments, in-vitro this, test-tube that, egg harvesting. Years wasted. Even calm and centered Ruth had pumped money and drugs into her uterus in a failed attempt to have her own bio-kid.

Ruth explained how infertility placed an enormous strain on her marriage, and how during treatments she fell into a deep depression. One day, at the end of her rope, she read about the side effects of an infertility drug she'd been taking. Third on the list was "mild insanity." She decided that having her own biological child was not worth her sanity, and stopped taking the drugs. This was how Ruth "arrived at" adoption, and her story was very similar to the others we heard that day as we went around the table telling our stories.

When it came time for Terry and me to introduce ourselves, what were we supposed to say? "Thrilled to be here, couldn't be happier?" We couldn't seem too upbeat, but we *were* feeling pretty up. When I came out, my straight friends told me I'd never have kids; a guy I knew to be gay in 1980 (we slept together) told me he'd never come out because he wanted a family. He died in 1986, never having come out, and never having that family he wanted. In Florida it's illegal for gays to adopt, and soon it may be illegal in other states. In some, our bio-kids are taken from us by homophobic courts in cahoots with homophobic relatives.

So sitting in this room, looking into adoption, living in a free state, being taken seriously by this agency—this was no defeat for us. This was a great, big, honkin' victory. A triumph. And while adoption was where the straight couples at the table ended up after a long and painful journey, it was practically where we began. So what did we say?

The wrong thing, naturally. When I'm under pressure and feeling awkward, my mouth opens and something idiotic, something totally Tourette's-y, drops right right out. This day was no exception. We were the next-to-last couple to speak, and we'd heard five very sad stories. Some wayward synapse in my pea-brain told me a joke might be in order, something to lighten the mood and cheer up the straight folks.

"Hi, I'm Dan, and this is Terry, and as you can see, we have some fertility issues of our own."

If there was any way to take it back, I would. No one laughed, no one smiled—and why should they? Thankfully, the couple after us, Carol and Jack, cracked a couple of jokes, too. Jack was an engineer, Carol a business executive. They'd spent years trying to get pregnant, to no avail.

"We're here, " Jack explained, "because I finally scored a zero on a test."

Heterosexual identity is all wrapped up in the ability of heterosexuals to make babies. Straight sex can do what gay sex cannot, make "miracles." The straights at our seminar had expected to grow up, fall in love, get married, make love for fun, and sooner or later make love to make life. Infertility did more than shatter their expectations; it undermined their sexual identities.

Straight sex can be recreational or procreational—or both—but gay sex can only ever be recreational. Gay sex is never a means, only an end, and the end is pleasure. Homophobes use this to justify their hatred of gays and lesbians: straight sex, since it can make a baby, is "natural"; gay sex, since it can only make a mess, is not. Babies make straight sex more important than gay sex, so straights are therefore more important than gays. Babies underpin all hetero-supremacism, from "Adam and Eve, not Adam and Steve" to "Gays don't have children, so they have to recruit yours." Even when straights are using birth control, procreation still sanctifies straight sex. Even when straights are having sex that couldn't possibly make babies (oral, anal, phone, cyber), the fact that these two people *could* make babies under other circumstances or in other positions legitimizes straight sex.

This is pounded into the heads of gay people and straight people alike. Gays grow up believing their desires, pleasures, and loves are illegitimate; and straights who fall for the hype believe they gotta work that magic, gotta make that baby, or . . . what? A straight person who can't make a baby isn't really a straight person at all. And if you're not straight, you must be . . . what? You're like my boyfriend and me. Suddenly your sex is all recreational, like gay sex, delegitimized and desanctified. Straight sex absent fertility has no larger significance. Oh, it's an expression of love—but so is gay sex, and that never made gay sex okay. No babies means no miracles, no magic. The sex you're having may still be pleasurable, but in a sex-hating (and consequently sex-obsessed) culture, pleasure is not a good enough reason, otherwise gay and lesbian sex would never have been stigmatized.

I sympathized with the straight people sitting around the conference table. I understood what they must have been going through. I had been through it myself, a long time ago. When I hit puberty, I got the news that I was functionally infertile. But the straight couples at the seminar had only recently gotten that news, and they were still adjusting to it. How much we had in common with them was driven home by the rhetoric the counselors used during the seminar. It was the rhetoric of coming out. The straight couples were encouraged to accept what they could not change. In time, they'd see their "problem" as a blessing. It was important to tell family and friends the truth, even if they might not understand at first. They might in their ignorance ask hurtful questions, but be patient and try to answer. And while it is possible to live a lie, possible to adopt a child and pass it off as your biological child, no one can spend a lifetime in the closet.

Now we all had some common ground.

While the straight couples at the seminar were getting a little gay by coming out to themselves and each other about their infertility, my boyfriend and I were getting a little straight. Terry and I would be giving up certain things that, for better or worse, define what it means to be gay. Good things, things we enjoyed and that had value and meaning for us. Like promiscuity. Safely and respectfully done, whorin' around, like travel, is broadening. One night in Amsterdam, I met a guy in a leather bar, a twenty-eight-year-old German student. We had a beer, left the bar, and went back to his apartment. We messed around, nothing serious, and when we were done, talked all night about German reunification, what it was like growing up in the East, and what his grandparents had been up to during the Second World War.

The next day, he showed me parts of Amsterdam I would never have found on my own; then he walked me back to my hotel, gave me a kiss, and said good-bye. I never saw him again, and I don't remember his name, but it was a beautiful experience. And certainly not one unique to gay people; heterosexuals have been known to get laid now and then while traveling, too. But this experience was made easier for both of us by certain assumptions we shared as gay men. On the basis of where we met, we knew about how long this relationship was destined to last (ten hours), what we were "into," and on what terms we would part.

My Amsterdam affair wasn't an experience I was prepared to deny or denigrate in an effort to make myself better parental material in the eyes of the agency, the court, or my mom. But I did know that by becoming a parent I was limiting myself, cutting myself off from similar experiences in the future. But who said I had to become a hypocrite, too? I inhaled all sorts of things: men, makeup, drink, drugs. Could I be honest about these experiences, treasure their memory, and still be a good parent? I thought so.

Terry and I wanted to adopt; we didn't want to hide or lie about who we were. But we did realize the kid meant no more Amsterdams, not for a while. Terry and I had talked about having a three-way sometime (actually, I talked about it, Terry listened, nothing happened), but once we had a kid in the house, it was unlikely we ever would. When sexually adventurous straight people go through this (the loss of certain sexual possibilities), I think it's called settling down. Probably, neither of us would ever have a good ol'-fashioned big-gay-slut phase again. I got sad when I thought about that, because I'd enjoyed my last couple of slutty phases quite a lot.

What else were we giving up? Well, it looked as if we were never going to make it to a circuit party. And if we ever did use recreational drugs again, it would have to be on a vacation, with the kid at home with my mother. For years, I'd indulged myself (once you've gone and kissed boys, there isn't anything you're afraid of), and I'd lived to tell the tale. If we got a kid, I'd be giving indulgence up, and so would Terry. So there were losses inherent in adoption for Terry and me, too, and perhaps we'd end up doing some grieving. But unlike the straight couples in the room, we chose this loss; it was not imposed on us.

The True Feminist Man

We weren't immune to the "dream" of our own bio-kid. Long before we found ourselves in a room full of straight people grieving our infertility, we'd looked into having bio-kids. Unlike the folks sitting at the table with us, however, we only wasted a little bit of time, and practically no money.

I'd started thinking about a bio-kid before I even met Terry, which was partly why we'd decided to go ahead and adopt even though we'd been together a relatively short time. Terry almost married into kids the day we met, so why not? The adoption process takes at least a year, so if things didn't work out we would have broken up long before we got the kid, calling a halt to the "lifelong" adoption process before it was too late. But if things were still going strong, the kid would arrive right around year threeish, which seemed like a reasonable time to start a family.

When I met Terry, I was in the middle of tense baby-making negotiations with three different lesbians. Two were a couple, one was single, and all were my kinda dykes: tough, smart, no-bullshit types, each with fully functioning senses of humor and just the right glaze of cynicism to take the edge off their people-united-can-never-be-defeated politics. All three wanted to get pregnant, none wanted to go the sperm-bank route, and all wanted to have a dad around. The lesbians would be the primary parents, but I would be "involved." And down the road, if things worked out, we'd make some brothers and sisters.

It was just what I wanted at the time. I was single and couldn't be a full-time or even a half-time parent, so the offers were very tempting. Sweep in, play dad, sweep out. Poopy diaper? Hand the kid to a lesbian. And since I like lesbians more than I like gay men, the idea of making babies with lesbians—and forming a large, happy, extended queer family—appealed to me politically.

So I talked with both Lesbian Couple and Lesbian Single. And talked. And talked. And talked.

This was my first personal experience with lesbian deep-process, and I can't say I cared for it. I especially didn't like how powerless the whole thing made me feel. Waiting for other people to make their minds up about something I was ready to do is not my idea of a delightful way to spend a year. But I couldn't force the issue, as that would have made me an asshole, and I understood that the decision had more serious consequences for the lesbians than it did for me, so I was willing to wait. For a while. I did my level altar-boy best to be patient as the talks dragged on. And on. And on.

As I soon learned, all three lesbians had approached me at the "beginning of their decision-making process," and none of them were even sure they wanted to have kids. They were "exploring" the possibility of parenting. Why they needed my balls along on their explorations, I don't know. If this was a purely hypothetical exercise, why not a hypothetical sperm donor? Lesbian Couple wasn't even sure who would be impregnated, though they were pretty sure they were going to take that step. They'd been together ten years, and parenting was the only new territory they could explore together. But then the talk of kids, the future, and the rest of their lives made mortality a little too palpable, I guess, and soon they were talking about breaking up.

Lesbian Single seemed closer to making a decision, but she was talking to another potential donor-dad. Even if she went ahead with the baby, I might not get to jerk off into her Dixie cup. I'm tall, with dark hair and eyes, and I look a lot like Lesbian Single herself. Her other potential donor, whom I met, was four feet tall and had white-blond hair. Apparently the Lesbian Single was having some difficulty deciding whether she would bring a tall, dark, handsome child into this world, or an albino dwarf.

Thinking one of these two scenarios was bound to pan out, I informed my delighted mother that she would have another grandchild within a year. Six months later, with talks still dragging on, I told my mother to forget it. Soon I was having a *feeling*, though because deep down I am a Catholic and not a lesbian, I didn't share this feeling with anyone. The feeling was resentment. Why had they bothered to approach me before they made up their minds? Why didn't they wait until after they'd come to what we boys like to call a decision before bringing me in?

While this was going on, I explained my frustrations to another lesbian friend, who didn't know any of the women involved. She was unsympathetic. "That's what it's like to be a woman," she told me. "You're learning what it's like not to have any power." I should embrace my powerlessness, she felt, and learn from it. When I told her I was thinking about adoption instead, she accused me of running back to my male privilege after a small taste of powerlessness women have had to endure for all of recorded human history.

"Your willingness to access your male privilege," she told me, "proves you're not really a true feminist."

"But," I protested, "I'm a feminist because I don't think anyone should have to put up with powerlessness—not women, not men, and certainly not me."

"The true feminist man," she corrected me, "would accept his powerlessness in a situation like this, and make a small payment on the enormous karmic debt men owe women."

Back at the negotiating table, things were getting ugly. Lesbian Couple had found out that I'd talked to Lesbian Single about doing for her what they had asked me to do for them (beat it, fill a Dixie cup, beat it). Because deep down I'm really Dan Quayle, Lesbian Couple was my first choice. Working in a day care for a couple of years left me of the opinion that two-parent homes are better than one-. But I talked to Lesbian Single, too, because I have a hard time saying no to people, especially lesbians, and I was hedging my bets. If things didn't work out with Lesbian Couple, I would go with Lesbian Single. It wasn't my first choice, but I reasoned that the kid would still technically have two parents, although in separate apartments. If Lesbian Single and I ever found partners, the kid could have four. Besides, the last time I talked with Lesbian Couple, they were thinking about breaking up. Why shouldn't I talk to Lesbian Single?

Lesbian Couple didn't see it my way. They hadn't broken up, that was just one option among many, and they were examining all their options during their decision process. While it was okay for them to examine all their options, it wasn't okay for me to examine all of mine.

Luckily, Lesbian Couple was angrier with Lesbian Single than they were with me. Lesbian Couple had let it be known on the Lesbian Grapevine that they had approached me about my sperm. Apparently, Lesbian Single knew they had dibs on my balls and had approached me anyway, fully aware that my balls had been spoken for. Add to this psychodrama the fact that Lesbian Single had once attempted to seduce half of Lesbian Couple away from the other half, and soon we were having meetings to process our anger and hurt feelings around these secondary issues, which delayed any further progress on processing our feelings around the primary issue, which was, as I understood it, the production of a human infant sometime before all three lesbians hit menopause.

While all this was going on, I met Terry and fell in quick, decisive, boyish love. Soon after we started dating, we had a conversation about kids. Reproduced for you here is a complete and unabridged transcript of that conversation, so that it may be contrasted with the discussions characterized above.

Dan: "You need to know I'm thinking about having kids."
Terry: "I love kids."

When the lesbians fell through, Terry and I started to examine our lesbian-free baby options. Which meant adoption.

But I had one more chance to embrace the role of powerless sperm donor and true feminist man. When Terry and I moved into an apartment together, our new next-door neighbor—whom neither of us had met—slipped a note under our door. She'd seen us moving in and wondered if either of us had ever thought about being a dad. Apparently, watching us heft Terry's ten-thousand-pound couch into our apartment convinced her we had the right genetic stuff. She'd been looking for a sperm donor for some time, none of her straight male friends were interested, and so she thought she'd take a chance. Would we be interested?

Thinking it odd to be asked by a complete stranger to make a baby, I immediately agreed to meet and discuss the matter. We had breakfast with our new next-door neighbor, and talked. She was straight, she was single, and she wanted kids. Straight Single didn't know us, but still, wouldn't it be great? We'd all be living next door to each other, the kid would have access to Mom and Dad, and I would have daily involvement, though she would be the sole legal guardian. She'd been trying to get preggers for some time and had done the frozen-sperm thing with no luck. Picking up the sperm, carrying it to the doc, climbing into the stirrups—the whole insemination thing was leaving her cold. And it wasn't working.

So after her last unsuccessful trip to the fertility doc, Straight Single decided she needed fresh spunk, and she needed it now. She was almost forty-five. If we were going to do this, it would have to be soon. While it would be nice if we could all get to know each other first, waiting a year might make it impossible for her to have a baby at all. This was a rush order. Before we left, we agreed to meet again and talk some more, this time over drinks.

When I got out of her apartment, and thawed out a bit, I couldn't shake the feeling that I was being sold a health club membership. The line about not being able to wait to get to know each other before we created a lifelong, everlasting bond was a little high-pressure. On the other hand, meeting someone who wanted to put a rush order on my sperm was a nice change. After a year spent talking to three lesbians who probably couldn't have agreed to rush out of a burning building, Straight Single's impatience had appeal. And I liked the idea of living right next door to the kid. Maybe with a drink in her, our next-door neighbor would seem less like a health club sales associate.

But there would be no next meeting. I had to cancel our first date to drink. Then I had to cancel our rescheduled date. Straight Single was a woman in a hurry, so she withdrew her offer and decided to adopt instead. Things were a little strained after that, as if we were living next door to a jilted lover. Eventually, Straight Single adopted a baby girl from China and moved away, and we were both happy for her and more than a little relieved.

Months later, we ran into Lesbian Couple at a Lesbian Event, a women's basketball game. They'd heard the news about us deciding to adopt. They congratulated us, but they were a little hurt that they hadn't heard the news from us directly, and hoped we could get together sometime and have a little conversation, to bring closure to the discussions we'd had more than two years ago about making a baby. Lesbian Couple was still thinking about kids, and was still thinking of me as their potential sperm donor. The news that my balls had been yanked off the market came as something of a shock.

The Real Reasons

There's a question I've been dodging.

Why were we having a kid? Or kids, plural, I should say, because Terry and I—younger brothers, remember—believed children should have siblings to torment. So, why kids? We were HIV-negative gay men living in America at the end of the twentieth century. Barring some social or economic disaster (like a Steve Forbes administration), we had a long, prosperous DINK future spread out before us. (That's "Double Income, No Kids," our by-default consumer demographic.) Remaining DINKs meant a future of travel, parties, cheap-if-not-meaningless sex, health clubs, and swank homes. Why would any gay man in his right mind trade DINKdom for dirty diapers?

"The middle age of buggers is not be contemplated without horror," Virginia Woolf is reported to have observed. I don't believe there's anything horrid about middle-aged gay men (provided they don't join men's choruses or the North American Man-Boy Love Association, watch *Deep Space Nine*, or display teddy bears in little leather harnesses in their living rooms). Nevertheless, at about age thirty, I began to contemplate my impending middle age with a degree of horror. What was I going to *do* for the next forty or fifty years? It didn't take me long to conclude I would need more in my life than money and men. I would want something meaningful to do with my free time, something besides traveling the world collecting Fiesta Ware and intestinal parasites.

So, kids.

Once upon a time, people had kids out of a sense of obligation to family, species, and society; and since they lacked birth control, most sexually active folks weren't in much of a position to prevent themselves from making babies. We've got birth control now, at least in most places, and we've got access to abortion, at least for now. While some couples feel pressured by their families or churches to have kids, for a large number of people in a large part of the world, having children is optional for the first time in history. Why do people have kids today? It's not to do the species a favor: the largest threat to our survival is our out-of-control breeding. The reason people in general (by which I mean straight people, since people in general are straight) have kids today is to give themselves something real and meaningful and important to do. Having children is no longer about propagating the species or having someone to leave your lands to, but about self-fulfillment. Kids are a self-actualization project for the parents involved. A lifelong Outward Bound. Something for grownups to do, a pastime, a hobby.

So why not kids? Gay men need hobbies, too.

Our other options as gay men at the end of the twentieth century—how to occupy our time over the next thirty years—were not at all appealing. Terry and I had, basically, three choices:

Option 1: Stay in the Game. Keep going to bars, and parties, and clubs, keep getting laid, keep drinking, keep taking drugs. This option leads, inevitably, to our breakup over some humpy young thing, who would in turn dump us for a humpier younger thing. Eventually we become a couple of fifty-year-old fags hanging out in gay bars full of men too young to care that we, you know, Marched on Washington in '93. To compete with and compete for the annual crop of just-out twenty-one-year-old gay boys, we have to go under the knife again and again, until we are so much scar tissue stitched to scar tissue. Then we die. Our corpses, drug- and silicone-contaminated superfund sites, are denied a decent burial. Distant relatives come to town, crate us up, and haul us to a toxic-waste incinerator.

Option 2: Go Places, See Shit. We stay together and spend our DINK dollars traveling the world. We take a lot of pictures, collect a lot of junk, have a lot of sex with the locals. Provided we don't succumb to Alzheimer's or some as-yet-undiscovered sexually transmitted disease, we have our memories to keep us company when we're old and gray. Then we die, our memories dying with us. Distant relatives come to town and haul us and everything else—photo albums, postcard collection, STD meds—off to the dump.

Option 3: Mr. & Mr. Martha Stewart. We buy a house and direct the passion we used to devote to sex to the renovation and decoration of our little manse. We spend the last years of our lives combing junque stores, yard sales, estate sales, and auction houses for that authentic Victorian/Edwardian/Art Deco/Fab Fifties nightstand/hall table/mirror/dinette set that will finally complete our beautiful-but-sterile home. Once we find it, our local newspaper's Sunday magazine does a photo spread of our to-die-for home. Then we die. Distant relatives come to town, sell the house and the furniture, and donate our ancient bodies to science.

I was already planning on having kids when I met Terry, so I'd already thought through all of this. After I walked Terry through what I saw as our options, he agreed that they were pretty depressing. Each ended with distant relatives coming to town and disposing of our remains in a tremendously unsentimental manner. And everything we would have DINKed so hard for—our possessions, our memories, our hair systems—would be busted up and thrown away. Mortality is unsettling, and the more we thought about having kids the more sense they made as hedges against depressing, lonely deaths. We didn't want to be anybody's forgotten old gay uncles.

Kids wouldn't keep us young, but they would keep us relevant, something other hobbies wouldn't do. If we had kids and they managed to outlive us, Terry and I would be hauled off to the dump when our time came by people who knew us and felt obligated to dispose of us.

So, kids.

Yes, I know: kids die, kids turn out rotten, kids grow up to be serial killers, kids abandon their parents, kids *kill* their parents. Adopted kids may decide their biological relatives are their *real* relatives and blow off their adoptive families. Kids are a crapshoot. But even if the only thing your kids give a shit about is getting their hands on your money or your Holden-Wakefield end tables, even if all your kids want is for you to drop dead, at least someone is giving a specific sort of shit about you. And if you have more than one kid who wants your end tables, you can have fun drafting and redrafting your will.

Sometimes, late at night, I'd sit up and worry that we might be adopting to prove a point. Were we doing this because we could? On some level, I think, we were. It wasn't the sole reason, but even if we were only doing this to prove something to the world or to ourselves, there are worse reasons to have kids. Straight people all over the world have kids for those much worse reasons every day. They fall down drunk and get up pregnant.

The same impulse that drives grown gay men to walk around holding hands could be pushing us toward this. For same-sex couples, taking a lover's hand is almost never an unself-conscious choice. You have to think about where you are, whether you're safe, and you have to look. By the time you determine you're safe, you're not even sure you want to hold hands anymore. The genuine moment has passed, but you've invested so much energy and angst that now you can't *not* take your lover's hand. You wind up holding and the only reason you take your lover's hand is to prove that you can.

Wondering whether we were doing this "just to prove we can," made us wonder about our motives. In that hesitation, the decision to adopt became more than "Let's have kids." Public displays of affection for gays and lesbians are political acts, and what could be a larger public display of affection than the two of us adopting a kid together.

I had a secret reason for wanting kids, one I haven't shared with my boyfriend. It's not an easy thing to write, and I hope you'll understand why I'd rather you didn't tell Terry. I'm not sure how he would take it. I wanted to have kids because I wanted to get fat. Actually, I should say, I wanted to have kids because I'm *going* to get fat.

Good Gay Men are not supposed to be heavy (though some gay men are allowed to be "bears" these days, if they're furry enough). We're expected to do our sit-ups, watch what we eat, and show up at family and high school reunions looking fabulous so that the girls can say, "What a waste!" and the boys can say, "What a fag!"

Staying fit is a crushing regimen, however, one that doesn't leave much time for anything else. In my twenties, I ran just far enough on treadmills and peddled just fast enough on stationary bicycles to stay fuckable. My fitness goal was to look good enough in clothes that I could get other people out of theirs. While my stomach looked flat enough with a shirt on, there was no six-pack under my slave-labor Gap-fag T-shirt. A two-liter bottle, yes, and one day soon, a keg. But a six-pack? Never. I was never enough of a gym queen to get comfortable getting naked in public. I never danced shirtless in a club or strolled around a bathhouse in a towel. I never even posed for porno Polaroids.

(Except on one occasion, when Polaroids were taken without my consent by a one-night stand. Since I didn't want them taken, I wasn't really posing for them. Sadly, I wasn't in a position to prevent them from being taken, if you follow my drift, and I didn't have the nerve to demand them back from from the scary freak who took 'em once I was, um, able to do so. These photos will probably surface after this book comes out, and my fitness to be a parent will be challenged by those who think kinky = crazy.)

Until I turned thirty, I made it to the gym at least three times a week. I fought getting fat long and hard, and when I went home for weddings and funerals the girls said, "What a waste," and the boys said, "What a fag!" But since turning thirty, I hadn't managed to get my rear end into a gym very often. This was not good. My gene pool is filled with fat, and an extreme kind of fatness it is. My people do not get pleasantly plump. We Savages do not "fill out," or "wear it well." We balloon. My family is inclined toward obesity, to thighs so large we're forced to walk like mincing three-hundred-pound Japanese ladies, hefting one leg around the other with dainty criss-cross steps. Our guts grow to enormous proportions. We get so fat we can't be cremated. Dead Savages are soaked in a vat filled with a particular enzyme that breaks us down into our composite elements—beer, brats, and cheese—which are then packaged and distributed to food pantries all over the Midwest.

My boyfriend was unaware of my impending enormousness, and I had no intention of bringing it to his attention. Once he was bound to my side by a web of car payments, shared possessions, and children, then I'd tell him what was in store.

Or I'd show him.

Unfairly, while I am destined to be fat, I am not in the least attracted to fat people. Not even to the slightly overweight. Lucky for me, my boyfriend is one of those hateful people who can live on deep-fried bacon, coconut milk, and crème brûlée and not gain an ounce. He could eat nothing but pork fat ten hours a day and you would still be able to count his ribs while he's wearing a parka. Terry is just skin and gristle stretched over beautifully proportioned bones. Naked, my boyfriend looks like a broad-shouldered Kate Moss with a dick. And this is how he is always going to look. His mother has the body of a twenty-year-old, and his grandmother looks pretty damn good for an eighty-year-old woman.

If Terry does gain weight, if he's got some recessive fat gene that blows up someone in his family every tenth generation, I will dump him. For while I am not destined to be slim myself, I do require slimness in lovers. Yes, I am a goose-stepping (good for the glutes!), black-shirt-wearing (so slimming!) body fascist. I believe people should have to get permits before they go shirtless in dance clubs, and that no one over the age of forty should go shirtless in public regardless of the shape they're in. One of the reasons I no longer attend gay pride parades is the inevitable belly-dancers-of-size contingent proudly heaving their guts down the street in a misguided effort to combat antifat prejudice. If one of these dancers were to drop dead from heat stroke, and sooner or later one will, her belly will go on dancing for half an hour after she hits the pavement.

I say these cruel things with full awareness that I will one day be heavy myself, for it is my genetic destiny. I would not make fun of black people or the disabled unless I woke up black or disabled one day. But I feel that I can in good conscience make fun of fat people, because I will one day be hugely fat. My family gets fat in middle age, so it could happen any day now. Every joke is just my sadistic way of adjusting myself to the future state of my body.

And when the pounds come my way, I don't want people—especially other gay people, who can be so cruel!—to look at me and say, "Wow, Dan really let himself go. Can't he get himself to a gym?" I want them to say, "Dan's priorities have changed. He has children. He doesn't have time for the gym. He has more important things to do."

That's why kids.

★ ★ ★

There's one more reason we decided to have kids early in our relationship, rather than waiting until we'd been together longer. And I'm afraid that, like having a hobby and getting fat, it wasn't a very good reason. But I want to be honest about everything that's shaped our decision.

I write a syndicated sex advice column. One day I was minding my own business, writing my column, when along came an agent, an editor, and a book publisher. They offered me a book deal, and I accepted. I signed a contract, and then I cashed an advance check with a lot of zeros before the decimal point. The problem with the book deal was that I didn't have the faintest idea what I wanted to write a book about.

There are thousands of writers out there with books they've already written who can't get book deals, much less deals with fourteen-gazillion-dollar advances, and it must pain them to read that someone got a book deal with no book. I don't know what it's like to have a book already written that you can't find a publisher for, and I assume it's hell. But having a deal and no book has to be at least as hellish. The sun comes up, you think about your approaching deadline. You stare at the computer, which stares right back at you. "Why are you surfing porn sites?" your boyfriend says every time he walks into your office. "Don't you have a book to write?" Every time you leave the house a friend asks, "How's the book coming?" Every time the phone rings, it's your mother. "I'm not pressuring you," she says when she calls to pressure you. "I just wanted to know if the book will be out by Christmas so I can give it to people as a gift." Having a deal but no book maybe isn't the deepest pit in writing hell, but it's close, and anyway hell isn't a contest. In hell everyone suffers.

If being asked by your lover, friends, and family how the book is coming is hell, getting calls from your agent, editor, and publisher asking for the manuscript is dirty rotten stinking can't-sleep-at-night hell. Having a book deal and not a clue as to what you want to write a book about is like standing in front of an open trench. There are Nazis standing behind you— No, that's a little extreme. Let's just say there are very insistent people with German accents standing behind you. If you don't fill that trench with words, hundreds of thousands of them, then one of those insistent people with German accents (your agent, your editor, your mother, your boyfriend) is going to march up behind you and put a bullet in the back of your head, filling the empty trench with your dead body.

With the deadline trench yawning before me, I asked myself what kind of book the world needed from a gay man right now. I'm not a complete idiot—I did get a book deal, after all—and I had some ideas. But I had wasted so much time surfing porn sites that other gay men with book deals and better work habits were coming out with books I might have written if I could have pulled myself away from bigcocks.com. The "Gay men should stop having sex" book came out, followed by the "Gay men should move to the suburbs" book, followed by the "Gay man giving sex tips to straight women" book, and then the "Gay men should get married" book. Anyway, by the time I was ready to write, the books I might have written were all on remainder tables at Barnes & Noble. Except one. Some gay men were writing books saying gay men should get married and have kids, but none had actually done it themselves—had the kid and written about it. So, I sat down and started writing the "Gay man actually having kids" book.

There was this book deal, and there was this squandered advance, and there was an approaching deadline. And I really did want kids, and I had almost made kids with lesbians before the book deal, and then the boyfriend started talking about adoption, and, well, why not kill two birds with one stone? Adopt a kid, and write the book about adopting the kid. That way, I wouldn't have to pay back the advance and I would get to write off every expense associated with the kid forever.

So while the adoption would have happened without the book deal, and the book deal happened without the adoption, I can't say that the book deadline didn't move the adoption deadline up just a tad.

Put This Book Down

That last chapter wasn't very pleasant to write, so I can't imagine it was very pleasant to read. When you write about kids, convention dictates that you go all mushy and magical: miracle-of-birth, new-life-created-out-of-love, proof-of-God's-existence, blah blah blah. But there are always practical considerations, and as people get better about planning their pregnancies, more people, gay and straight, are applying a kind of *Wall Street Journal* hard-nosed cost-benefit analysis to timing when they have kids.

But let me emphasize this: the book deal that destroyed my carefree sex-columnist lifestyle (open the mail, read the letters, cash the checks) was not why were adopting. For the record, Terry and I began the "lifelong adoption process" before it even occurred to me that I could make it the subject of the book I was contracturally obligated to write. I need to write this to avoid offending the kid Terry and I will wind up adopting. Even when children are brought into this world as a result of practical, less-than-magical reasoning, or when children are brought into the world by accident, their parents usually don't share that info with them. Our kid would, we hoped, be able to read eventually, and if this book was one day required reading in all American high schools—as it should be—he would run across it, and one day be exposed to information that most kids are spared.

"My father never loved me," he'd tell his therapist one day. "He just adopted me because he spent his advance."

So you'll forgive me if I do something I swore I wouldn't when I decided to write about becoming a dad. I'm going to address my as yet unborn child, assuming that he can read.

Sweetheart, if you're reading this, rest assured that I was kidding when I wrote that last chapter. Kidding and drunk. Don't believe me? Ask your other father. We wanted a kid before I got a book deal, though once I decided to write about how we got you, kiddo, we moved your adoption to the front burner. Deadlines are deadlines, after all.

My advice for you would be not to read this book. It can be hard to put down a book that's all about you. God, for example, likes to have the Bible read to him every Sunday in church, as you would know if we had ever taken you into a church, and he never seems to tire of it. If you insist on reading this book, I'll understand. But take everything in it with a grain of salt, just as I assume God takes everything in the Bible with a grain of salt.

This advice I'm giving you—to put the book down and slowly back away from it—comes from experience. You see, my mother, your Grandma Judy, kept a journal all through 1964, the year she was knocked up with me. Her journals were never published, but I did manage to find them while digging around in her dresser. I stole them and read them, and it was a mistake. I learned things that I didn't need to know and things I would have been happier not knowing, risks you're running by reading this book.

For instance, my parents had sex, with each other, and quite a lot of it. For years before I found my mother's journals, I'd suspected my parents were sexually active, but I had no proof. Having my suspicions confirmed, in my mother's handwriting no less, was too much for my fifteen-year-old head! Suspecting something is different than reading all about it, especially in the same handwriting that signed "Mom & Dad" to all my birthday cards. Even more disturbing than the news that my parents had sex was reading about my parents having sex while my mother was pregnant with me.

But most disturbing of all was reading that my mother and my couldn't-keep-his-filthy-paws-off-a-pregnant-lady father were hoping and praying that the baby she was carrying—me—would be a girl. My parents already had two boys (your uncles, Billy and Eddie), and Mom and Dad wanted a girl this time. Mom lit candles, said Hail Marys, and buried saint statues upside down in the backyard. I guess my father had read somewhere—*Esquire*? *Everything You Always Wanted to Know About Sex (But Were Afraid to*

Ask)? Field & Stream?—that if he screwed Mom while she was pregnant—over and over again—this would turn me into a girl.

Now, back when I found my mother's diary, I was just beginning to understand that I might be gay; I was a little too excited whenever the Hardy Boys got tied up on TV. Not knowing what made boys gay, I wasted a lot of time wondering if I was gay because Mary, Mother of God, was only half-listening to Judy, Mother of Dan, when Judy prayed for a girl. Or because my mother had buried Saint Jude facing the wrong direction. Or because Bill, Father of Dan, had endowed me in utero with a taste for what he was giving my mom every damn night. Reading my mother's journals led me to believe I might be gay because of some Catholic technicality, or as a result of floating in a pool of my father's semen for nine months.

I know now that it wasn't Mary or Judy or Bill that made me gay, but genetic predisposition, Catholic school, high-tension wires, and sitting too close to the TV. But I could have saved myself years of anguish had I respected my mother's privacy and not read her journals when I was fifteen. So, kid, you might be be better off if you didn't read this book. Just as I learned things about my parents I didn't need to know, there are things you'll learn about your dads from reading this book that you'd be better off not knowing. Like about those Polaroids, or how your other father once looked like Kate Moss with a dick.

If you put this book down now, you won't get to the chapter in which I discuss your father's and my sex life in detail. Being able to live your entire life in denial about your parents ever having had sex is a distinct advantage that you, the adopted child of two gay men, have over biological children raised by straight parents. Bio-kids can't live in denial forever about their parents' sex lives, because they're living proof their parents had sex at least once. But you, kiddo, you can live out your days without having to wrestle with the mental image of Daddy crawling on top of Daddy and drilling away, provided you put this book down before you read this paragraph.

Open and Closed

Negotiations with Lesbian Couple and Lesbian Single were just starting to fall apart when I first learned about open adoption. I wasn't immediately interested, being convinced at the time that the commingling of gay and lesbian genetic material was a beautiful, transformative, progressive notion, and an appealingly subversive way in which to breed. But a good friend felt differently. When I told my lawyer, Bob, that I was trying to get a lesbian pregnant, he said, "Why would you do something so stupid?"

Not the reaction I'd anticipated.

Bob didn't have anything against lesbians, the commingling of gay and lesbian genetic material, or progressive or subversive notions. As a lawyer, Bob had something against legal nightmares, which he was sure this plan of mine would become. When he got it out of me that I wouldn't be the legal parent, just a donor-dad, that the lesbians would have custody but that I would get to be "involved," Bob promised me we would all wind up in court.

"What happens if they want to move out of state or out of the country?" Bob asked. "You're all friends now, but what if you have a falling out and they decide not to let you see 'their' child anymore? What if they want to send your beloved offspring to a vegan anarcho-syndicalist commune in Eastern Nevada? What if they break up? How are you going to work out custody and visitation among three adults? And if the lesbians die in a car accident or a plane crash, who gets the child? You? Their families? Some other lesbians?"

I confessed that I hadn't given any of these issues much thought.

"Well, give them some thought. If you do this, be prepared to take your lesbian friends to court, and be prepared to spend a buttload of money to win the right to see your kid."

"I don't think we'll wind up in court," I lamely offered.

"No one ever thinks they're going to wind up in court. But when people do stupid things, that's just where they find themselves. Don't do this," he implored me. "If you want kids, adopt."

I promised Bob I'd think about adoption, and decided I wouldn't tell him about my recent talks with our next-door neighbor.

Bob and his wife, Kate, have three kids. When Bob and Kate had difficulty getting pregnant, their first impulse was to head to a fertility clinic. After one unsuccessful, intrusive, stressful, high-tech procedure (involving Dixie cups), they figured they weren't able to make bio-kids, accepted their infertility, and didn't waste more time by extracting eggs or implanting fetuses. First they adopted Lucy, and then, just after bringing home their second child, Gus, Bob and Kate discovered they weren't infertile after all. Kate very suddenly got very pregnant with Isobel.

Months later when I finally lost patience with the lesbians and things with our neighbor fell apart, I asked Bob for more information about adoption. Where had he and Kate adopted Lucy and Gus? What agency did they go through? Was the agency any good? How much did it cost? Did he think the agency would work with a gay couple?

"I know they've placed kids with lesbians," Bob told me, "but I don't know if they've managed to place any with gay men." The only gay couple he knew who had attempted to adopt through the agency "had a disruption," agency-speak for having an adoption fall apart at the last minute. This was a newish agency, founded in Oregon, and Bob had helped open a branch in Seattle. It was organized around a radical new way of doing adoptions, and Bob felt confident they'd want to work with us.

"Open adoption may not be as subversive as gay men and lesbians making babies," Bob said, "but it's still pretty subversive."

Open adoption? I'd never heard the word adoption qualified before. Adoptions were adoptions, I thought, and all adoptions were alike. You could adopt at home, go overseas, go through an agency, go through a lawyer, or go through the state. A woman who couldn't take care of her kid handed it over or had it taken away; then an agency or the state handed her kid over to a straight, married, middle-class couple. The records were sealed, the woman was encouraged to forget she ever had a kid, and when or whether to tell the kid it was adopted was left to the straight, married, middle-class couple to decide. That's adoption. Openness only came into play if an adult adopted child wanted her records unsealed, or if she went looking for her biological parents.

"Open adoption means the adoptive parents know their kids' birth mothers," Bob explained. "The birth mom picks the adoptive parents from a pool of wannabe adoptive parents. We know Lucy and Gus's birth mothers. They met us before deciding to place the kids with us. They can visit us and the kids; we have an ongoing relationship."

Open adoption sounded a lot more complicated than what I had wanted to do with lesbians. It sounded more complicated than even my deal with the next-door neighbor. The birth mom chooses? She comes to visit? What if she's a drunk or a drug addict? Won't the kid be confused? What if she wants her kid back?

Bob listened to my questions, told me I had it all wrong, and invited me and Terry over to dinner. He and Kate would explain things for us.

A week later, over pizza, Bob and Kate told us about open adoption.

In an open adoption, the birth mother selects the family her kid will be placed with out a pool of prescreened couples. Then the agency introduces the birth mom and the couple. If they hit it off, the agency helps them come to an agreement about the amount of contact they're going to have after the adoption takes place. Everything is negotiable. The agency works with the birth mom and the adoptive couple on an adoption agreement that sets out a minimum number of visits per year. If a birth mom wants more contact than the adoptive couple does, she's not the right birth mom for that couple. Before the adoption goes forward, the agency makes sure the birth mother and the adoptive couple are on the same page. Doing an open adoption ensures the birth mom an ongoing relationship with her child. She doesn't have to pretend she never had a baby or that her baby died, as birth moms who do closed adoptions are still encouraged to do. Ironically, while the subject of visits is a touchy one initially for the adoptive couple, Bob and Kate told us that it's usually the adopting couples who want more contact once the adoption is final.

Fears about birth moms using drugs or showing up trying to reclaim their kids are rooted in false assumptions about the kind of women who give up their children for adoption.

"They say that women who have the least to offer as parents are likelier to keep their kids," said Kate, who is also a lawyer. "Women who see that they have a future and who have something they want to accomplish in life, they're the ones who tend to place their kids for adoption. Women with little to look forward to tend to keep their kids. What else have they got, who else to love them?"

"But what if the birth mom sees the baby and decides she wants him back?" asked Terry.

"Apart from the fact that birth moms have no legal rights to have their kids 'back' once the adoption is final, women who place their kids in open adoptions are much less likely to *want* them back," Bob said, picking up another slice of pizza. "Women who don't know where their children went, who adopted them, or how they're doing are the women who wind up regretting doing an adoption."

"Think about it," Kate said. "You're a woman, you're pregnant for nine months, you feel this little person growing inside you, you go through the incredibly emotional experience of giving birth and seeing your baby emerge from your body. If you chose closed adoption, your baby disappears. All your life you're going to wonder, 'Is my baby okay? Is my baby happy? Who are his parents?' The only way you can ever answer these questions is by trying to get him back. In open adoption, the birth mom can come and see that her baby is okay, and go on with her life. She is empowered by her decisions and soothed by the information she has about where her baby is. She knows, she doesn't have to worry. This isn't to say that there is no grieving or even remorse. But the birth mom doesn't have to deal with her emotions in a vacuum."

I asked if open adoption confused their kids, Lucy and Gus.

"No, it only confuses adults," said Bob.

And a two-minute conversation with five-year-old Lucy and three-year-old Gus made it clear that they weren't confused. They knew they were adopted. They knew who their birth-parents were. They knew who their real parents were. And they knew the difference.

At the seminar in Portland, we were learning more about open adoption, but thanks to our dinner with Bob and Kate, we had a leg up on some of the other couples in the room. Still, we had some things to learn.

A lawyer who specialized in adoption spoke on the first after-noon, and we learned that open adoption was legal in only three states: Oregon, Washington, and New Mexico. For an open-adoption agreement to be legally binding, either the birth mom or the adoptive couple had to live in one of these three states. Birth moms and adoptive couples in other states had drawn up open-adoption agreements, but these were not legally binding.

"The birth moms in these cases have no legal recourse, as their adoption agreement is just that, an agreement, and not a legally binding contract," the lawyer said. "There have been cases of adoptive couples entering into open-adoption agreements, sign-ing the papers, and then disappearing with the baby. These adop-tive parents will, I hope, spend an awful long time in hell."

The mood in the room was not much more relaxed than it was at the start of the day. The only couple sitting at the table that didn't seem so fragile that a loud noise could shatter them were Jack and Carol, who were sitting to our left. They were quick to laugh at the small jokes the lawyer made during his presentation and, sensing that we, too, had a sense of humor about this, they smiled at us conspiratorially.

The lawyer went on. In most states, before an adoption could be finalized, the agency had to make a good-faith effort to find the birth dad if he wasn't in the picture. Once he was found, the agency had to convince him to sign away his rights, which in most cases wasn't a problem. But some birth dads threw a wrench in the works.

"Birth fathers who deny consent aren't required to raise the baby themselves, and the child can wind up in legal limbo, not wanted by his biological parents and yet not adoptable, either. It's a real problem in most states—but not in Oregon."

Oregon's adoption laws were radically different from those in most other states. If a birth dad wasn't around, if he wasn't providing emotional and financial support during the pregnancy, under Oregon law he had already signed away his rights. The law in Oregon recognized that guys have orgasms and women have babies. Ignorance of pregnancy was no excuse: if a birth dad wasn't aware that the woman he'd screwed was pregnant, that was an indication he didn't have much of a relationship with her. Again, he had an orgasm, she was having a baby. Being present at the moment of conception didn't entitle a guy to much in Oregon.

"The best-case scenario," the lawyer told us, "is that the birth mom who picks you lives in Oregon—or, if she lives in Washington or another state, that the birth father is supportive of her decision to adopt."

Unfairly, if a woman decides to keep her baby, that guy who only had an orgasm could wind up making child-support payments for eighteen or twenty years. If the law in Oregon were consistent, guys should have had the option of accepting or rejecting paternity. That would have required a change in the law, which would have opened politicians to charges of being soft on deadbeat dads, so the law wasn't likely to change. My impartial advice to guys having one-night stands in Oregon would be to have them with other men.

As a consequence of eliminating the birth-dad problem, Oregon was widely considered the best American state in which to adopt. Those high-profile adoption disruptions of the last few years (which resulted in kids being taken from the only homes they'd ever known) were the result of birth fathers surfacing after the kid had been adopted. The twin specters of Baby Richard and Baby Jessica haunt couples adopting children, which is why when you flip through adoption magazines you'll see agencies advertising themselves with this line: "We specialize in Russian, Chinese, and Oregon adoptions."

After the lawyer's presentation, some birth mothers were going to visit the seminar. Before they arrived, one of the agency's "adoption specialists" talked with us about the kind of women who put their children up for open adoption.

"Adoptive parents tend to confuse women who have their children taken away from them by the state with women who make the choice to place their child for adoption," said Jill.

We weren't supposed to say "put their kids up for adoption," we learned. This expression was frowned upon in adoption circles, as it comes from the practice of loading orphaned urban children onto "orphan trains" and sending them out of cities and into rural areas to be "adopted." When an orphan train arrived at a station, the children would be placed up on a platform for farmers to look over. Children who looked like they'd make good farmhands were "adopted," and the rest got back on the train and headed for the next station.

"Culturally, there's a great deal of prejudice against women who place their children for adoption," Jill continued. "Anyone who's doing an adoption should rid themselves of these prejudices, but it's especially important for people doing open adoptions to root them out, since you will be in contact with your birth mothers."

The couples in the room asked the same questions of Jill that Terry and I asked of Bob and Kate months ago. What if the birth mom is a drug addict? What if she wants her kid back? Won't the children be confused?

Jill explained that women who place their children for adoption usually have a lot going for them:

"They've imagined futures for themselves, and a child doesn't fit into their plans at the moment. Playing a role in selecting a family for their child is powerful. The woman doesn't feel that she abandoned her child, or acted irresponsibly. Open adoption is about honesty, and about what's best for birth moms and their children.

"Open adoption means ongoing contact between birth mom and child, and between birth and adoptive families. Openness means no lies, and an adopted child who doesn't grow up wondering who his 'real' mom or dad is, or why they gave him up. If the child has a question about why his birthparents couldn't raise him, he can ask his birth mom."

The agency believed open adoption was the best option for

adoptive couples, too, though not everyone in Lloyd Center's conference room seemed convinced.

Adoptive couples were the only people who lost something, and what they lost was a measure of control and autonomy. "Traditional" closed adoption only came into being about fifty years ago, when adoption laws were rewritten all over the country. What had been open (and in many cases informal) arrangements were regulated and "closed," with records being sealed to protect adopted children from the stigma of illegitimacy and single pregnant women from the stigma of premarital sex. Even now, when an adoption was finalized, the court permanently sealed the child's original birth certificate and issued a new one, with the adoptive parents' names listed on it as "father and mother." This was how it was done everywhere, even in progressive Oregon.

("I want to be listed as the father," Terry whispered. "You're the one with birthin' hips." If we'd been alone somewhere and Terry had taken my hips in vain, I'd have punched him in the shoulder. I wasn't sure how hitting would play in a room crawling with social workers who'd be assessing our fitness to parent, so I had to kick Terry under the table instead.)

Closed adoption also provided adoptive parents with something not every adoptive couple wanted though some did. Closed adoption made it possible for adoptive parents to pretend the child they'd adopted was their own biological child, and for many years adoptions were arranged to match the looks of adoptive parents and their adopted children to facilitate this pretense. Closed adoption made allowances for lies.

Needless to say, this was not something Terry and I could have taken advantage of even in a closed adoption. If we got our families and friends to play along, we could fool the kid for a few years, or longer if we home-schooled, but even the kid would catch on sooner or later. Two men can't make a baby.

But I could take comfort in knowing there was one fundamentalist Christian out there who thought Terry and I should be able to raise our children believing they popped out of our butts. I was interviewing a woman in Seattle who was trying to get books about gays and lesbians out of the schools. She felt homosexuality was something that only parents should discuss with their children, and that it was up to parents whether a child ever even learned that such things as homosexuals even existed. I pointed out that she was arguing for the right of parents to keep their children ignorant; she responded brightly, "That's right, I am. That's my right as a parent. My children shouldn't know things I don't want them to know."

I told her I was about to become a parent. Should I have the right to raise my child in complete and total ignorance of "such things" as heterosexuals?

"Oh, yes. You see, this isn't a gay or straight issue, or a Christian issue," she said, reaching for common ground. "This is about parents' rights. If you have children, you should raise them how you see fit. If you don't want your children to know about heterosexuality, you shouldn't have to teach them about it."

To make the telling of lies possible, the birth mother naturally had to disappear. Terry and I couldn't hide heterosexuality from our child if this woman was coming around asking to see her baby. Some women who placed their children for adoption through the agency did want to disappear, and were only doing an open adoption because they wanted a hand in selecting the family that adopted their baby.

"They care about their kids, and want them to be happy and well taken care of, which is why letting them play a real role in shaping their kid's future is just so right. Most of the women who come to this agency tell the counselors that if they couldn't do it this way—pick the family, have ongoing contact—they wouldn't place their kids for adoption. Some would raise them themselves, but most indicate they would have an abortion before doing a closed adoption."

When abortion was declared a woman's constitutional right in 1973, the number of children available for adoption plummeted. Abortion is a tough choice for some women, but so is carrying a baby to term, giving birth, and then being told to pretend your baby died or didn't happen. Perhaps there are women who can walk away from a baby, and not wonder all their lives where that baby is or how it's doing. At least if she has an abortion, a woman doesn't have to wonder. She knows. Why pretend your baby "didn't happen" when you have the option of actually making your baby "not happen"?

★ ★ ★

We took a break, then listened to a presentation about the mountains of paperwork we'd all have to do in order to adopt. We learned about the home study and the other hurdles we'd have to jump before we could join a pool of couples for birth moms to select from. Then two birth moms were shown in and took seats at the conference table. We'd been talking about birth moms all afternoon, so actually laying eyes on two of them was like having Madonna and Cher join us.

The paranoia that plagued me earlier in the day had subsided, and I was feeling pretty at ease. We'd had a chance to ask a few questions, make eye contact with the other couples in the room, and be taken seriously. I wasn't feeling like one of "the gay guys," but more like one of nine wannabe dads. Until the birth moms opened their mouths.

"It was so important to me to find a family that would bring my child up a good Christian," said one. "Yes, that was important for me, too," said the other.

They said other stuff, too, stuff about finding adoptive couples they felt comfortable talking with, the amount of contact they wanted, how important it was to them to play a role in shaping their child's future, how wonderful it was to have a relationship with their child, how neither had ever doubted their decision, and how both regarded their biological children's adoptive parents as the "real" parents. None of that mattered, of course, because all I heard was that "Christian homes" were important, and important to both birth moms. Terry and I were wasting our time.

During the next break, Terry and I rented skates, tossed our shoes in a locker, and went around and around Lloyd Center's ice rink. We were quiet for a few minutes.

"Maybe we should go home," Terry said. "We know lots of single lesbians. Let's see if one wants to be a surrogate mom. No birth mother will ever pick us."

"Paying someone to be our surrogate mom will probably cost less than doing an adoption," I responded. "Did you see the fee schedule?"

"I think we're kidding ourselves being here," said Terry.

Before I could answer, Carol and Jack waved us over to the side of the rink.

"You two are so lucky," Carol told us. Terry and I looked at each other, and then asked her what she meant. "You're so differ-ent! Everyone in the pool is exactly the same. Everyone's white, suburban, middle-class, and straight. You guys will stick out, birth moms are going to notice you in the pool."

"Yeah," said Jack. "You two will get picked before anyone else."

DG Kids

If Carol and Jack were wrong—if we weren't picked right away or if we never got picked at all—Terry and I had other options. Talking with Bob and Kate made quick converts of us, and we'd come to view closed adoptions as unfair to birth mothers and adopted children. That meant traditional closed agency adoptions were out. But if we weren't picked by a birth mom in an open adoption, we would have to consider some other route to parenthood. We could do a foreign adoption, but we'd have to be "discrete," i.e., closeted, something neither of us do well. Or we could adopt an abused or neglected kid from the state, some poor kid languishing in foster care, and attempt to undo the damage done by the kid's biological family. We called this route, indelicately, our damaged-goods adoption option.

Without exception, children in the custody of the state were abused or neglected by their heterosexual parents. When straight parents beat, rape, or abandon their biological children, the state steps in. If the kids can't be returned to their biological parents, the state goes looking for homes for these kids. In adoption-speak, these kids are called "hard-to-place" or "special-needs." They are hard-to-place because most couples doing adoptions want the same thing: the Great White Infant. Couples want a healthy baby, one without emotional and physical scars. DG kids are generally not healthy, often not white, and by the time their biological parents have been stripped of their rights, they're usually not infants. When Terry and I started talking about adoption, we concluded that—as shameful as it sounds—we wanted the same kid everyone else wanted. We weren't hung up on race, but we wanted that healthy infant.

But when you read in straight newspapers about gay couples who've adopted, it's almost always a damaged goods adoption: Good Gay Couple plays foster parents to Damaged Goods Kid, nurses DG kid back to health, and having grown attached, moves to adopt DG kid. GG couple saves DG kid from the system. The subtext? If not for the GG couple, this DG kid wouldn't have a home at all, so . . . if gay men aren't taking optimal babies (healthy white infants) from optimal homes (straight white parents), why not let the fags keep the baby? Gay men are damaged goods, too, so why shouldn't they settle for damaged goods?

Admitting we were just as selfish as every other straight couple trying to adopt wasn't easy. Besides the ease and relative rapidity, there were other perks to adopting the DG kid: First, it's tremendously good karma, and that has to count for something. Also, gay men are constantly told we're morally inferior, so any opportunity to claim a chunk of the moral high ground would be tempting. In addition to being told we're morally inferior, gay men are accused of being a danger to children. Adopting a child endangered by straight parents would allow us to refute that particular lie more dramatically than any citation of child abuse statistics demonstrating that it's straight-identified men who sexually abuse children, not gay-identified men.

Not too long ago, a Good Gay Couple made news in New Jersey. GG couple wanted to adopt Adam, a DG kid born addicted to drugs, with lung damage and heart problems. GG couple had been Adam's foster parents, and under their care, Adam made a remarkable recovery, and wasn't a really a DG kid anymore. Then GG couple sued for the right to adopt Adam as a couple rather than going through the expense of doing separate single-parent adoptions. The court ruled in their favor, placing gay couples in New Jersey on the same legal footing as straight couples (which already was the law in Oregon and Washington, and other states). After their victory, "Good Gay Couple Adopts Damaged Goods Kid" stories ran in papers across the country.

Christian conservatives weren't pleased by the news about Adam, but it was difficult for them to argue that gays were a danger to kids when two gay men were fighting to adopt a kid no one wanted—especially a kid that had been so spectacularly endangered by his heterosexual parents. So when the anti-gay

Family Research Council spat out a press release about Adam, there was nothing in it about gay men being a danger to children, or morals, or gerbils, or anything else. Instead, there was only a deep concern for little Adam.

"A child placed with two fathers will never be able to call out the word, 'Mom,' " said FRC cultural studies director Robert Knight in the FRC's press release. While conservatives are typically opposed to the creation of new rights, the FRC read a brand new "right" into the Constitution: the right to a mommy. "The state is abrogating that child's right to a mother for the rest of his life."

When Elizabeth Birch, head of the gay-rights group Human Rights Campaign, adopted twins, Jacob and Anna, with her girl-friend Hilary Rosen, the Family Research Council spat out an-other press release, this time complaining about children being denied their right to daddies. "Placing babies in a lesbian house-hold deliberately deprives these children of a father's love. . . . What kind of image of manhood and fatherhood will little Jacob obtain being raised by two lesbians? How will little Anna, who will never know the love of a father, relate to men someday?"

There are many arguments Christian conservatives could make against gay adoption—Leviticus, Romans, Timothy—but the one they're opting to make these days is this every-child-has-a-right-to-a-mommy-and-daddy argument. Yet plenty of healthy chil-dren are raised in environments where they never get to call out "Mommy" or "Daddy." Children are raised by their grandparents or aunts or uncles; they're raised by single dads and single moms. No FRC press release was issued when my next-door neighbor adopted a little girl who will never know the love of a father. The FRC isn't really all that interested in making sure every child has one parent of each gender. They're interested in preventing gays and lesbians from enjoying any of the rights straight people take for granted, and, of course, raising money by scaring little old ladies in Omaha with nightmare visions of children brought up in creepy, queer single-sex environments: little Adam's play group meeting in a gay bathhouse; little Anna having her hair braided by shirtless wimmin at the Michigan Women's Music Festival.

Children adopted by gay or lesbian couples may not get to call out "Daddy" or "Mommy," but they don't grow up in a single-gendered gay universe either. Gay men have mothers, sisters, and aunts; we have female friends, coworkers, and neighbors. Lesbians have fathers, brothers, and uncles, male friends, coworkers, and neighbors. Conscientious gay parents, like conscientious straight single parents, take steps to ensure their children have male and female role models.

Opposition to gays and lesbians becoming parents isn't about kids, of course, it's about politics. While it's currently illegal for gays and lesbians to adopt only in Florida, the Christian right has pushed for bans on gay adoption in Texas, Indiana, Utah, Oklahoma, and Arizona. Governor of Texas George W. Bush went on the record in support of a ban on gay and lesbian adoptions in Texas, saying he believed "a traditional home with a mother and a father present should be the first choice for a child in need of home." At the same time Bush endorsed mothers and fathers, Jeanne Shaheen, governor of New Hampshire, signed a bill repealing her state's twelve-year-old anti-gay adoption ban. Undoing the gay adoption ban "was good for New Hampshire and good for our children," Shaheen said. On gay adoption, America could quickly break down into slave states and free states.

Yet while gay adoption garners less support in public opinion polls than gay marriage, passing anti–gay adoption laws will be harder than passing anti–gay marriage laws. The Defense of Marriage Act, passed in 1996, prevented hypothetical marriages from occurring some time in the murky future. But gay adoption isn't hypothetical: gay men have been adopting children for years; lesbians have been adopting and making babies forever. The National Adoption Information Clearing House, a federal agency, estimates there are between six and fourteen million children being raised by gays and lesbians. A fight to ban gay adoption would not be over hypothetical children and optimal homes, but a fight over real children in real homes. The question wouldn't be, "How will kids do in gay homes?" but instead, "How are kids already in gay homes doing?"

The limited research that exists shows that kids with gay or lesbian parents are doing fine. They're just as well adjusted as kids with straight parents, just as likely to identify themselves as straight when they grow up, and just as likely to have positive relationships with other children. There isn't much of a measurable difference. Since gay men and lesbians don't have children by accident—it's hard to get drunk one night and do an adoption, or slip and fall into the stirrups at an artificial insemination clinic—all our kids are wanted kids, planned for and anticipated. All parenting experts agree that a wanted child is usually a loved child, and a loved child is a well-looked-after child.

In deciding to push ahead and do an open adoption—or try to, anyway—Terry and I decided against the DG adoption option. It takes a special kind of parent, we were told, to adopt a child with a physical or emotional disability. We weren't sure for how long the satisfaction of sitting on the moral high ground, knowing that we were better than abusive straight parents, would keep us going. There's always the chance you'll adopt a child who's fine, like Adam, or a child who can be repaired, but there's a chance you'll wind up with a kid past help, one who can't be fixed. We didn't want to start parenting at a disadvantage, not with our first kid. We didn't want to adopt a kid someone else had messed up. No, we wanted to mess up a kid all by ourselves.

And if we did an open adoption and went for that healthy infant, maybe Robert Knight and the Family Research Council would leave us alone. If their opposition to gays adopting is really just about depriving children of their right to a mommy and a daddy, Knight and the FRC could take some comfort in what Terry and I were trying to do. Whatever child we would adopt— provided we got picked—would have a relationship with his birth mom. He'd get to call out "Mommy," and he'd know a mother's love. Knowing the FRC would be on our side made us feel a little bit better about pressing on with open adoption.

So what if we weren't going to be the Good Gay Couple? We were going to be a Selfish Gay Couple and go for that healthy infant, and if that made us assholes, well, we had a lot of company— most of it straight. I felt tremendously guilty about all of this, naturally, and reminded myself that even the healthiest of infants can become a DG kid in a moment. One fall from a swing, one moment alone in a bathtub, and we could find ourselves raising a child with severe disabilities. Should this happen, we would, like good parents, rise to the challenge. But we wanted to start even, though we knew there was no guarantee we would stay even.

Friends and Family

Telling friends and family that we'd decided to adopt was harder work than we thought it would be. We were unprepared for the most common reaction: "Why?" Instead of giving the long answer over and over again (lesbians, next-door neighbors, lawyers, birth moms, etc.), I'd just answer, "Because it's illegal to steal children," or "We need a hobby." I told a few friends the truth: "I want to get fat." Now when people ask I say, "Buy the book."

"Why?" is not a question straight people having kids are required to answer. Everyone understands why straight people have kids: they get drunk, they get naked, they get pregnant, and someone has to milk the goats or be the next King of England. You're having kids 'cause that's what straight people do. We don't call you breeders for nothin'.

Straights who don't want to breed, or are unable to do so, are the ones who have some explaining to do. My brother Billy, who doesn't want kids, has to explain himself to our mother three or four times a week. Mom had some therapy in the late seventies, which left her convinced that everything means something other than what it appears to mean. To Mom, the fact that her firstborn doesn't want kids of his own means something, and the obvious answer (Billy doesn't like children) simply won't do. If Billy doesn't like kids, it means Billy didn't like being a kid, which means he didn't like how he was raised, which means he must be angry with his parents, which means he needs therapy. Billy isn't at all unhappy and doesn't want therapy. But to therapy fans, personal happiness is not proof that someone doesn't need help. In the hands of a trained professional, my brother could discover that he is deeply unhappy.

Both Terry's family and mine are constituted almost entirely of straight people, but our families had different reactions to the news that we were setting out to become parents. I come from a large, loud, downwardly mobile, urban Irish-Catholic family. I have about two dozen aunts and uncles at any given time (depending on who's divorcing whom at the moment). I have three thousand cousins, one useless grandparent, two brothers, one sister, two parents, two stepparents, three stepbrothers and -sisters, and four stepcousins. Letting all these people know I was going to adopt would take too much time and effort, so I told my mother and let her spread the word.

At first Mom was a confused.

"What happened to the lesbians?"

I explained that the lesbians weren't sure if they wanted kids after all, and I didn't want to wait. My mother suggested we see a therapist, "to talk things over," before we went ahead, and I assured her we'd be talking things over with the counselors at the agency. Fifteen years ago, when I told my mom I was gay, she didn't suggest therapy. She told me a joke. Our late-night exchange went something like this:

"Mom . . . I'm gay."

"Really? Did you hear what happened to the woman attacked by two gay men in the park?"

"No, Mom."

"One held her down, the other did her hair."

She seemed to take the news rather well, but two days later she had a little breakdown. She'd always thought I would make a good father, and now that I was gay, I would never get to parent (her verb, not mine). Luckily for Mom, she managed an office for a bunch of shrinks back then, and was able to get counseling gratis. Since my adopting undid the only thing that pains my mother so far as my homosexuality is concerned, she was thrilled by the news and started signing her letters "Grandma Judy."

My brothers and sister and stepfather, Jerry, were also thrilled. Billy was mostly thrilled because the more kids his siblings have the less pressure he's under to breed. My sister Laura loves kids, and wants very badly to have kids of her own, but has yet to meet a man who meets her high Oprah-influenced standards. She's always dumping some very nice guy who worships the ground she walks on because he doesn't "love himself enough to be in relationship." Until she meets the man who loves himself to pieces, I fear, Laura will remain single. My mom told her the news, and she promptly called Terry and offered to fly out and baby-sit whenever we needed her to. She was hoping we'd get a girl, and was excited about becoming an aunt.

Not that she wasn't already an aunt. My brother Eddie has a son named Mars. My nephew lives in Montana with his mother, Eddie's ex-wife. Eddie married during a short stint in the Air Force (hence Mars, for the Roman god of war). After the divorce, Eddie moved home to Chicago. Staying in touch with Mars has been difficult, and my mother doesn't get to see her grandchild as much as she would like. Eddie was happy for me and Terry, but he called up to warn us.

"You don't know what you're getting into, bro," he said, laughing. "Kids are great, but man, they're a lot of fuckin' work."

Terry's family seemed to have doubts, not that they would communicate those to us. While my family communicates too much and too loudly, Terry's family communicates too little. Terry was raised in Spokane, a small town with a large desert on one side and Idaho on the other. Like good Episcopalians, Terry's parents had two children and then stopped. Claudia, Terry's mother, remarried after his father died, and Terry's brother, Tom, joined the Promise Keepers not long after we met. Terry's relatives, in contrast to mine, are quiet, deliberate people, who think long and hard before they speak. Coming from louder, more opinionated stock, at first I found the funeral-parlor ambiance at Miller family gatherings unnerving. Having dinner with Terry's family is like having dinner in the "Modern Humans" diorama at the natural history museum: nobody says much or makes any sudden moves. While I've gotten used to it, the first time I met Terry's mother, her silence spooked me.

Meeting the mother of the boy you sodomize is one of those situations in which homos are likely to interpret silence as disapproval. After ten minutes of Terry's mother staring at me—

unsmiling, unblinking—I was convinced that she hated my boy-buggering guts.

My family is aware that silence can be interpreted as disapproval, and they don't want to seem disapproving. My family was so noisily welcoming whenever I brought a new boyfriend home that some left with the impression that my family strongly approved of my being sodomized. A few got the impression that my family, especially my sister, would approve of my being sodomized right in front of them.

After a few more visits with Terry's mom, it became clear that she *did* approve of our relationship. Terry's mom, like his brother and his stepdad (Dennis), are just very nice, very quiet people, and my relationship with Terry's mom continues to evolve. There was one unfortunate setback when I used a metal spatula on one of her nonstick pans, but we've managed to put that behind us and rebuild. Anyway, after our first meeting, things had nowhere to go but up. Claudia and Dennis like to fish, and they recently shipped us two hundred pounds of halibut, caught by Claudia on a trip to Alaska. Our freezer is filled with fish. She may not have much to say, but she has made it clear she doesn't want us to starve.

When Terry told his mother that we were adopting, he wasn't sure what to expect; he thought she might be excited by the idea of grandkids. But Claudia only said, "Oh." She didn't ask any questions about how we were adopting or when. We weren't sure how she felt, but she seemed underwhelmed by the idea.

A few months later, when we were in the middle of the paperwork, the annual Miller Christmas newsletter arrived. Terry's mother wrote at great length about her oldest son. Tom was getting married the following June to Pam, a very nice woman he met at his fundamentalist Christian church. Reading the newsletter, you learned that Tom was very happy, that his fiancée was very sweet, that they met six months ago, that they became engaged after just three months, and that everyone was very excited about the wedding. On and on, for four paragraphs.

As for Terry, "Terry works in a bookstore, and enjoys his job." That's all. Nothing about the guy Terry has been with for two years, nothing about the fact that we're adopting a child. Maybe we could have snagged a line or two in the newsletter if we were adopting a Promise Keeper. When the Christmas newsletter went out, we'd already done the weekend seminar, and were hard at work on our paperwork. Claudia knew we were getting close to acquiring the kid; she had even written a letter of recommendation to the agency.

Maybe she wanted to surprise folks with the news of our baby in the next Christmas newsletter, but not even Terry thought that. He believed the letter was a subtle communication from his mother. She disapproved. When someone "isn't very verbal," you read their feelings into their actions, and this was an omission that spoke pretty loudly. Terry was upset, but unwilling to ask Claudia about it.

"It wouldn't do any good, and it would make her feel bad," he said.

"The letter made you feel bad, so why not talk to her about it?" I asked.

Terry thought for a minute.

"When she sees the baby, she'll come around."

Our friends, gay and straight, were supportive. But some of our older gay and lesbian friends were mystified that we would want kids at all; when they came out, kids were a spring in the heterosexual trap. A few looked on having children as a betrayal of gay and lesbian liberation. A gay male friend in his sixties told me that he's amazed by the demands made by younger gay men and lesbians (he means anyone under fifty), and he worries that some of us may go too far, demand too much, and create a backlash that harms all of us. When he was young, all he wanted was the right to suck dick without having to worry about getting arrested. When I first told him we were thinking about adopting, he looked like I'd announced we were moving to Jupiter.

A gay academic friend jokingly accused me of adopting a "heteronormative" lifestyle, and a gay Communist accused me of selling out.

The other objection we've heard from some homos is that my boyfriend and I are not the kind of gay men who should be adopting. When word of our plans went out in Seattle, a local gay activist/idiot called me: Had we given any thought to the political aspects of what we were doing? He felt Terry and I should wait. It was important, he said, that gay people adopting right now be safe and unthreatening. Gay parents should be men in their forties, together at least eight years, monogamous, professional, irreproachable, and unassailable. With the religious right making an issue of gay adoptions, gay dads were going to be under a lot of scrutiny. He felt it was important that they be as unthreatening to straight people as possible. Gay men like me and Terry, gay men closely identified with "the urban gay lifestyle," should wait.

Most of my friends involved in gay politics have been very supportive; few would suggest that a gay person wait to do anything out of deference to the religious right. But more than one person told me we weren't the kind of guys who should adopt. You know, for political reasons. I'd written too much, and too frankly, about my sex life. The religious right wants to ban gay adoption, and is probably looking for gay parents it can use to scare those little old ladies in Omaha.

Until the first really juicy example of an evil gay parent comes along, the first gay dad or lesbian mom to rape or kill their kids, the religious right will have to make do with whatever "unfit" gay parents they can find. Of course, straight people rape and kill children every day. Child abuse is so common that unless the circumstances are unique or compellingly gruesome (six-year-old beauty queen, heavy-metal prom night, kids tossed out windows), the deaths of children at the hands of their straight parents hardly make the papers. And naturally, they're never held up as examples of the unfitness of heterosexuals to parent.

But for gays and lesbians, having children, like everything else, is regarded as a privilege, not a right. And privileges can be taken away.

Misrepresenting Our Relationship

We left the seminar in Portland with everything we needed, except confidence. We had a stack of forms to fill out, and should we decide to pursue open adoption even though most birth mothers seemed to want Christian homes for their babies, we had a stack of checks to write. Unlike most agencies, ours does not demand a lump sum up front but instead staggers payments over time. This makes the cost less burdensome, according to the head of the agency, making it possible for po' folks to adopt. But adoption's still expensive. The seminar cost $350. Next up was the Application Fee, $600, followed by the Family Preparation & Homestudy Fee, $2,175. Then there was the Pool Entry Fee, $3,080, and, if a birth mother picked us, the Adoption Mediation & Planning Fee, $4,650. If we got the kid, there was a Placement Fee, $2,100. The agency fees would add up to $12,455, but the fee schedule warned additional costs: "travel, medical expenses, legal fees, and birth-mother adoption-related living expenses when appropriate and desired by all parties." We could expect to spend somewhere between $13,000 and $15,000.

Looking at the payment schedule, it was hard not to get the feeling we were buying a baby on the installment plan.

We also left Portland with a stack of handouts. The most helpful, though not in the way the agency intended, was "10 Reasons Not to Adopt a Child." I read it aloud to Terry as we drove out of Portland ("Never to return, hopefully," said Terry), and from it we learned what not to say in any of our upcoming meetings with agency counselors. For example, we shouldn't say we'd been growing apart and hoped a child might bring us closer together, or that we wanted someone in our lives who had to love us. And we shouldn't say we wanted a child so he could accomplish things in life that we hadn't, and we shouldn't say we were adopting because we felt sorry for orphans. There was nothing in "10 Reasons Not to Adopt a Child," however, about adopting kids because you wanted to have a hobby, prove a point, or get fat.

Our next appointment was a final intake interview. A week after the seminar, we sat down in a small office with the agency's Seattle-based counselor, Marilyn. Marilyn told us that the agency was willing to work with us, that we seemed like good candidates for open adoption, and that she was sure there was a birth mom out there for us. As we left, she advised us to get cracking on the paperwork.

And there was quite a lot of paperwork to crack. In addition to a homestudy written by the agency, we would have to fill out application forms, compile health histories, sign releases for financial information, authorize criminal background checks, obtain letters of reference, and write our autobiographies. The end of the seminar was really just the beginning of the paperwork. During the home study, an agency counselor would come to our house, sit down with us, and ask us what the hell we thought we were doing. If our relationship outlasted the paperwork phase of the adoption process, our final act before entering the pool would be to write a "Dear Birthparent . . ." letter.

When it was time for a birth mom to select a family for her baby (after she was six months pregnant and had had some counseling), she was given "Dear Birthparent . . ." letters to review. Writing our letter, Bob and Kate had warned us, would be the hardest part of the paperwork. Each birth mother got a personalized set of the "Dear Birthparent . . ." letters. That way, if she was carrying a multiracial child, she wouldn't be shown letters from couples not interested in adopting such a baby. The birth mom then picked out one or two couples from the "Dear Birthparent . . ." book and got their home studies to read, as well as their autobiographies. She then selected one couple. The agency called the couple, set up a meeting, and introduced the birth mom to her first-choice couple. The birth mom or the couple could say no; when that happened, the birth mom moved on to her next choice, and the couple went back in the pool. But if the birth mom liked the couple, and the couple liked the birth mom, three months later they adopted her kid. Simple.

It wasn't always that simple, though. Sometimes women contacted the agency from the hospital after they'd given birth. In these cases, "Dear Birthparent . . ." letters and an agency counselor were hustled over to the hospital. The birth mom picked a family, and the counselor called and asked the couple if they wanted to take this child. If you did a hospital placement, you didn't get to meet the birth mom before the birth, which was a drawback. You were going to be in touch with this woman for the rest of your life, so compatability counted; also, she hadn't had any counseling and might not be completely comfortable about her decision to "make an adoption plan."

"Once your paperwork is finished, your home study is done, and your birthparent letter is written," Ruth told us during the seminar, "it's pretty much out of your hands. Once you're in the pool, the average wait is about nine months. Some couples have waited as long as two years."

Apparently, the wait could be stressful: along with "10 Reasons Not to Adopt," the agency gave us another handout listing ways couples could keep from going crazy while waiting in the pool: redecorate; travel; read; learn to bake. What you weren't supposed to do, however, was buy baby furniture, diapers, or booties, or decorate the nursery. Looking at an empty nursery every day for two years could drive a couple crazy. Since all indications were that Terry and I would have to wait a long time, we decided not pass the time we were in the pool painting bunnies on the ceiling of our spare bedroom.

"Anyway," Ruth told us on the seminar's first day, "everything you need for the first few weeks, you can pick up on your way home from the hospital."

But before the hospital, there was the home study; a counselor from the agency would visit our home, ask us questions, and write up a report for the agency and the state assessing our fitness to parent.

I didn't mind the idea, but it was clear at the seminar that the straight couples minded it very much. In the first Q&A session most of the Qs were about the home study: how it was conducted, how intrusive it was, what the agency was looking for, were they trying to "bust" couples, how often did couples fail. Ruth assured us that there was nothing adversarial about the home study, and that while they would be visiting us at home and asking a lot of personal questions, they weren't out to "bust" anybody. There were no unannouced visits, no white-glove tests, no poking around in drawers or closets. And as for personal questions, they couldn't be avoided. The agency would have to vouch for us the state and our birth moms, and to do that they would have to get to know us.

It seemed sensible that before the agency handed anyone a kid, they'd have someone drop by and ask a few questions. It would be in everyone's best interests for the agency to make sure we had smoke alarms, indoor plumbing, and a good reason for wanting a baby. Likewise, if we had pentagrams painted on the walls and dead chickens scattered around the living room, well, the agency might want to take that into consideration. The home study made sense to me.

But I'm not straight.

I haven't lived all my adult life with the expectation that when I decided to have children, only one other person would be in on the decision. Terry and I didn't regard having babies as our inalienable biological right. Even before we decided to adopt, we were having to answer a lot of questions from the people who could've made us dads: lesbians and next-door neighbors.

But the straight couples had expected to make the decision to have kids with absolute autonomy. When they tried to get pregnant and couldn't, they sought out fertility treatments. They lost some physical autonomy, and judging from what some of the couples subjected themselves to, they lost a little dignity. But they were still in charge, and when and how they had kids was still a decision they got to make.

When they gave up on bio-kids and started the process of adoption, the loss of any sense of autonomy must have come as a shock. The agency called all the shots, and unlike doctors and insurance companies and functioning reproductive systems, the agency made you prove you were fit to raise children before they'd help you have a baby. You had to open your home, your bank accounts, your criminal record, and your skulls for agency inspection. And in open adoption, the birth mother called the final and most important shot: she decided who got her baby.

Fertile couples have complete autonomy. They can have as many pentagrams and dead chickens as they like, with no agency standing in judgment. They can prove themselves unfit *after* having a baby, but no one tells fertile straight people they can't have babies in the first place. Twelve-year-olds have babies, insane people have babies, drug addicts have babies, dirt-poor people have babies, drunks have babies, people who've had their babies taken away from them have more babies. None of these people would get through an adoption agency's home study. Only adoptive parents have to prove themselves fit. For the couples at the seminar, this double standard heaped one more insult on the pile of injuries and indignities of infertility.

Our home study was more complicated than we thought it would be. It wasn't one visit at home with an agency counselor, but four: one visit with both of us present, one visit each alone with the counselor, and a follow-up home visit with both of us. After we sent in our completed application, we got a call from Ann, who was going to do our home study. The day before our first appointment, Terry and I took steps to deceive Ann, misrepresent our relationship, and conceal the truth about our living arrangements.

We cleaned.

Terry's a slob and so am I. We don't live in filth; there's no rotting food in our fridge or black slime growing around our toilet seat. But we do let things pile up. We don't hang our coats up, we don't throw newspapers away when we're done reading them, and our bedroom is basically a dresser, with dirty and clean clothes piled up on the floor. Pretty much every flat surface in our apartment was covered in change, receipts, notes, clothes, books, and empty shopping bags. The place was a mess, and we liked it that way. It was comfortable. We worried, though, that the agency wouldn't like it, so we decided to clean up just a little bit before Ann was supposed to come over. It was probably anxiety, but we wound up cleaning things that no one but my mother and other obsessive-compulsives would even think of cleaning. We washed the windows, rolled up the carpets, and swept under the rug. We dusted the plants. When Ann walked in, our living room looked like a showroom at Ikea.

Ann was an older woman, fifty-ish of the radiant variety. She wore chunky amber jewelry and elegant earth-toned clothing. She had an open, honest face, and complimented our taste in, oh, everything before she'd even sat down.

"Oh, this is nice. Where did you get this?" she said, picking up a large crucifix I keep on our coffee table. Ann wasn't the kind of person that anyone would feel comfortable telling lies to, and after a few short minutes we broke down and confessed.

"We're not this neat," I said. "Usually the place is a mess."

Terry glared at me.

"We would be neater, but Dan's a slob and I don't like picking up after him." Terry lied. He's at least as much a slob as I am, and if anyone picks up after anyone, I pick up after him. If he cares to dispute this, he can write his own book.

"Oh, you don't have to be neat to be good parents," Ann broke in. "In fact, the opposite is often the case. Well, let's talk. Why do you fellas want to adopt?"

"Well, Terry and I have been growing apart," I said, looking serious, "and we think a baby will bring us closer together. And I'm hoping a child can accomplish the things we didn't, and we feel sorry for orphans."

Ann looked a little stunned, then laughed out loud. She'd read "10 Reasons Not to Adopt," too. Terry apologized, but Ann said there was no need.

"Usually when I ask that question, the answer is a very sad story, and there are tears. Most couples don't have a sense of humor about adopting at this point, so this is a nice change of pace.

"But now, down to business. What are your real reasons?"

We told Ann about the lesbians, the next-door neighbor, and the long road that brought us to open adoption. We even told her about wanting a hobby. Ann was open, and so were we.

But we did wind up telling Ann a lie. We couldn't avoid this one, since we'd already told it to a room full of people from the agency. When we went around the table introducing ourselves at the seminar, I said Terry and I had been together three years.

During our first home-study meeting, when Ann asked us

how long we'd been together, I looked at Terry. We left the seminar feeling as if we hadn't needed to lie about how long we'd
been together, but we'd already done it. I felt bad lying to Ann,
but we had already told the head of the agency we'd been together three years, and we couldn't change our story now. How
long had we been together?

"Three years," said Terry. "We've been together three years."

"How did you meet?"

Terry and I looked at each other, and there was a long pause.
We both must have blushed, because before either of us could say
anything, Ann said, "Well, there must be some wonderful story
about how you met."

We told her everything: the gay bar, the drag queen, "You've
got a pretty mouth," and the bathroom. Ann loved it.

Rutherford B. Finger

I'm bent over an examining table. Behind me, the great-great-grandson of a nineteenth-century American president snaps on a rubber glove. We've arrived at the business end of the full and complete check-up required by the agency—complete with full digital penetration. The agency wants some assurance I won't drop dead the day after the kid arrives, and my prostate gland apparently holds the answer to that question.

We adopters must have cash on hand, health insurance, smoke alarms, friends and relatives willing to vouch for us, a roof over our heads, and, most important, the ability to fill out forms and enclose checks. The finger is yet another way in which we are required to prove ourselves worthy and breeding couples or singles are not.

Now here I am, ass cracked open, waiting. We've already looked in my ears, checked my eyes, listened to my heart, and reviewed my health history. Now, the deluge: Dr. Finger, having pulled on one rubber glove, starts talking to me in hushed and soothing tones. This-lubricant-may-feel-cold, you-may-experience-some-slight-discomfort, we'll-take-it-slow.

Less highly evolved readers probably assume that I'm digging this—that for gay men, any opportunity to stick something up our butts is welcome. While I can now brag that I've been fingered by an American president's great-great-grandson—how many people can say that?—a rectal exam is not my idea of a thrill. Being gay does not mean you enjoy anal penetration at all times and under all circumstances. Personally, I don't enjoy rectal exams or colostoscopes any more than straight women enjoy speculums or suction abortions.

Gay men do *fear* the finger less than straight men, though. After all, we're not worried a prostate exam will make us gay. We arrive gay.

I'm still bent over at the waist, ass cracked open, and all I want—all I really, really want—is for Dr. Finger to stop reassuring me and get the fingering over with. I would like to pull up my pants. I don't enjoy being naked, not in front of strangers—not even in front of Terry. Exposing myself like this is not working any sex magic for me.

But it *is* bringing back memories. . . .

The first time I had a finger in my ass was also a less than magical experience. One day in July 1979, when I was fourteen years old, I started having cramps. About an hour later, I started bleeding. Buckets of blood were pouring out my ass, filling the toilet as fast as I could flush it. I should have called in the Feds—Mom and Dad—right away, but I stalled, hoping the bleeding and the cramps would just . . . stop.

As I sat on the toilet bleeding to death, I wondered what could be wrong. Nine years of Catholic education kicked in: this had to be the result of something I'd done. Could just thinking about getting fucked in the ass do this? Had I harmed myself? Or was God punishing me? He was my heavenly Father, and I was his child, but I'd been jerking off a lot lately. Maybe my heavenly Father was firing a warning shot.

But when I did think about doing things with my butt—bad things, things that might anger my heavenly Father—it was always with dread. I understood I was attracted to men, but I didn't really want to be this way. I didn't *really* want to get fucked in the ass. When I masturbated about it, about getting fucked in the ass, it always happened in circumstances where I couldn't stop it from happening. I would be taken by force, against my will. I was never a willing participant in my late-night masturbatory fantasies, so why was God punishing me? I was the victim!

Or maybe God had me all figured out. It's not as if I was doing a very good job of fooling myself. Somewhere, deep down, I knew that as much as anal sex might repulse me, I was masturbating about getting fucked in the ass because getting fucked in the ass was the logical, if wrath-of-God-provoking, implication of my desires.

When I first figured out that I was gay, the thought of a guy touching me *back there* revolted me. I was attracted to other boys, but I was not immune to the cultural prejudices that my family, friends, and classmates swam in—I was soaking in them, too. Being attracted to boys meant I was going to have to sleep with gay men. And gay men were boofooing, fudge-packing butt pirates. If I was going to be sleeping with gay men, I would have to learn how to do this disgusting thing. I didn't have to *like* the idea of anal sex, and I was sure I never *would* like it, but the gay men I would sooner or later be sleeping with would expect it of me. And so, to acclimate myself to the idea, I jerked off thinking about it.

So sitting in the toilet, bleeding, I figured I was being punished. But I'd also jerked off thinking about the blow jobs I would be required to give. Why couldn't God curse me with bleeding gums instead?

I started making deals. Maybe if I promised never to think about my mother's best friend's son kissing me, God would stop the bleeding. So I promised. Maybe if I swore to throw away the *Playgirl* magazine I'd hidden in the basement, the bleeding would stop. So I swore. Maybe if I solemnly vowed to jerk off about girls and only girls from now on and forever after, amen, God would stop the bleeding. I solemnly vowed.

But the bleeding didn't stop. When I started feeling faint, I called in the Feds.

"Mom?"

I told her I had the shits. She took one look in the toilet and screamed, "Jesus Christ!" I'd tried appealing to him already, but Mom didn't know that. She did know this wasn't the shits, not even ambitious "bloody stool." This was serious. She asked when it had started, and when I told her three hours ago, her jaw dropped. Why hadn't I called her right away? "I don't know," I muttered. Had the blood been coming out of my nose, or shooting out of my eyes, if I'd had a sunburn or a hangnail, I would've screamed for my mother right away. But screaming "Look what

my ass is doing!" seemed as good as screaming "Guess what I've
been thinking about doing with my ass!" In my mind, there was a
straight line from my ass to my secret.

Soon we were on our way to the hospital.

Now, let's remember that this was 1979. At the time, my father
thought Anita Bryant was a right-on sister, and my mother was a
lay Catholic minister. I didn't think the your-third-son-is-a-fag
news would go over well with the Feds. All the way to the hospital,
I kept wondering what my mother was thinking. No man had
been anywhere near my ass, nor had I done any what's-this-gonna-
feel-like probing on my own. If what I'd read about homosexuality
in my parents' copy of *Everything You Always Wanted to Know About
Sex (But Were Afraid to Ask)* was at all accurate (it wasn't, not at all),
my first boyfriend (whom I would meet in a bowling-alley bathroom) would expect me to give it up, so I had contemplated fingering myself, but I couldn't bring myself to do it.

My mother was sitting beside me in the ambulance, holding
my hand and smiling. I worried that her smile meant she was
connecting the dots between my wanting to see the national tour
of *A Chorus Line* on my thirteenth birthday and my bloody ass.
My mother wasn't stupid, as she liked to remind us.

At fourteen, I lived in a constant state of panic; the monotony
was broken only by moments of terror. Fear of discovery ruled
my life. My bloody ass wasn't my first fear-of-exposure moment.
I'd been caught looking at underwear ads, staring at older boys in
locker rooms, and watching *Solid Gold*. At a party a couple of
months before my ass started to bleed, I found a copy of *Playgirl*.
The party was at a bad girl's house when her parents were out of
town. She'd invited the entire St. Jerome's Teen Club over to
drink beer and make out. On the way to get another foul-tasting
beer, I spotted it. *Playgirl*. In the dining room, on the floor, almost
under the table, partly obscured by the tablecloth. My first impulse was to grab the magazine and run, but if a gay adolescence
leaves you with anything, it's an ability to squelch first impulses.
My first impulse in freshman swim class was to get a boner, but
did I let that happen? No.

The magazine could be a trap. Someone might have put it
there to see who'd pick it up. Two or three of my awful peers
could be watching from inside the kitchen, or hiding under the

dining room table, ready to jump out. The girls would chant,
"Faggot! Faggot! Faggot!" while the boys beat me up, and I
would have to go home and blow my brains out.

I was cautious. For an hour, I cased the dining room. I tallied
heads and tried to account for everyone at the party, to make sure
no one was missing and possibly hiding under the table. I peeked
inside cabinets. It wasn't a trap, I finally realized, it was an opportunity. So I did the bravest thing I had ever done in my life up to that
point: I dropped my coat on top of the magazine. Two hours later,
I topped that act of heroism: I picked up my coat—and the magazine—and walked out the front door. I was trying to look cool.

I probably looked like I was having a seizure.

Getting that magazine out of the bad girl's house was only the
beginning of my troubles. I lived about eight blocks from the
bad girl's house, and it was a short walk home. But what if I got
stopped by a cop? I mean, I looked pretty guilty sneaking down
the street with a magazine under my shirt. If a cop stopped me, he
would find the magazine—and he would probably know my father. I slunk down side streets, terrified. Once I made it home, the
first thing I had to do was find a hiding place. Well, actually, the first
thing I had to do was masturbate. The centerfold was an oiled-up
guy with lots of body hair, sweaty-looking balls, and a really ugly
mustache. Not my type at all, but he was naked and I wasn't supposed to have this magazine, and that was exciting enough.

When I was done, I looked around my bedroom for a spot
where the magazine, and my secret, would be safe. Soon I found
the perfect parent-proof hiding place: I slid the magazine between my mattress and box spring. For the first few weeks the
magazine was in my possession, all I could think about was where
I'd hidden it. Was someone going to find it? What if there was a
fire, and the firemen pulled my mattress out the window, the way
they'd done when a house down the street burned down? They
would find the magazine. Or what if, for some reason, the Feds
looked under my mattress? Soon, I couldn't concentrate on anything else. It got so I couldn't leave the house; if anyone went
near my room, I would run in and lie on my bed. I was a nervous
wreck.

Now, I knew my brothers had porn hidden in their rooms,
too, magazines that they didn't want the Feds to find, either.

While I'm sure those mags caused my brothers some low-level anxiety, their suffering couldn't compare with mine. If the Feds discovered my brother's magazines, at least they were filled with pictures of naked ladies. Billy's and Eddie's mags didn't give them away as perverts. Oh, they might be punished, but they wouldn't be *found out*. In fact, about this time, my mother found *Playboys* in Billy's room. As she lectured him at the dinner table, my father said, "Well, at least they're pictures of girls."

The anxiety of keeping that magazine in my room soon over-whelmed me. So one day, when no one was home, I removed the magazine from its hiding place in my bedroom, sneaked across the hall, and hid it in my sister's bedroom. If it was found in there, Laura would get in trouble—mere trouble—but Mom and Dad wouldn't think she was a pervert. I could hear my father say, "At least they're not pictures of girls." Getting Laura in trouble was a risk I was willing to take.

But Laura's room wasn't a very good hiding place, either. My sister slept in her bedroom, which limited my access.

I considered hiding it in one of my brothers' rooms, mixing it in with their other porn mags. But what would happen when my brothers found it? They would figure it was mine, and take it straight to the Feds. So I opted for the basement. At first, it seemed there were a million places to hide my *Playgirl* magazine in the basement, but almost everywhere I looked someone had some occasional cause to poke around. My mom was always coming down and "organizing" things. Shelves were stacked with stuff my father used around the yard. But there was one place no one but me knew about. It could only be a temporary hiding place, but it would get me through the summer. The furnace—an enormous old cast-iron monster with a two-foot-wide iron door—was creepy, but it would do. The heat wouldn't be coming back on for months, by which time I would find a new hiding place. I opened the furnace, leaned in, and laid the magazine on the flat metal surface beneath the unlit burners.

When my mother and I arrived at the emergency room, the nurse on duty turned out to be my aunt Peggy's best friend. More panic: I was sure she'd be on the phone with my mother's sister in no time. "Your effeminate nephew is here—the one who wanted to see *A Chorus Line* on his thirteenth birthday. His ass is bleeding like someone stuck something in it."

My father wasn't at the emergency room. He might have been at work, or maybe he was away, or maybe he figured he had sons to spare. I don't remember, but considering what was about to happen, wherever he was, I'm glad he wasn't in the emergency room with Mom and me. After the nurse filled out her forms—bleeding profusely from the anus, check; brought this on himself, check; going to hell, check—the intern on duty came in. And he was beautiful. Guest-star-on-*The-Love-Boat* cute, with straw-blond hair, dark eyebrows, and a jaw made for clenching. He wore V-neck scrubs with no shirt on underneath, and when he leaned over me, pressing on my stomach, I could see down his shirt. He asked my mother some questions, she answered them. He was concerned, he said, very concerned. This wasn't *normal*. The cramps could indicate appendicitis, but the bleeding was not *normal*, not *normal* at all, not even with a burst appendix. Just not *normal*.

I wanted to die.

I wanted to die before the beautiful intern said, "I'm going to have to check . . . inside." Mom nodded, and the doc—the handsome *Love Boat* doc—pulled on a rubber glove and walked to one side of the bed. I'd probably lost fifteen or sixteen gallons of blood at this point, and I was still having cramps. I wasn't sure when the next gush was going to come shooting out of my ass, but I was praying it would happen before the beautiful intern got his finger in me, and I would be dead before he could "check inside."

The same folks who think I should enjoy Dr. Rutherford B. Finger poking around my ass as an adult will also think that I was secretly thrilled at the impending loss of my fourteen-year-old third-base butt-cherry to the *Love Doc*. Wrong. I was hoping I would just bleed to death so I could go home. In a box.

But things weren't going my way. The Love Doc rolled me on my side. I started to go into a panic-attack meltdown: *Did* I stick something in my ass and forget about it? What if I did it in my sleep and left it up there? He pulled my shorts and underwear down *to my knees*, exposing my rear to him and my full frontals to mom. More cramps. I was now in a white-hot panic. Delirious, I convinced myself there was something in my ass—a chair leg,

Legos, a Number 2 pencil. He'd stick a finger in, pull out a Lincoln Log.

The panic must have shown on my face—I mean, how could it not? I could scrounge up a closet-case poker face most of the time, but this wasn't high school gym. This was an exceptional circumstance.

My mother had been sitting in a chair on the other side of the room, low enough that I couldn't see her. But I guess she could see me, or she sensed how distressed I was, because she did something that, while it was well intentioned, I will never, ever be able to forgive her for, not if I live to be a hundred thousand years old: she stood up, walked over to the bed, took my hand, and looked me deep in the eyes with an expression of motherly concern on her face . . . just as the beautiful intern in the V-neck scrubs stuck his finger in my ass.

There was nothing in my ass, and I didn't have appendicitis. I had ulcers, dozens of bleeding ulcers in my colon. I was rushed to surgery, I was chopped up, and I lived. No one could figure out why I had ulcers, or why they were gushing blood the way they did, or why a nice, polite, calm, well-liked kid—so even keeled, so well mannered—would suffer from such stress-induced ulcers as I had. I was fourteen years old, my father asked when he got to the hospital, what on earth was I stressed out about?

Dr. Finger is still talking. I wish he'd stop telling me about it and just do it. He'll be gentle. When the day dawns that he does put his finger in my ass, would I be so kind as to push against his finger as if I were having a bowel movement? Okay, now we're going to start. . . .

Jesus, I wish the first guy who *fucked* my ass had been this considerate.

Dr. Finger is wasting a lot of tender bedside manner on me. He's probably violated hundreds—thousands!—of men in his career. But the vast majority of those men were probably straighter, older, and much more married than I am, the kind of men who've never had a thing in their asses that they hadn't chewed up and swallowed first. Exit types, never entries. I, on the other hand, have had things in my ass that would make a Thai bar hostess blush.

I look back at Dr. Finger and say, "Look, dig in, would you? I can take it."

And he's in . . . and he's past the sphincters, he's going deep . . . this way and that . . . and he's on my prostate . . . and he's out! It's over in less than ten seconds. He pronounces my prostate slightly larger than normal—wear and tear?—but healthy, nothing to worry about. While I get dressed, Dr. Finger fills out the form I brought with me from the agency: "Dan is in excellent health and would make an excellent parent."

Oh, incidentally, while I was in the hospital that summer when I was fourteen, recovering from surgery for my stress-induced ulcers, Chicago had a cold snap. The temperature fell to the low fifties. The furnace kicked in. I never saw my *Playgirl* magazine again.

The Susan Scenario

According to the agency, it was possible for a couple to go from seminar to pool in eight weeks if they were diligent about getting their paperwork done. We were not diligent. We kept our appointments with Ann, but the stack of paperwork sat on my desk, slowly disappearing under newspapers and magazines. It was on my desk because Terry felt paperwork was my responsibility, "since you're the writer." In the end I even wrote Terry's autobiography.

It wasn't until six months after the seminar that we turned in the next-to-last bit of paperwork and, shortly after Thanksgiving, sent off a package to the agency, along with another large check. Our backgrounds and finances and prostate glands had all checked out, and our meetings with Ann together and alone had gone well. Phase one of the adoption process, the paperwork, was almost over. Phase two, the wait, was about to begin.

We had only one thing left to do before we entered the pool. Well, two things: we had to write our "Dear Birthparent . . ." letter, and we had to write another large check.

Terry, as I've mentioned, didn't want anything to do with the paperwork. But there was some stuff he had to do alone and some stuff we had to do together. We had to write detailed family health histories, and there were forms to fill out about what level of "special-needs risk" we were willing to accept. I didn't want to make *that* call alone; but for months, we would say, "We have to get this stuff done," then never actually sit down and do it.

With the rest of the paperwork, the problem was me. Getting

letters of recommendation from our neighbors, for example, was a major stumbling block. We tried to beg off, explaining to the agency that we were *urban* people. The suburban couples the agency usually dealt with might be on speaking terms with their neighbors, but we were not. (Especially not with the one who'd asked to borrow a cup of sperm the day we moved in.) We'd lived in our courtyard apartment building for almost two years, and had made no effort to get to know our neighbors. We couldn't just ask them to write us a letter of recommendation.

We pleaded our case to Ann, who agreed that requiring a letter of recommendation from a neighbor might not be fair to urban people. She checked with the agency, but we had no choice. A letter of recommendation from a neighbor was required by law. There are things only the people living next door to you know. Letters from friends and relatives in far-off cities only tell the agency and the state that your friends and relatives like you. My mom wouldn't know if Terry and I shot guns off at night or sold crack out our back door, but our neighbors would. I sat down and wrote a note to our neighbors begging them for this favor. "All you have to do is write, 'Dan and Terry do not sell crack or shoot guns,' put your note in the enclosed stamped, pre-addressed envelope, and drop it in the mail," I wrote. "We'd be eternally grateful."

In the middle of the night, I stuffed my notes, along with envelopes and stamps, in our neighbors' mailboxes, and slunk back into our apartment. I didn't want to risk having to talk to our neighbors, and I wasn't sure any would take the time to vouch for us: Terry and I weren't exactly Mr. and Mr. Congeniality. Some of the folks in the building had little barbecues and impromptu dinners, and when we first moved in, we had to deflect a few invitations. We weren't interested in dorm living, and soon the invitations stopped. Now we crossed our fingers, hoping someone would do the neighborly thing, which was more than we'd ever done.

Seven of our neighbors wound up sending in letters, six more than we needed. We were the first couple in agency history to get seven letters of recommendation specifically noting that the people in question did not deal crack out their back door.

★   ★   ★

There was no waiting list at our agency. Once your paperwork, home study, and "Dear Birthparent . . ." letter were done, you were in. Some adoption agencies limited the number of couples in their pools to better the odds for couples who'd been waiting a long time to adopt. Our agency was committed to "maximizing the number of choices available to each birth mother," so there was no limiting the number of couples in the pool.

The final hurdle we had to jump was the "Dear Birthparent . . ." letter: five hundred words and a picture with which to introduce ourselves. We'd been warned at the seminar and by Bob and Kate that the letter would be the most difficult part of the paperwork, and when I finally sat down to write it, I learned they were right. What did we want to say? We'd been told in not so many words that a good birthparent letter could get you picked right away, and a bad one meant languishing in the pool.

The pressure was intense.

Once the letter was written, we would have it laid out on agency stationary, print five hundred copies, and deliver it to agency HQ in Portland. The agency didn't let birth moms pick adoptive parents for their babies until they were at least six months pregnant. Birth moms met with counselors and discussed all their options, including what help was out there if she wanted to keep her baby. If, after all these initial counseling sessions, the birth mom wanted to go ahead and pick a family, a special "Dear Birthparent . . ." book was assembled just for her.

Unable to get started on the letter, I called Bob and asked for his advice.

"You know, people worry too much about the birthparent letter," Bob said. "They say most birth moms flip through their books and wind up selecting adoptive parents without reading the letter at all. They take one look at a picture and say, 'That's them.' It's like they have a picture in their heads of the parents they want for their kid."

Bob's advice did not set my mind at ease. How many birth moms had a picture in their heads of two gay men? Who was going to look at Terry and me and say, "That's them"?

We'd been given an old "Dear Birthparent . . ." book at the seminar, and when I finally sat down to write our letter, I dug it out from under the stacks of paper on my desk and started flipping through. Everyone was so white, so middle-class, and oh so straight-looking that I felt as if I was back on Lloyd Center's ice rink. Maybe this was a waste of time. Talking with Ann during our home study made us believe this actually might happen; she was so upbeat and positive. But after five minutes looking at the pictures in our "Dear Birthparent . . ." book, I was having doubts. Maybe we should've gone to China, or offered a female friend the money we were paying the agency to have our bio-kid.

This was truly a waste of our time.

If looking at the pictures filled me with doubt, reading the letters themselves filled me with despair. Like the couples in the pictures, the letters were all remarkably similar. He worked; she didn't, or didn't plan to once the baby came. He liked to tinker on the car; she liked to garden. They lived in a big house in the burbs. They had a dog. And almost everyone seemed to be a close friend of Jesus Christ. "We are both Christians," read one letter, in a passage that could have been lifted from any of them. "And we're active in our church. We feel our faith affects the way we view other people and makes us more patient and understanding. Our children will grow up in a Christian home which emphasizes Christians values and faith."

What were Terry and I going to say? "We're both cynics, we're active in our bedroom, we believe Stephen Sondheim is a genius, have faith in Björk's next CD, and sometimes walk past churches?" Both birth moms who spoke at our seminar picked couples who shared their faith in Jesus Christ. Judging from them and from the letters in front of me, birth moms were going to take one look at our picture and flip past us without bothering to read our agonized-over letter. So why bother?

There *was* one same-sex couple in the book we'd swiped. The two women didn't blather on about Jesus, and Ann told us they'd been picked. Another couple in the book, straight, did a fair amount of spiritual blathering, a lot more than any of the Christian couples, but it was of the New Age variety: "We believe that we are one with the earth goddess, and that we are all on a mystical journey." Even this couple had been picked.

These were good signs, Ann assured us. We would be picked, too, "but not until you get that birthparent letter done."

We'd known going in that the agency had yet to do a successful placement for a gay male couple. There was one gay couple that got through all the paperwork, wrote all the checks, got into the pool, and was picked by a birth mom. Bob and Kate told us about them months earlier. Then at the last moment, after the baby was born, their adoption was "disrupted."

It turned out that Ann had worked with the men, too, and we brought it up during our final home-study meeting. Ann made a concerned face and dipped her head to one side.

"It was sad," she said. "The birth mother changed her mind, and the couple went back into the pool for a short time." Ann didn't remember all the details. "They seemed pretty angry about the whole situation, and it was sad for everybody."

The two guys whose adoption had fallen through happened to live in Seattle, and when they heard that Terry and I were thinking about adopting, one of them called me at work. Doug wanted to warn me about the agency. Their adoption fell apart when the birth mom's mother, a practicing Catholic, talked her out of giving her baby to a gay couple. Birth moms have the right to change their minds, but if the birth mom wavers after the baby is born, an agency counselor is supposed to be on hand to walk her through the original decision to place the child for adoption. The agency respects the birth mom's right to change her mind, and drills it into adoptive couples that they must respect that right. But immediately after the baby is born, most birth moms have a moment of doubt, and may forget the reasons why they didn't think they could keep their baby. The agency is supposed to be there to remind them.

Doug told me that no one from the agency showed up when their birth mom's mother burst in screaming about Jesus.

"She gave birth at home, not in a hospital, and we were in town at a hotel. She'd already called us and said, 'Your son is healthy, he's beautiful.' She said she would call the next day, and then . . . nothing. We tried to get someone from the agency to come down, but no one did."

Doug and his boyfriend had made the mistake of filling their house with baby stuff, decorating a nursery, and having a baby

shower. After their birth mom told them "their" son was beautiful and healthy, they called their friends and families to announce
they were dads. When they came home without the baby, they
had to get on the phone again, calling everyone they knew to tell
them they weren't dads after all. Some of their friends had already
sent gifts, and they dreaded the mail coming. And they had to
walk past the empty nursery every day.

"It was like we had a child and he died. It tore us both apart,
and our relationship didn't survive." Six months after the adoption was disrupted, Doug and his boyfriend broke up.

This was a very bad sign.

With bad signs outnumbering good, I was unable to write
our "Dear Birthparent . . ." letter. Instead of sitting at the computer writing the letter, I sat at the computer surfing porn sites.
I even shelled out cybercash for an AVS (adult verification system) I.D. so I could get into some really naughty web sites. Getting an AVS made me a geek in my boyfriend's eyes, but the
temptation of restricted web sites jammed full of dirty pictures
was too much for me to resist. As I shortly thereafter discovered,
most restricted web sites were full of photos I'd already found
on nonrestricted web sites, so I could have saved myself the
money and the geek status.

When I wasn't in front of the computer surfing porn sites,
Terry and I would sit in bed and talk about the baby. One night,
he rolled over and gave me a sad look. "I want to name our baby
after my dad."

I had thought of some names, too, but what could I say in response to *that*? I wanted to name the baby Morris, after my dead
cat. But the beauty of Daryl, Terry's father's name, was that it
would work for a boy or a girl. I gave in without a fight. Since
Terry got the first name, he let me pick the middle one. I chose
Jude or Judith, for my mother. Daryl Jude or Daryl Judith.

D.J.

It worked.

The last name was more problematic. Would it be mine, since I
was writing the checks? Terry's? How about D. J. Miller-Savage?
Or Savage-Miller? We put off making that decision.

Of course, there would never be a D.J. without a birthparent letter, which I was making no progress on. We did make an appointment to have pictures taken. In the photo we chose, we're sitting side by side, looking at the camera. Just like the lesbian couple we'd seen in the "Dear Birthparent . . ." book, we aren't touching. Most of the straight couples, by contrast, are draped all over each other in the "Dear Birthparent . . ." book.

So with all our paperwork done, our pictures taken, a name picked out, and our checks cashed, the only thing we were waiting on was the letter. We were waiting on me. But I couldn't write it.

"What if the one woman who *would* consider giving her baby to a gay couple is sitting in the agency's office right now?" Terry said, one night in bed. "What if we end up not getting a baby because we didn't get our letter in soon enough for her to see it? Write the damn letter!"

I got out of bed and sat down in front of the computer, determined not to get up until I finished the letter.

It was a very long night.

Someone once told me that when I was having trouble writing, I should get a clear mental image of one very specific person. Then I should write as if I were speaking to that person, and the words would come. Now when I'm stuck, I picture a person and . . . the words come.

But I couldn't picture a birth mother, and the words didn't come. I sat down in front of my computer determined not to get up and not to surf porn sites, until I finished. Trying to picture the girl I was writing for was impossible. My mind's eye had a hard time conjuring up the girl who'd turn a page in her "Dear Birthparent . . ." book, find a picture of me and Terry, and shout, "Yes, of course! Fags! I want to give my baby to fags!"

The girl who picked us would have to be politically progressive, not acutely Christian, and she'd have to be inconveniently pregnant. I could picture all that; I've known plenty of nice knocked-up hipster girls. The problem was, whenever I pictured a politically progressive, not acutely Christian girl who found herself inconveniently pregnant, it was hard not to picture her at an abortion clinic with her feet up in stirrups. Unable to conjure up a mental image of a birth mom who would choose life *and* fags, I started surfing through porn sites.

Nothing was coming. So to kill time, I wrote the definitive anti–"Dear Birthparent . . ." letter. Putting this letter in the "Dear Birthparent . . ." book would ensure that Terry and I never got a kid. Of course, we'd already been told very few birth moms actually read the letters, so what would it matter if we turned in a fake?

Dear Birthparent,

We are Terry and Dan. Yes, we are both men, and we would like to adopt your baby! If you have a problem with homosexuality, please know that we have a problem with teenagers who go out, get themselves knocked up, and then think they can sit in judgment over others. We have been with each other for three months. We hope to adopt a baby soon, as gay relationships don't usually last longer than six or seven months.

We are both atheists.

Dan is an overworked, undersexed sex-advice columnist. He is writing a book about adopting a baby, but we promise we're not doing this just for the fourteen-figure advance. Dan is fifty-nine years old, has heart trouble, smokes three packs a day, and will be the sole means of support for our little family.

Terry is seventeen years old and emulates Martha Stewart in every possible way, including Martha's emotional distance and passive-aggressiveness. After the baby comes, he plans on working a few hours a week in a bookstore that sells a great deal of homosexual pornography.

We live in a cramped apartment filled with dangerous and sharp-edged tchotchkes perched high atop unstable shelving units purchased at an Ikea seconds sale. We have a funky Brady basement, and a killer sound system that will blow our baby's head off if we're not careful! In our kitchen, Terry bakes pies and cookies in effort to make Dan so fat no other gay man will want him.

Our home is near a large park frequented by homosexuals in search of anonymous sexual encounters. There our child will enjoy many hours of unsupervised play. Most of our friends are in the music industry and addicted to hard drugs. They are all very excited about baby-sitting! As most of them use only heroin and not dangerous hallucinogenics, the odds that one of them will pop the baby into the microwave are pretty low.

Dan will be too busy to say hello to the baby until he is old enough to fetch his morning *New York Times*. Terry will be the primary caregiver, and not letting the baby die will be Terry's top priority! Allowing the baby to die would reflect badly on gay men everywhere, including those gay men in the park having anonymous sex, and would harm the sales of Dan's book. Especially if the baby died during the book tour.

We are looking forward to becoming parents, though we don't like the idea of changing diapers. We welcome frequent visits, so maybe you could come over and change the baby's diapers. We hope to provide a home full of love where a child can grow and thrive in an atmosphere of wonder, stability, and respect, but we know this probably won't happen.

Dan & Terry

While I was working on our anti–"Dear Birthparent . . ." letter, a picture of a girl who might give her baby to fags popped into my head.

Susan is sixteen years old; her parents are fundamentalist Christians. Susan gets pregnant, and her parents refuse to allow her to have an abortion. They insist that Susan choose life. Susan can't raise the baby herself and has no interest in marrying the baby's father. She was sleeping with him only because her parents hated him, not because she found him at all attractive. Giving her baby to her parents to raise was not an option. They were willing, but Susan wouldn't condemn the kid to a childhood like the one she'd suffered: home-schooling, Christian summer camps, prayer meetings, youth retreats. Susan decides to put her kid up for adoption instead. Short of the increasingly popular infanticide, what choice does she have? Her parents give their blessing.

By some miracle, this politically progressive, inconveniently pregnant sixteen-year-old girl contacts our agency. A counselor assembles a "Dear Birthparent . . ." book for her. Flipping through it, she finds our picture. Three months later, Susan gives birth, and we adopt her baby. "Mom, Dad," Susan says when she gets home from the hospital, "I GAVE IT TO FAGS! I HOPE YOU'RE HAPPY! YOU WOULDN'T LET ME HAVE AN

ABORTION, SO I GAVE YOUR GRANDCHILD TO FAGS! FAGS!"

For Susan's parents, giving the baby to fags is the only thing she could have done that is worse than having an abortion. They would have preferred to see Susan give their grandchild to a couple of wolves to raise. This being my fantasy scenario, Susan's fundamentalist Christian parents get so worked up, they both have strokes and die, and Susan comes to live with Terry, little D.J., and me.

The Susan Scenario, as I came to call our best hope, was deeply satisfying. Once we went into the pool, whenever we were asked who we thought might pick us, we laid out the Susan Scenario. We knew it would be better not to adopt a child given to us out of spite or in an act of adolescent rebellion, but if that was the only way we were going to get a baby—and it did seem likely that it would be the only way we would—we were ready and willing. We talked about Susan constantly, in hopes that repetition would transform our fantasy birth mom into a living, breathing, knocked-up sixteen-year-old with fundamentalist Christian parents, sitting alone on the sofa at the agency's office flipping through birthparent letters, about to turn the page and find our picture.

This was a girl I could write to. I sat laughing and saying, "I gave it to FAGS!" over and over, and a *real* birthparent letter finally flowed out of my pin head, through my fingers, and onto my computer screen. The letter is almost too sentimental and embarrassing to publish. Though my mental image was of a bad girl, our birthparent letter wound up being about as bland and inoffensive as any of those in our book. If you added a line about Jesus Christ and Photoshopped a girl into our picture, you wouldn't be able to tell it from any of the others:

Dear Birthparent(s),

We're Dan and Terry. We are very excited about adopting a child, and we look forward to building a healthy, respectful relationship with you, the child's birthparent(s). We are committed to the concept of open adoption, and welcome a high level of contact. We understand that the decision to place your child for adoption is difficult. We admire you for considering adoption, and would be grateful if you would consider us as possible parents for your child.

Dan is thirty-three years old and a writer. Terry is twenty-seven years old and works in a bookstore. Very early in our relationship we began discussing the possibility of starting a family. Before we met, Dan explored having a baby with some female friends, but decided against it, as he wanted to play a more active role than this would have allowed. When it became clear that Terry was also eager to have children, we began exploring our other options. When we learned about open adoption, we decided this was the route we wanted to take.

We live in a two-bedroom town house on a quiet street, close to parks, schools, movie theaters, museums, and playgrounds. We are city people, and any child we're lucky enough to raise will be brought up in a diverse and interesting urban environment. While we're comfortable in the home we're in now, we have started looking for a larger house, and hope to move at the beginning of next year.

We both come from large families. Our families are excited about us becoming parents. Dan's mother lives in another part of the country, but visits regularly, and Terry's mother lives nearby and visits often. Dan has three siblings, and Terry has one older brother, so there will be lots of aunts and uncles and cousins. We also have a large circle of close friends who want to help us in our new roles, and want to be involved in the life of our child.

We are voracious readers and are very excited about sharing our love of learning with a child. Terry has already started a collection of children's books. We spend most of our free time going to movies, concerts, and plays, or reading. We have traveled widely, and hope to travel with our child once he or she is old enough.

Dan's work keeps him very busy. Terry will be the primary parent, and will be staying at home to take care of the baby. While Dan's work keeps him busy, he sets his own schedule, and is able to work from home. We're excited about the challenges that raising a child will present, as well as the great joy that can come from parenting. We would love to hear from you.

Dan & Terry

Eesh.

★ ★ ★

A friend scanned in our photo, laid out the text, and printed our five hundred copies. Terry took the stack of letters to the bookstore where he works, packed them in a box, and shipped them to the agency. We forgot to keep a copy for ourselves as a souvenir. We sent another check to the agency, this time for the pool entry fee, and a week later a letter came in the mail. We were officially in the pool.

Now we had to wait.

It was two days after Christmas. We walked around a Baby Gap in downtown Seattle later the same day, admiring cute and inexpensive kiddie duds probably made by cheap child labor in far-off sweatshops. We tried to keep from buying anything, and wondered if we'd be in the pool longer than the nine months we'd been told was typical. Some couples waited as long as two years. I predicted we'd set a new record. Terry was more optimistic, predicting we'd wait about a year, maybe a little less. Either way, the itty-bitty flannel shirt we bought at Baby Gap wouldn't swaddle anything for a good long time.

When you'd been picked, the agency would call. If your birth mom was six months pregnant, you got two calls: that first "You've been picked!" call, and another one when your birth mom went into labor. The first call was to adoptive parents what "Congratulations, you're pregnant," is to bio-parents. The second was the equivalent of your water breaking; it sent adoptive parents rushing to the hospital.

On the other hand, you might get a call from the hospital, with no warning, and have to make an immediate decision about a baby that had already been born.

"Since being picked can happen at any time, day or night, this minute or a year from now," Ruth had said at the seminar, "every time the phone rings couples in the pool tend to jump." Waiting couples, we were warned, go a little nuts.

We wouldn't be like that, we told ourselves. Since we didn't expect to be picked for a long time, we didn't think we'd start getting jumpy until at least a year had passed. It would take a while for a Susan to come along, and we were sure we wouldn't turn into basket cases when we got in the pool. But from the day the letter came announcing that we were officially in, we were both a mess. Every time the phone rang our hearts stopped.

To help couples stay sane while they wait in the pool, the agency runs support groups. Unfortunately, we don't own a car and the Seattle group meets too far away for us to take the bus. Even if the support group had met nearby, or if we'd owned a car, we wouldn't have gone to many meetings. We're not the support-group type. Also, we'd misplaced the handout the agency gave us on things-to-do-to-keep-from-going-nuts-while-you're-in-the-pool. So we were really on our own.

Every time the phone rang, we glanced at each other. *Maybe this is it, maybe Susan picked us.* We could barely sleep at night, we were so excited. We would sit up and talk about where the crib would go, what we would do with D.J.'s room, what school he'd go to, how Terry's mother would get better about this. Taking the agency's advice, we didn't start putting a nursery together, buying baby furniture, or stocking up on diapers. We would have plenty of time to do that after the call came—hopefully, we would have the three full months to max out our credit cards.

Thursday night, the phone rang.

It wasn't the Call, but Jack of Carol and Jack, the straight couple from our seminar who'd predicted we would be the first from our group to be picked. They wanted to meet for dinner. They lived out in the burbs, but would be in town a week from Tuesday for the pool parents' support-group meeting. Did we maybe want to come to the meeting and then go get some dinner? "We'll show you our birthparent letter if you show us yours."

When I got off the phone with Jack, I told Terry we should think about joining the support group. It might help to be around other couples going through the same things we were.

"No, it would be awful," Terry said. "Every other couple in the group will get picked before us. There'll be new couples every week, and couples leaving the group because they get picked, and we'll be there forever. It'll make waiting much worse."

Terry had a point. We were going to be in the pool a long, long time.

Gestation

Picked

Two days after Carol and Jack called to invite us to the pool parents' support-group meeting, we were picked.

Not only wasn't our wait as long as we had anticipated; frankly, it wasn't as long as we would've liked. Expecting a long wait, we'd behaved as if our wait would be long. We hadn't drawn up plans, laid in provisions, or made lifestyle changes. The night before we got the "You're pregnant" call, we'd gone out drinking. Terry and I had pretty much stopped going to gay bars soon after we met, but with diapers and day care looming, we suddenly wanted to spend more time where the boys were, wanted to take one last lap around that dog track while we still could.

It was a Saturday morning in January when the call came. I was at home in bed, reading *The New York Times* and waiting for my hangover remedy to kick in. Aspirin with codeine can be purchased over the counter in Canada, and every once in a while we head to Vancouver to stock up. When the phone rang, I ignored it, letting voice mail pick up. Ten minutes later, it rang again. I ignored it again. It's bad luck to get out of bed before the codeine does its job. Then the phone rang once and stopped. That was Terry's pick-up-the-goddamn-phone-you-lazy-asshole signal, so I slumped out of bed and sat by the phone.

It was about ten-fifteen, and Terry was at work. Seven years younger than I, he could still go out drinking all night, get completely smashed, and jump out of bed the next morning and go to work. I could drink only when I had nothing to do the next day. I'm three-quarters Irish, which should have blessed me with a high tolerance, but the infrequency of my drinking has lowered my defenses. As my eldest brother remarks whenever we go out for a drink, I am a *lightweight*. The word sits in his mouth like a spoonful of spoiled mayonnaise. The fact that I can drink only one beer to his three is pitiable. How I struggle through life with this infirmity, he can't fathom.

Terry, on the other hand, is made of more absorbent stuff. I was in bed with a hangover, and I'd had three beers; Terry'd had eight beers and he was at work, listening to Madonna's new CD.

When the phone rang, I picked it up and said, "What is it, honey?" In our relationship, "honey" is code for "You're annoying me, but I love you; what is it already?" I have pet names for Terry, but if I revealed them he'd kill me, or reveal his pet names for me, and we can't have that. The tone of my voice made it clear that I was not thrilled about being dragged out of bed before the codeine I'd had for breakfast undid last night's damage. If this was something that could wait, I was gonna be pissed.

"Terry's on the phone with the agency." It wasn't my honey, it was Dave. He's one of Terry's coworkers, and a friend of mine, and he's no man's honey. "You've got a kid! Terry will call you as soon as he gets off the phone. Don't go anywhere."

Then Dave hung up.

I sat there by the phone, thinking, *Got a kid?* Dave didn't say we'd been picked, or we had a birth mother. He said we got a kid.

"Oh, my God," I said out loud. "It's a hospital birth."

That would mean the kid had already been born. A birth mom called the agency from the hospital, they rushed over a "Dear Birthparent . . ." book, and she picked us. We were going to be dads.

We were going to be dads *today*. Right away, no mediation, no three months to get used to the idea, no time to go shopping. As I sat by the phone waiting for Terry to call, I imagined myself having to change diapers with this hangover. All we had in the house was that flannel shirt from Baby Gap. We had more women's underwear in the house from when I used to do drag than we had baby clothes.

I tried to stay calm waiting for Terry to call back. I drank some tea. I took some codeine. I ate some cereal. I about had a stroke. When was he going to call?

After twenty minutes, I called the bookstore.

"He's still on the phone with the agency," said Dave, and I hung up.

And I waited.

We didn't have a crib, we didn't have a single diaper, and the only bottle in the house was the nearly empty bottle of codeine in my hand. It was too soon. We weren't ready, we didn't have anything we needed. I had a hangover.

Pretty soon we wouldn't even have a place to live. Earlier in the week, we'd sold our condo. We had to be out in two months, and were just starting to look at houses. We wanted to escape the courtyard, buy a house somewhere else in town, and be moved in and settled before the baby came. We'd have time, we'd thought, to find a new place, sober up, and get rid of my old drag. Now I found myself wondering if we would able to get everything we needed on the way home from the hospital, the way they told us at the seminar.

Finally, the phone rang. It was my mother.

"Can't talk, Ma. I'm waiting for Terry to call about—"

Do I tell her? No. Don't want to jinx things, and what did I know anyway? If I told her what I knew—"We got a baby"— she'd have a million questions. I had no answers.

"—something important. I gotta get off the phone."

"Is it a baby?" Mom asked.

"No, it's a—job," I lied.

"What job? Whose job?" Mom asked.

"Um a different one, for Terry. Mom, I gotta get off the phone."

"Terry doesn't want to work at the bookstore anymore?"

"Mom, I gotta go."

"All right, but call me later."

"I will," I lied.

The phone rings.

"Her name is Melissa." Terry sounds as freaked out as I am. "She lives in Portland, and we need to get down there as soon as possible."

"Did they call from the hospital? Did she give birth already?"

"No," Terry said, to my relief and disappointment. In the half-hour I'd spent in a panic about a baby coming right way, I'd started to like the idea. Maybe being spared the three-month build-up was a blessing.

"She's a little over seven months pregnant, and it's a boy," Terry said.

"It would be Daryl Jude, then" I said.

He'd been talking with Laurie, Melissa's counselor and the agency counselor who would take over from Ann if we decided to adopt Melissa's baby. They'd been on the phone a long time because there were, as they say in the adoption biz, *issues.* Terry told me to get some paper and a pen, sit down, and take notes.

Melissa was homeless. She was "homeless by choice," Laurie had explained. She wasn't a bag lady, she wasn't crazy, she wasn't a prostitute or a drug addict. She wasn't what we've been trained to think of when the media talk about "the homeless," even if she was technically homeless. She was a smart, resourceful, intelligent kid who, for reasons of her own, chose to live on the streets in the company of other smart, resourceful, intelligent kids. She could find a job and a place to live if she wanted to, but she didn't want to.

"She's a gutter punk," Terry said.

The gutter-punk stuff wasn't the only issue, though.

Laurie explained that we were not Melissa's first choice; she had picked two other couples before us. Her first-choice family was nabbed by another birth mom before Melissa was six months pregnant. Her second choice turned her down because she drank for the first four and half months of her pregnancy. And she'd taken LSD a couple of times while she was pregnant. And she smoked some pot. As soon as she'd found out she was pregnant, she'd stopped drinking and using drugs, but her second-choice couple didn't want to risk adopting a baby that might have fetal alcohol syndrome (FAS).

Melissa was pretty upset about the rejection, Laurie told Terry. Finally, Melissa came in for a counseling session with Laurie, and she spotted our home study sitting on top of a stack of files in a corner of the office, and we were her third choice.

"She told Laurie she would have picked us first, if she had seen our birthparent letter, but we weren't in the pool when she started looking at them," Terry said.

Since Melissa was seven months pregnant, Laurie was anxious for us to come down and meet her. If we didn't want her baby, then she'd have to pick another couple, and she'd have to do it soon.

The drinking was a problem. We didn't know much about FAS, but we knew enough to know it wasn't something you put in the plus column. But what if we said no to Melissa and then never got picked again by another birth mom? Buggers can't be choosers. . . .

I took some more codeine.

Things were even more complicated than simple drinking. Melissa had started having contractions earlier that week; she went to the hospital, where she almost gave birth prematurely. Tests all indicated that the baby was healthy. The ultrasound showed that he was a boy, and that his head and limbs were all normal. When Melissa was released a week later, her doctors ordered her to get bed rest. Melissa didn't have a bed to rest in, though, so the agency got her into emergency housing. But emergency housing didn't allow animals, and Melissa wouldn't be separated from her cat and dog. Melissa needed to get into an apartment, and if we went ahead with this adoption we would be expected to pay her rent as a "reasonable birth mother expense."

A birth mother is expected to pay back these costs if she decides to keep her baby. To protect her from feeling obligated to give her baby up, and to avoid running afoul of anti-baby-selling statutes, the agency tries to keep the expenses as low as possible. If a birth mom wants to change her mind and keep the baby, she should be able to make that choice without having to worry about paying thousands of dollars back to the couple she jilted.

Laurie told Terry that if after meeting Melissa we decided to go ahead with the adoption, we would be expected to pay for an apartment. Melissa didn't want anything fancy, just a studio apartment somewhere downtown, close to where her gutter-punk friends hung out. The agency had already helped Melissa get Oregon's health care plan and her food stamps. Melissa told Laurie she'd die before she put on maternity clothes, so besides the apartment there would be no expenses.

Since Melissa was going to be on the streets until we made our decision, Laurie wanted us to come down to Portland as soon as possible and meet her. First we'd see Laurie, who would help facilitate that conversation. She'd been working with Melissa for about a month, and knew her pretty well, and when she read our home study she thought we'd be a good match for Melissa. Birth moms and adoptive couples will sometimes meet two or three times before the adoptive couple makes a decision about going ahead, but we had time for just one meeting. Melissa was seven months pregnant and living on the street. If we weren't going to adopt her baby and pay her rent, Laurie needed to find a couple who would.

We rented a car and drove to Portland the next day.

Driving down to our first "mediation," a meeting that could potentially alter the course of both our lives forever, what did Terry and I do? Read up on fetal alcohol syndrome? Flip through Dr. Spock? Talk about the future? Of course not. We fought about music. We may have been on our way to meet the woman carrying the baby we might adopt and raise as our own, but that didn't mean we had to act like grown-ups. When Terry was packing the rental car, he grabbed fifteen of his CDs, none of which I would ever want to listen to unless I were listening to them being snapped in half. When we were too far from home to turn back and get any of mine, he popped in a CD and told me that it was my fault for not grabbing a few of my own.

By the time we got to Portland, we weren't speaking to each other.

Our first stop was the Mallory Hotel, our base camp in Portland. We checked in, dropped stuff off, and headed over to the agency. We'd never been to the agency's offices before; the seminars, meetings, and interviews we'd been to were all held elsewhere. We felt as if we'd been called to the principal's office. We would only be there for a few minutes, time enough to meet Laurie, go over what she'd told Terry on the phone, and then drive to Outside In, a drop-in center for street kids and gutter punks. And there we'd meet Melissa.

We got to the agency early, so we walked around the neighborhood. We found a Starbuck's and got some coffee for Terry and some tea for me, then spent half an hour picking over used Christian records in a church thrift shop. I once heard a recording of Anita Bryant singing "Over the Rainbow," and I am determined to find that album one day. It is my quest. Terry and I both love resale shops and junk stores, we find them soothing. But this resale shop didn't have the usual calming effect. Not today, at least. We were so nervous we even started speaking to each other again.

Anita Bryant's "Over the Rainbow" was nowhere to be found, and it was time to head over to agency HQ. I'd spoken on the phone with people from the agency so many times that I'd developed a detailed mental picture of the place; a homey little office in a funky old building, with wainscoting, rag rugs, gingham curtains, and a room full of kids waiting to be picked up by adoptive couples.

The agency shared the second floor of a creepy, two-story glazed brown brick office building with a travel agency. On the wall opposite the single elevator in the lobby was an enormous oil painting of a fishing village at sunset, rendered in inch-thick blobs of orange and brown and dark red paint. The painting was easily three feet high and fourteen feet long. It was absolutely hideous, and if it had been for sale I would have bought it. A chrome light fixture hung in the lobby, with two dozen clear-glass lightbulbs on chrome spikes radiating from a large center ball. The building was about as welcoming as the Nixon-vintage county courthouse.

We took a seat on one of two couches in the agency's cramped waiting area. There was a coffee table, some toys, and a wall of smiling children, kids, alone or with their adoptive parents. They seemed to say, "We're in the kids biz. We can get you kids, lots and lots of kids."

Laurie came out, said hello, and showed us into her office. Like everyone at the agency, she was extremely nice in that professional way, and she was dressed like a mom, in a loose denim skirt and white turtleneck. On her desk were pictures of her own kid, a little boy, and as we sat talking I wondered if it was her own bio-kid or her own adopted kid, but I didn't think it would be polite to ask. We sat down on a couch in her office, and she sat at her desk. She turned to us, made an empath face—lips pursed, eyebrows up, head tilted to one side, a polished look of engaged and upbeat concern—and asked us if we had any questions.

We did.

What was Melissa like? Where was she from? Who was the birth father? What should we expect at this first meeting? Was she being honest about how much drinking she'd done, and about having stopped?

Melissa was a nice-looking young woman, Laurie told us, but she was homeless. "She doesn't have access to a shower or a bath, so she smells a little. And you have to look through the dirt to see it, but she's a pretty young woman." Melissa was from a small town outside Portland, and she was committed to placing her child for adoption. A friend of Melissa's had had her baby taken away by the state. The kid was in foster care, and Melissa's friend was probably going to be stripped of her parental rights. She wouldn't be able to see her kid after that happened, which was part of what was motivating Melissa to do an open adoption. Melissa knew she couldn't take care of her kid, but she wanted to be a part of his life.

The birth father was not in the picture: he was another homeless street punk, and he didn't know Melissa was pregnant. Since Melissa was living in Portland, this would be an Oregon adoption.

"Melissa says he usually turns up in Portland or Seattle in the summer," Laurie said, "which would be well after the baby was born."

As for the drinking, we had no way of knowing for sure how much Melissa drank, and there was no way of knowing for sure that she had stopped.

"But Melissa comes across as a very honest, straightforward person," Laurie said, "and I really think she's telling the truth. She's been very reliable and responsible about coming to her counseling appointments, and I don't think she would be so reliable if she were drinking on the streets."

Laurie also reassured us that, while we were Melissa's third choice, we would have been her first choice had we been in the pool sooner.

Why did she pick us?

"Melissa said you looked like real people, like people she might know," said Laurie. "All the other couples looked phony to her. She really liked your home study, and really wanted to meet you guys."

★   ★   ★

There were two issues Laurie felt we should think about while making our decision. First, the drinking and the drugs; second, Melissa's lifestyle. Melissa planned on going back to the streets after she had the baby, and that would create special "challenges" for us in our relationship with our child's birth mom. Laurie was a little concerned that Melissa was different from the birth moms we'd met at the seminar, so she wanted us to brace ourselves. We didn't tell Laurie that, as far as we were concerned, the less Melissa was like those birth moms the better. Laurie kept calling Melissa homeless, but we knew what Melissa was: she was a gutter punk, one of those kids who travel around the country looking like punks and smelling like hell, sleeping on downtown streets and driving business owners crazy. Seattle's full of them in the summer.

Seattle's too cold and wet for anyone other than the truly homeless to live on the streets year-round; as soon as it gets cold, the gutter punks who come up here in the summer head south, to Arizona, southern California, and Mexico. A few damp gutter punks can be found in Seattle in the winter, but it's the summer when they return in force, tanned, rested, and ready to hit us up for change. Terry works at one end of Broadway, Seattle's hip/queer shopping district, and I work at the other end. Walking from Terry's bookstore to my office between May and October means wading through clumps of gutter punks. Two or three stand or sit at almost every corner, with huge backpacks, bedrolls, and punked-up hair. They wear sweatshirts, baggy army pants, boots, and white T-shirts. From sleeping on grass, in alleys, and under overpasses, gutter punks tend to take on a uniform greenish-gray-grime color. Some travel with dogs. Most of the punks are pretty harmless, but a run-in with one suffering from some major psychological damage or on too much acid can ruin your whole day.

In addition to rejecting mainstream American values, like cars, homes, and jobs, gutter punks also reject mainstream personal hygiene, like toothbrushes, soap, and shampoo. When you're living on the streets and begging for change, you're not going to pour what money you do come by into hair-care products and dental floss, or pump quarters into washing machines at Laundromats.

Consequently, two gutter punks standing together can create quite a stink.

The kids hit you up for change as you walk by. They need the change for food, forty-ouncers, and dope, and they'll tell you as much. Run-of-the-mill bums or drunks will give you a line of crap about needing a dollar to get on the bus, but gutter-punk culture has an almost Holden Caulfield–like reverence for honesty. Gutter punks don't give you a sob story about needing exactly forty cents to get on the bus; they tell you they need another dollar to score some dope, and could you help get them high?

But after you've been asked for change six or seven thousand times in one day, you can get pretty tired of gutter punks. Even the bleedingest heart eventually hardens. Some will sneer at you as you race to work, without acknowledging that they depend on your job, as well as your guilt and empathy, to move change out of your pocket and into theirs. On some level I envy gutter punks and think the circuit they've created is a kind of wandering Woodstock. One day, I suspect, kids who are in their teens and early twenties right now and who don't run off to be gutter punks for a few years will feel the way all the sixties kids who didn't go to Woodstock now feel. They're missing out on their generation's defining cultural experience. Twenty years from now, we'll all be reading the great novels of the Gutter Punk Generation, and people who weren't gutter punks will claim they were, just like people who didn't make it to Woodstock claim they did.

But while I look forward to the novels they're going to write, living in Seattle it's easy to get sick of the gutter punks and their shtick. They especially drive Terry crazy. He's always having to throw gutter punks out of the store. They come in, stink up the place, and shoplift books in order to resell them at a used-book store down the street. The summer before, while we were doing our paperwork, Terry'd had a confrontation with a clearly tripping gutter punk that almost turned violent. At a party a few days later, he joked that the gutter punks should all be herded together and gassed.

No one objected.

We were relieved Melissa was a Portland gutter punk and not a Seattle gutter punk. It would be a little awkward if she turned out to be one of the gutter punks I said no to when she hit me up for spare change, or one Terry had thrown out of the bookstore. Or wanted gassed.

We followed Laurie through downtown Portland to the drop-in center.

Meeting the woman carrying the baby you might adopt is an unusual situation, not just for gay men. We had no idea how we were supposed to behave when we met Melissa. We hadn't watched this scene play out in movies or on television, and we hadn't thought to ask Bob or Kate about what meeting their kids' birth moms was like. We had a better idea about meeting aliens than birth moms.

How were we supposed to behave? How did she feel about giving up her child? Odds were good she wasn't feeling too upbeat. We couldn't go in all smiles. But we didn't want to walk in looking as if we didn't want to be there either.

At the seminar, all the birth moms and the couples who'd adopted told us about their first meetings. They all said they hit it off right away, that there was an instant connection, and ten minutes after they met they were like old friends.

"It'll probably be that way for Melissa and us," said Terry. "I mean, why not?"

Outside In is three old wood-frame houses facing the freeway that cuts through downtown Portland. When we walked up to the building, two gutter punks were sitting out front with a dog. They checked us out, looking us up and down, and seemed to know who we were. We smiled and nodded and walked by, grateful they didn't ask us for change.

Inside the door was a long hallway filled with backpacks, lockers, safe sex posters, and punks. On one side, a stairway went up; on the other, a doorway opened into a living room. Kids in their gray-green-black clothes were sleeping on couches, milling around, and eating instant soup and ramen noodles.

Standing next to Laurie was a short girl with long black hair, dark eyes, and a wary look on her face. She was obviously pregnant.

Melissa.

Melissa gave us a quick "Hey," and turned away. She called to one of the Outside In's staff and asked if we could use one of the upstairs counseling rooms.

We were both staring at Melissa; we couldn't help it. She was wearing a grimy white T-shirt, fatigue pants covered with patches and cut off below the knee, and knee-high Doc Martens boots. A Swiss Army knife, some tools, and a cup hung from her belt. She wore a black zip-up sweatshirt that hung from her shoulders to her knees and made her look smaller than she was.

As we started to walk up the creaky staircase, Melissa smiled at a friend coming in the door. *Dental work,* I thought to myself, catching a glimpse of her teeth. Any son of Melissa's is going to need dental work.

In the first few moments we were together, I caught myself assessing her in the crassest possible way. It was hard not to look Melissa over as if she were a horse we were about to bet on. Was she good stock? How do those teeth look? Any hint of inbreeding in the slope of her forehead or the shape of her eyes? Would her offspring be strong? Did she have the right genetic stuff? If we went with Melissa were we betting our $15,000 on the right horse? And there was the birth father to think about, too. What did he look like? We were not, in all likelihood, ever going to meet him. All we had to go on was Melissa, and except for the teeth (which were no more crooked than mine, actually), she looked good.

Down a short second-floor hallway, a small room had been carved out of a larger one. Woodwork and baseboards disappeared into the wall. A brown sheet was tacked over the only window. Melissa sat down in a low stuffed chair, Terry and I sat on a couch, and Laurie sat in a chair. No one said anything for what seemed like a very long time.

"Well, Melissa, this is Dan and Terry," said Laurie, "and Dan and Terry, this is Melissa."

It's hard to remember that first conversation, but we weren't chattering away like old friends in ten minutes. Melissa stared at the floor, and Terry and I stared at Laurie. Melissa gave one-word answers to Laurie's ice-breaking questions, and when Laurie asked Melissa if there was anything Melissa wanted to know about Terry and me, she shrugged and said no.

It didn't feel as if things were going well, and I wondered if

Melissa had taken one look at us and decided we weren't the parents she wanted for her baby.

When Laurie asked us if we had any questions for Melissa, Terry asked Melissa about the baby's birth father.

"Everyone calls him Bacchus," Melissa said, "but his real name is Kevin. We were traveling together, and I got pregnant, I guess." They hadn't seen in each other in months.

"It's not like he could take of a baby," Melissa said, "so I wouldn't worry about him wanting to take the baby away or anything."

Melissa didn't know much about Bacchus's family or his health history, since they'd only hung out for a month.

"It's not like we talked about that sort of stuff," she said. "And, anyway, we were high or drunk a lot, so even if we did talk about it, I wouldn't probably remember. He was a normal guy; I don't think there was anything wrong with him."

"Dan and Terry have some concerns about your drinking and drug use," Laurie said.

"We've both used drugs, and we both drink," I said, trying a little too hard to put Melissa at ease and coming across like a boomer talking to his teenage kid. "It's not like we have anything against drinking or drugs, but we're a little worried about it, with the baby and all."

Melissa ran us through the drinking and drugs she did before she knew she was pregnant. She had three or four beers a day, four or five days a week, for the first four and half months.

"It was usually beer, but we got a space bag every once in a while."

All three of us looked at Melissa, and said, "A space bag?"

She pushed her hair behind her ears and clued the squares in: "The bag inside a box of wine is silver and shiny. It's, like, Mylar or something from outer space. You take it out of the box and pass it around. It's a space bag. We didn't drink until we passed out, just enough to stay warm and get a buzz."

She'd also taken acid twice, and smoked some pot. She'd stopped drinking when she found out she was pregnant, and had smoked some pot maybe once since. She rattled this information off, seeming upset at having to talk about it at all. Her drinking was what made the last couple she met pass on her baby.

"Why did you stop drinking?" I asked.

"Some kids with dogs on the street think it's funny to give their dogs beer and get them drunk," Melissa said. "I don't do that; it's not good for dogs, they shouldn't drink. Neither should babies. So I stopped."

"Drinking is not always good for adults, either," said Laurie.

Melissa looked at Laurie as if she just didn't get it.

"Yes, but adults get to choose, and that's different. Dogs don't choose, and babies can't."

Melissa didn't want to talk about drinking or Bacchus anymore. Laurie steered the conversation to Melissa's recent stay in the hospital and her reasons for leaving emergency housing.

"It wasn't just that they wouldn't let me have my animals there," Melissa said. "It was filthy, and there were bugs, and the place was dangerous and full of crazy people. It's safer on the street than in a place like that."

Laurie had another birth mom to meet at the office. She got up to leave. "Why don't you all go out for a walk or get something to eat?" she said. "Get to know each other better."

Standing outside after Laurie left, Terry asked Melissa if she was hungry.

"Not really."

Did she want to get something to eat?

"I don't care."

I said that I was hungry, and I cared very much about getting something to eat.

"What's good around here?" I asked.

Melissa looked at me as if I were crazy. "I don't eat in *restaurants*," she said.

"Well," Terry said, making a beautiful recovery, "if you did eat in restaurants, what restaurants would you eat in?"

Melissa suggested Rocco's, a pizza place across the street from Powell's, Portland's huge independent bookstore, in the middle of Portland's hopelessly depressing strip of gay bars.

"I don't have money," Melissa said when we got up to the counter. This wasn't a spare-change request, and there was no self-pity in her voice. It was just a fact, like "dogs shouldn't drink." If we wanted to eat with her, we'd have to buy.

We got some slices, sat in a booth next to a pinball machine, and, over the racket, talked about the agency and Laurie.

Melissa didn't like Laurie. Laurie was nice, and all, but Melissa thought she was square. It didn't help that it was Laurie's job to ask Melissa a lot of questions about her feelings and the future at their weekly counseling sessions. "Everytime I go, it's like, question after question."

When we asked her what she wanted to know about us, she said she'd read our home study and knew everything she needed to know.

Terry made a comment about the music at Rocco's, and he and Melissa started talking about bands they liked. Melissa was opinionated about music, and soon she and Terry were chattering away like . . . not quite old friends. The music conversation led to talk about Seattle.

Melissa didn't know where we lived, and didn't know our last names. The agency doesn't give any "identifying information" to birthparents until the adoptive couple decides to go ahead with the placement. Talking about Seattle bands, Terry looked at me and asked if we could tell Melissa where we were from. I nodded and said of course.

"We live in Seattle," said Terry.

"I was in Seattle all last summer," Melissa said. "With Bacchus. That's where I got pregnant."

FAS

Two hours later we were back in front of Outside In.

We were even less prepared to say good-bye to Melissa than we'd been to meet her. We had anticipated the meeting, imagining what we would say, what Melissa might say, and how she would smell. But this moment sneaked up on us. Melissa looked at me and then at Terry. She looked us in the eyes, which was unsettling. Except during the music conversation with Terry, she hadn't made eye contact with either of us. In our meeting with Laurie, she looked at the floor; eating, she looked at her pizza; walking around, she looked at the ground. As one hour stretched into two, Melissa had become chattier. She told us about growing up in a small town, which didn't sound like much fun, and she shared what she considered the worst part of living on the streets: you never got to have steak, only hamburger. But even when she got chattier, she wouldn't look at us.

At the pizza place, Melissa dropped another bomb, just as startling as the fact that the baby boy she was carrying had been conceived steps from where we live and work. The hospital where Melissa spent a week after she went into early labor, the hospital where her baby would be born, was OHSU. If we adopted this child, our son would be born not only in the city that Terry hates, but in the same hospital where Terry's father died.

When Melissa mentioned OHSU, I stopped chewing my pizza and looked at Terry. He had stopped chewing his pizza, too, and was looking at me. I raised my eyebrows to say, "Will you be okay with that?" and he shook his head and shrugged as if to say, "Not really, but whatever." We resumed chewing. Melissa had finished picking all the pepperoni off her slice and eating the pieces one at a time, and was starting to pick off the cheese. When there was nothing but sauce and crust left, she ate her slice proper.

"I hate that place," Melissa said, of OHSU. "They wouldn't let me keep my dog in my room. I didn't see what the problem was. My dog is clean."

Standing in front of Outside In, Melissa suddenly became very quiet. She was waiting for Terry or me to say something, and we knew what she wanted to hear. Did we want this baby or not?

When someone offers you her baby, it seems only polite to say, "Thank you," smile, and take the baby. But even if we wanted to say yes, Laurie had recommended that all three of us refrain from making any commitments today. She wanted Terry and me to be absolutely sure before we said yes to Melissa; she would be crushed if we said yes right away and changed our minds after we gave it some thought. It would be better to wait two days and give Melissa a firm yes, Laurie advised us, than to put her through that.

Anyway, I couldn't have told Melissa we would take her baby, because I wasn't sure how Terry felt about Melissa, or even how I felt.

"It was nice to meet you," Terry said.

"We'll call soon," I said. "We'll be in touch through Laurie, I guess."

"Okay," Melissa said, shrugging. She looked up at her dog, chained to the railing on Outside In's porch. Melissa pulled her lips between her teeth and bit down on them, and slowly nodded her head. She turned and walked up to the porch, and sat down with her dog. She didn't look at us as we got back in our car. Clearly she was certain she'd never see these two fags ever again.

Driving back to our hotel, which was a few blocks from Outside In, I asked Terry what he thought.

Terry didn't respond. He swung the car into the Mallory Hotel's parking lot, pulled into an open space, shut off the car, and turned to face me. He looked somber, and I thought he might be worried about having to drive up that hill and return to the place where his father died.

"Here's what I think," he said, looking very serious, placing his hand on my shoulder. "After talking to Melissa I'm convinced of one thing: she has much better taste in music than my boyfriend."

I punched him on the shoulder—a little-brother punch, not an abusive-spouse punch—and held up my fist.

"She's nice, a little weird, like a gutter punk, but nice. She doesn't seem crazy or anything. But I don't know what to think," Terry conceded. Then he hit me back a little harder than I'd hit him, just like a little brother, and jumped out of the car.

I didn't know what to think, either. The gutter-punk thing wasn't the problem for us that it might be for a suburban couple. We were familiar enough with street kids not to fear them. The drinking was a problem, though. The number of beers Melissa had told us she had every week during the first four and half months of her pregnancy was considerably more than the number of beers Laurie had told us about. Laurie'd said two or three beers, three or four days a week; Melissa'd told us four or five beers, four or five days a week. We didn't know what to think about Melissa's drug use, but we'd never heard of babies being born addicted to acid or pot, only to crack or heroin, and we both assumed the drugs weren't much of a problem. But we needed to check.

And when it came to drinking, how much buzz was too much buzz? Was there a significant difference between nine to twelve beers a week and twenty to twenty-five? Was twenty-five beers too much? Or nine? Was one beer too much? And while we knew FAS was a Very Bad Thing, we only had vague ideas about what FAS did to kids exactly. Did it make a kid temporarily stupid but fixable? Or was he stupid forever? If we said yes to Melissa what were we risking?

When we got up to our room, the message light on the phone was blinking. Laurie wanted to know if we could make up our minds by Wednesday. It was Sunday, and she hated to rush us, but Melissa needed to get off the streets.

Sitting in our room later that night, we decided we couldn't decide. We needed to learn more about FAS before we could give Melissa an answer. Laurie had already given Terry the numbers of an FAS specialist in Seattle, and had faxed us a copy of Melissa's ultrasound, which she told us showed that everything was normal. Judging by the ultrasound, Laurie thought the risk of FAS (or anything else) was very low.

"But you're the guys who would be adopting the baby, not

me," Laurie had told Terry in that first phone conversation. "Call these doctors; ask them what they think."

We were quiet for a while; then Terry finally said, "If we took the beer out of the picture, if Melissa hadn't drunk during the first part of her pregnancy, we would say yes to her, right?"

"I would, yeah. But you're the one who wanted to have all the street kids gassed a few months ago. And is having to go to OHSU a problem for you?"

"The street-punk thing is not a problem. The dog is not a problem, the smell is not a problem, and OHSU isn't really a problem, either. Only the booze is a problem."

We had dinner in the Mallory's dining room, a restaurant with no name, where we had to remove our baseball hats. We didn't know what to do with ourselves after we ate, so we drove to Lloyd Center and saw a movie. On our way back to the hotel, we passed the pizza place Melissa had taken us to, parked the car, and walked around. In Powell's, we found some books on FAS, but we couldn't process any more information. We put the books back on the shelf.

We wandered up the street and into one of the gay bars. At the PDX Eagle, we each ordered a Coke; we got some quarters and played some pinball. The Eagle is a leather bar, painted black on the inside with chain-link-fence accents. There's a sling hanging from the ceiling, and gay pornography of the soft-core SM and hard-core sex variety was playing on television sets set all around the bar. A couple of older men, guys in their sixties, sat at the bar drinking beer and watching the videos. As we played pinball, I wondered if Terry and I would be sitting in leather bars when we're sixty, watching porn, sipping beer and laughing with the bartender.

I hoped so.

Before we left Portland Monday afternoon, we called the FAS specialist Laurie had recommended, leaving a message asking her to call us at home. We drove straight to Bob and Kate's. Bob and Kate were having fun playing adoption experts to our adoption neophytes, and over wine and pizza we told them about Melissa. Lucy, Gus, and Isobel were upstairs in the attic, watching a Disney video.

"Before we had kids we swore we wouldn't park 'em in front of the TV," Bob said. "But, oh, you start to feel different about the TV when you've got 'em. Then there's McDonald's."

We told Bob and Kate about Melissa's drinking, the absent birth father, the Seattle connection, and the weird way she ate her pizza.

"We're under all this pressure to make a quick decision," I said. "Melissa is living on the street right now, and will be until someone agrees to take her baby and pay her rent."

"And if it wasn't for the drinking," Terry added, "we would say yes right now. But we aren't sure we're up for an FAS baby, and that makes us feel awful."

"Everyone wants a healthy baby," said Bob, "there's nothing wrong with wanting a healthy baby, so you have nothing to feel awful about."

"If we were pregnant, we could eliminate the risk of FAS by not drinking, right?" I said. "But under these circumstances, to eliminate the risk of FAS, we have to eliminate Melissa. We'd be the third couple to reject her."

"And she's on the street right now, waiting for us to make up our minds," said Terry.

"You can't think about that," Kate said. "You have to make up your minds based on what's best for you. It sounds nasty but you can't adopt a kid for life because you feel sorry for that birth mom this week."

We pulled out Melissa's ultrasound and passed it around.

"One of our birth moms had a lot to drink when she was pregnant," Bob said, "and we were very worried, but we went ahead with it, and we're all fine. Sometimes you have to take chances and keep your fingers crossed. Every kid—bio or adopted—comes with issues and uncertainties."

"Is that your legal opinion?" asked Terry.

"I advise all my clients to cross their fingers," Bob said, opening another bottle of wine. "And I'd advise us to have some more wine."

"Terry, if you had to decide right now, what would you do?" Kate asked. When Terry looked at me, Kate said, "No, don't look at Dan, look at me. What would you do?"

Bob is a real estate lawyer; Kate's a county prosecutor; and here you see the difference.

"I don't know—it depends on what the risk is," Terry said. Kate rolled her eyes, and turned to me.

"Dan, if you had to decide right now?"

"We might not get picked again ever, and maybe a baby with half a brain is better than none," I said, "so maybe we should say yes."

Terry put his head down on the table and said he didn't want to think about it anymore. Bob filled Terry's wineglass back up.

"We could offer to pay for her apartment," I said, "whether or not we take the baby. That way she'd be off the streets, and we wouldn't be worrying that by saying no we were abandoning Melissa to the streets, and we could take more time to make our decision. It's not that much money."

"No," Kate said. "First, it would be unfair of the agency to put you in that position, and second, the fact is that girl had a place to stay and walked away from it over a dog—"

"And a cat," Terry said. "She has a cat, too."

Kate looked at Bob, and threw her hands up.

"If she can't be separated from her dog and cat," said Kate, "what do you think is going to happen when she lays eyes on her baby? Forget about the FAS stuff. Think about that dog! Once she sees her baby, she's not going to want to be separated from him, either. You feel guilty now, but how will you feel when you're sitting in a hospital and she decides to keep that baby? That will feel a lot worse. I'd say no, don't go with Melissa."

It was Bob's turn to throw up his hands.

"Don't tell them what to do—they have to make their own decision!"

"I didn't tell them what decision to make," said Kate. "I just said, 'I'd say no.' They can say yes if they want to, but if it were me, I'd say no."

Bob and Kate gave us the number of the doctor they'd talked to about FAS before they adopted. We called and left a messages for Bob and Kate's doc, and then made the biggest mistake we would make in the entire adoption process.

We got online.

There must be information on the Internet about FAS, we

figured, so we typed "Fetal Alcohol Syndrome" into a search engine. Fifteen million sites popped up.

"Fetal Alcohol Syndrome is a pattern of mental and physical
defects which develops in some unborn babies when the mother
drinks too much alcohol during pregnancy," read one site. "A
baby born with FAS may be seriously handicapped and require a
lifetime of special care. . . . Alcohol in a pregnant woman's blood-
stream circulates to the fetus by crossing the placenta. There, alcohol interferes with the ability of the fetus to receive sufficient
oxygen and nourishment for normal cell development in the
brain and other body organs. . . ."

On another site, this:

"The fetus is most vulnerable to various types of injuries depending on the stage of development in which alcohol is encountered. A safe amount of drinking during pregnancy has not
been determined, and all major authorities believe women should
not drink AT ALL during a pregnancy." Several sites quoted God
as an authority on the subject. When someone got knocked up
in the Old Testament, an angel of God instructed her to avoid
"strong drink." One site had this flashing warning on every page:
"EVEN ONE DRINK PUTS YOUR UNBORN BABY'S
HEALTH AT RISK."

All the sites were scary; most featured a lot of medical jargon
and a few featured New Age bullshit: "The alcohol affected child
is like a garden. Some seeds need to be planted year after year, like
the carrots and radishes. The seeds the birds carry away have to be
replaced almost immediately. But there are bulbs that grow in the
garden and every year they come up almost without tending. It
can be too easy to see what failed to come up this year and step
on crocuses close to the ground. The important thing is to be
thankful there is a garden."

An FAS web site brought to you by *Martha Stewart Drinking*.

In addition to fetal alcohol syndrome, we also had to worry
about fetal alcohol effect. While FAE is milder than FAS, the lists
of FAE symptoms were just as long and just as terrifying as the
nearly identical lists of FAS symptoms.

We sat at the computer in silence, clicking through pages,
soaking up the bad news.

The symptoms of FAE and FAS included brain damage, mental

retardation, a pointy chin, a flat nose, behavior problems, and the inability to learn or retain information. IQs in FAE/FAS babies range from 20 to 130, and these children are prone to hyperactivity, attention deficit disorder, oddly shaped ears, heart defects, small bones, and misaligned teeth. Drinking in the first half of the pregnancy, when Melissa was sucking down space bags, damages the brain; drinking in the second half results in physical abnormalities. Every site said that even one drink during a pregnancy was risky. Melissa had twenty-five drinks a week for the first four and half months, when alcohol damages the brain. That's three hundred and seventy-five drinks. An hour online convinced both of us Melissa's baby would be born without a head.

"Okay, I've had enough," Terry said, and walked out of the room.

I shut down the computer. We got undressed and crawled into bed—or climbed up into bed, I should say. A week before the call came and just before we had to move, we'd bought a new bed. A famous furniture designer we'd met built it for us at cost (he also did Jay Leno's desk, and Sandra Bernhard's bed, too, which Terry managed to work into just about any conversation), so after twenty years of sleeping on a mattress on the floor, I was suddenly sleeping four feet off the ground. It was rather disconcerting; in fact the first night we were in the bed, I didn't sleep at all. I was too afraid of rolling out and tumbling to my death. Now, sitting in bed with Terry, I wondered how any kid we adopted would ever manage to crawl up into this bed on a stormy night.

"I don't want a stupid kid," I said. "That makes me terrible. If we had a bio-kid and he was born stupid, I'd love him. But if we can avoid a stupid kid, I want to avoid it."

"But if we say no," Terry said, "will we ever get picked again?"

"We could go to China, or pay a surrogate to have a baby," I said. "We don't have to do an adoption; we're only out a couple of grand at this point."

"So we say no, then, I guess." Terry turned off the light.

"This is what I'm afraid of," I said in the dark. "We get picked again, and the next girl is smart enough to lie about whether she drank, and we adopt her baby. And this other baby has FAS. Or if it doesn't have FAS, we're at a park when he's two years old and God says, 'There are those fags who didn't want to take a chance on an FAS baby and broke that gutter punk's heart.' And God makes our kid fall backwards off a swing, cracking his head open, and leaving him a vegetable for the rest of his life. That's what I'm afraid of."

"Jesus, I am so glad I wasn't raised Catholic."

After a long silence, I said, "So, what do we tell Melissa?"

"We tell her no, right? And we go back in the pool. That's what you want to do, right?"

"Yeah, I think so. What do you want to do?"

"Whatever you want to do," Terry said, rolling over, "is fine with me."

Two hours later, I was back in front of the computer.

Terry fell right asleep, as usual, but I couldn't sleep. I got out of bed, turned the computer on, and started surfing through more FAS sites, hoping to firm up my resolve. If we were going to tempt fate by saying no to Melissa, I wanted to be certain it was the right decision. To be certain, I needed to be absolutely sure that Melissa's baby would have FAS.

Every site was gloomier than the one before. FAS kids can't learn anything, they can't remember anything, they can't think. And as they grow, their problems don't get better, they get worse. FAS children grow into FAS adults, and in adult situations, their inability to learn or control their impulses magnifies the severity of their condition.

At about four in the morning, I clicked to one last site, "Personality and Learning Traits of FAS/FAE Children," promising myself it would be the last one I'd read tonight. After this, I would go back to bed or surf some porn. But first, I would read about the personality traits of FAS children. At the top of the page, the site warned that FAS/FAE children may exhibit one or all of these personality traits, and that some FAS/FAE children showed symptoms that weren't yet listed.

"Kindergarten through 6th grade: easily influenced by others; difficulty separating fantasy from reality; temper tantrums; lying, stealing, disobedience; delayed physical/academic/social development; memory loss; impulsiveness; inappropriate social behavior; need for constant and consistent reteaching and repeating."

I read that paragraph again. Temper tantrums? Impulsiveness? Disobedience? Sounds like me at five. What five-year-old doesn't have at least one of those symptoms? Or all of them? I had a very hard time separating fantasy from reality until I was twelve. For the first time that night—or rather for the first time since reading aloud to Terry the extended FAS-child-as-garden metaphor—I laughed. When I was five years old, apparently I had FAS/FAE, as did every other kid in my kindergarten, *and no one knew.*

I scrolled down the page. Under "Personality Traits of High School Age FAS Kids" was this list:

"Poor sequencing; lying, stealing, cheating; poor reasoning; memory loss; self-centered; high level of frustration; unwanted pregnancy/STDs; low self-esteem; poor motivation; depression; alcohol involvement . . ."

Depression? Lying? Self-centeredness? Apparently, I had FAS in high school, too, as did my brothers and my sister and everyone else who's ever been a teenager. Who wasn't depressed or self-centered or unmotivated in high school?

I clicked onto a dead-porn-star-shrine site and flipped through some photos of the late, great Matt Gunther. I looked Matt over, trying to think about something other than FAS, but my mind kept wandering in a disturbing direction toward my mother. She drank a little when she was pregnant. So did Terry's mother. So did everyone's mother. Despite displaying almost every last one of the FAS/FAE symptoms on the list I'd found, I was pretty sure I didn't have FAS. My siblings didn't, and my boyfriend didn't, and no one we knew whose mom drank did.

I tried to concentrate on Matt Gunther, but my mind wandered off my mother and onto that absurd list of FAS/FAE symptoms. When did drinking during pregnancy become so self-evidently dangerous that women shouldn't have even one drink for fear of pickling their unborn baby's brain? Every FAS site made it sound like spilling a beer in a pregnant woman's lap was more dangerous than kicking her in the stomach or throwing her down a flight of stairs. One site recommended that sexually active women obstain from drinking at all: If a woman was pregnant and didn't realize it, whatever drinking she did during the first few weeks could seriously harm her baby.

If this was all true, how come I didn't have FAS? My maternal grandmother was an honest-to-God miserable Irish Catholic drunk—my mother used to pull her head out of the oven once a week—but none of my grandmother's six kids, my mom or any of my aunts and uncles, had FAS/FAE. How come we were all fine?

Tuesday morning, Laurie called. She was just checking to see where we were in our "decision-making process." We explained that the more we learned about FAS, the more concerned we were about Melissa's drinking. We were also concerned about the inconsistencies in her story. She'd told Laurie the low figure—nine to twelve beers a week—and told us a higher figure—twenty to twenty-five. Which set of numbers was correct? Melissa was coming in that day for a regular counseling session; Laurie would nail her down on the drinking and call us back later today. I told Laurie that we still had to talk to the doctors she and Bob and Kate had referred us to, but that after looking at stuff on the web we weren't feeling very positive.

Then one of the docs we'd left a message with called us back. When I told her we had a copy of Melissa's ultrasound, she asked me to fax it to her. Twenty minutes later, she called back. Terry had left for work, so I took notes.

"Judging from the amount of alcohol we're talking about, the drinking pattern you've described, and the ultrasound report, I would say that the risk of this baby having FAS is very low. The head circumference, the estimated body weight—everything on this report indicates normal fetal development."

What about the stuff on the web? What about the warnings that even one drink could damage an unborn baby? What about FAE?

The doctor, a leading FAS researcher, sighed, and there was a long pause. Then, slowly, she began to undo the damage the Internet had done.

"I'm not convinced there *is* such a thing as FAE," she said. "Out of every thousand births, fifteen children have learning disabilities. If a child has a disability and there was any drinking during the pregnancy, any drinking at all, the temptation is to blame the drinking. But honestly, we don't always know the cause."

There was still more doctors didn't know: for reasons not understood, she explained, firstborn children almost never have FAS regardless of the amount of drinking the mother did. Same goes for children born to women under the age of twenty-one.

The kind of drinking Melissa described—sharing several beers over a period of hours—was also a good sign. "It's in children of women who binge-drink, who have five or more drinks in a very short period of time and then black out, that you're likelier to see FAS. But looking at this ultrasound, and considering this woman's age, and that this is her first child, and that she stopped drinking when she did, I would have to say that it is highly unlikely that this baby will suffer from FAS. Does that mean this child absolutely won't have a learning disability? Or some other problem? No. Any number of things could be wrong. But there's no indication from this ultrasound that anything detectable at this point is wrong. But if something *is* wrong, it probably has nothing to do with the drinking. There's always a risk of something, you understand? I can't give you a guarantee. But I can tell you that, in my professional opinion, you shouldn't say no to this adoption on account of the drinking."

I was stunned.

"Why were the web sites all so scary?" I asked.

"A lot of the information out there about FAS is designed to scare pregnant women away from alcohol, not to provide them with an accurate picture of what we do and do not know about FAS. The people who put those web sites together have a public-health agenda, not a medical agenda. You have to read them with a grain of salt."

Laurie called back as soon as I hung up the phone. Melissa was with her. I asked Melissa to give us all the details of her drinking. We needed to know everything. She drank when other people bought beer, but she didn't spend money on it herself. Some weeks, she drank five or more days a week, and some weeks she drank less. She almost never got drunk, she never blacked out, and she never threw up. Two weeks during the first or second months, she didn't drink at all. Melissa was traveling at the time, riding the rails, and didn't have access to beer. That was all she remembered.

I thanked Melissa and Laurie and said that Terry was getting off work at ten tonight, and we would sit down and make a decision.

"We'll call you tomorrow morning," I said.

A few hours later, Bob and Kate's doctor called. Terry had already faxed him the ultrasound results, and he listened to me describe Melissa's drinking.

"The risk for FAS, I would say, is minimal. Considering everything else you know about the mother and the father, you should worry more about this baby being predisposed to depression or mental illnesses than about FAS. Most people on the street are mentally ill, a lot are schizophrenic, and there's a hereditary predisposition to many mental illnesses. That's what you should be concerned about."

I didn't want to take the time to explain gutter-punk culture to Bob and Kate's doctor, so I told him we'd think about it and got off the phone.

Ten minutes later, the phone rang. It was my mother.

"Where have you been? I've called a million times."

Should I say anything now?

"We were in Portland, doing some stuff with the adoption agency."

"Did you get picked?" My mother was already hip to the open-adoption lingo.

"No, we had to go and do one more interview. We're in the pool now."

There was a pause.

"You told me you were in the pool two weeks ago. Did you have to get out of the pool and get back in?"

Now what do I tell her? I could tell her the truth, I supposed, but telling my mother meant telling everyone else on earth, and I wasn't ready to do that. I didn't want gifts to start coming in the mail, and I didn't want to jinx anything.

"We forgot to sign something," I lied. "So we went down and signed it. Now we're in the pool, officially."

There was a longer pause.

"Mom, when we get picked, I'll call you right away, okay? You'll be the first to know, I swear."

Considering the headaches alcohol had given us over the past few days, the last thing you'd expect Terry and me to want set down in front of us was a drink. But, as Homer Simpson once said, beer is at once the cause of and the solution to all life's problems. I walked down to the bookstore and met Terry out front as he was locking up. We walked down the street to Cafe Septième, the last place I'd waited tables and one of the few places with soul left in a Seattle rapidly filling up with Planet Hollywoods and Wolfgang Pucks.

Stephanie, Seattle's best waitress, put a big bottle of Chimay and a couple of glasses on the table. Terry pulled Melissa's ultrasound and some things he'd found in the store about FAS out of his bag and handed them to me. I pulled the notes I'd taken during my phone conversations with the FAS specialists out of my bag and handed them to Terry.

We read.

We drank.

But neither of us said anything.

Stephanie saw that our bottle was empty and dropped another off. We were done reading; while Terry poured us each another beer, I broke the silence.

"The good news is that no one thinks Melissa's baby will have FAS. The bad news," I said, holding up the list of FAS/FAE personality traits I found online, "is that you and I have FAS."

Terry read the list out loud, and laughed. "Temper tantrums, impulsiveness, inappropriate social behavior; I didn't know it, but it looks like I had FAS as a child."

"If that list is correct, you still have FAS."

Terry dipped his fingers in his beer and flicked them at me.

Even while I was wiping the beer out of my eyes, it seemed obvious we'd already come to a decision. My mind had been pretty much made up after I spoke to the FAS docs, and I could tell Terry was making up his mind while he was reading my notes. Last night's Internet-induced gloom was gone, and each of us sat waiting for the other to go first. We were both suppressing smiles, as if somehow the importance of the decision we were making required us to look serious while we made it.

"I talked to my boss about it," Terry said. Barbara was a lesbian who didn't understand why anyone would want kids. "Her mother had three martinis a night, every night of her adult life, during all her pregnancies, and none of her kids was born without a head."

There was a pause.

"What's your worst-case scenario?" Terry asked.

"The baby has FAS."

If we said yes, and the baby turned out to have FAS, I pointed out, well, adoptive parents could change their minds at the last minute, too. Birth moms weren't the only ones who could disrupt an adoption. We could say yes to Melissa, and if the baby was born with FAS or any other problem we could back out at the hospital, and the agency could find another couple for Melissa's baby.

"We have that right, you know. If the baby is born messed up, we don't have to take him."

Terry looked at his beer.

"We wouldn't be able to do that, and you know it. We wouldn't show up and say, 'Oh, sorry, pointy chin, no thanks.' "

"It's just a hypothetical."

"No way would you, Mr. Guilt, be able to back out at the last minute. And once I see that baby, no matter what's wrong with him, I won't be able to just walk away. So it's not even a hypothetical, really. You're too Catholic, I'm too sentimental."

Terry was right. If we said yes to Melissa, that would be that. We'd be pregnant, too, and we'd love that kid no matter what was wrong. We wanted a healthy baby, and this was the moment to decide whether we thought the odds were good that Melissa was carrying one.

"If we think she's going to have a healthy baby, we should say yes right now," Terry said. "And if we think she isn't, we should say no. So . . . what do you think?"

"I think even if the kid turns out to be the healthiest newborn baby on earth, there are still swing sets, *E. coli* hamburgers, and car accidents to worry about."

There was a long pause, and we sipped our drinks. We looked at each other.

"What if we say yes, and Kate's right and Melissa changes her mind after she sees the baby?" Terry asked. "This is the girl who can't be parted from her dog and cat."

"If she changes her mind, we go back in the pool. In the meantime, we don't let ourselves get carried away. We don't fill the house with baby stuff or have showers."

"So, what do you want to do?" Terry asked.

"No, you go first."

"If you were going to say yes," Terry said, "well, then, I would say yes. But if you don't want to . . ."

"I was going to say yes if you were," I said.

"So it's yes?"

"Yes."

"Okay."

We both let out loud sighs, and sipped our drinks. I held out my arm for Terry, showing him the gooseflesh. Terry picked up my notebook and walked over to the pay phone. It was almost midnight, and when Terry called the agency he got someone at their live twenty-four-hour answering service. He left a message for Laurie, telling her we wanted to go ahead with this placement, and that she should tell Melissa yes. Then he came back to the booth and sat down beside me.

Kurt, Septième's owner and my old boss, came over to say hello.

"What's the news?" he asked.

We both looked up at Kurt, and then one or the other or both of us said:

"We're pregnant."

Getting Close to Melissa

The agency encouraged birth moms and adoptive couples to get together as much as possible before the baby came. Melissa was seven months pregnant when she picked us and we accepted, so we had to squeeze as many of these meetings in quickly as we could. We didn't have to meet in the presence of an agency counselor; only the initial introductions were stage-managed. Since birth moms have less money than adoptive couples, poverty being one of the top reasons women give their children up, the adoptive couple was expected to travel to the birth mom. Over the next few weeks, Terry and I would be seeing a lot of the dull, flat highway between Seattle and Portland, and getting to be regulars at the Mallory Hotel.

A few days after Terry left a message for Laurie telling her that, yes, we would adopt Melissa's beery baby, we were back in Portland to meet with Melissa on our own. This time, without Laurie, there would be no net. After we dropped our bags at the Mallory, we drove the few blocks to Outside In. At the seminar and during our home study sessions with Ann, all the counselors had emphasized that in an open adoption the stronger the bond between adoptive couples and birth moms the better for everyone involved, especially the kids. "Think of your birth mom as a relative," said Ruth during the seminar. "You will be related to each other through the baby you adopt. She will forever be your child's birth mother, just as you will forever be your child's parents. You don't get to pick your relatives and, as adoptive parents, you don't get to pick your birth mom. But you should make the most of your relationship with your child's biological mother, one based in respect, trust, and love."

Getting close to Melissa was not going to be easy, but since she would forever be part of our family, we were going to try. At that first meeting, Melissa had hardly looked at us. She wasn't hostile, just standoffish, her early-onset world-weariness leavened by traces of adolescent awkwardness. Only when she and Terry started talking about music, or when I asked some polite questions about the logistics of living on the street, had she opened up. Talking about spare-changin' or avoiding cops, Melissa could get very chatty. But she didn't have any questions for us.

There was more we needed to know about her, though, and we didn't have a home study to refer to. And I was curious what role, if any, our being gay had played in her decision to pick us. Why did she want two fags to raise her son? I'd wanted to ask the question at our first meeting, but it seemed . . . a little self-involved. "Oh, enough about you already, Melissa, let's talk about how gay Terry and I are; gay, gay, gay." When we were with Laurie at Outside In, or later at Rocco's eating pizza with Melissa, I just couldn't bring myself to say, "You're homeless and pregnant, Melissa, and that's very interesting, but how do you feel about us being cocksuckers?"

Still, it seemed an important issue, practically the defining issue in this particular adoption. We were fags; no other fags had successfully adopted through the agency before, and it's not so common for gay men to have kids at all. For gay men to adopt children is controversial—in a few places, illegal. So why Melissa chose us seemed important, and it seemed like something the three of us should discuss before the baby came. Had she given it any thought?

On our way down to Portland, I told Terry I was going to ask Melissa about all this.

"She didn't seem to care that we're gay," Terry said, leaning over to turn down the car stereo. "Why should it matter to us if it doesn't matter to her? It's a nonissue."

Terry had a point. But as we drove through Olympia, I told Terry it didn't seem possible that Melissa hadn't thought about the fact that we were gay.

"But if she didn't, asking her about it might make it an issue," Terry said.

"If it's gonna be an issue, it'll become one sooner or later," I replied. "Wouldn't you rather get it out of the way before the baby is born, instead of having it all blow up in our faces later on? And aren't you at least a little curious what this twenty-year-old from Small Town, Oregon, thinks about homosexuality?"

"She's giving us her baby; I think that's a good indication that she likes us, Dan, she really likes us. Leave it alone; if it were an issue she wouldn't have picked us. She saw our picture, she read our home study, she met us. She knows we're gay. The end."

Our second meeting was less awkward than the first. Melissa's dog was chained up on the porch of Outside In, and she was inside arranging for someone to watch her cat while she visited with us. Today her belly was noticeably larger, and when we walked up the porch steps she looked us up and down before she said hey. She didn't smile, but she didn't seem upset either. She seemed businesslike. Her twelve-thirty had arrived, and she was clearing her schedule for the rest of the afternoon.

We'd come so the three of us could get to know each other better—in the best interest of the kid—but Melissa didn't come across like a person who wanted to be known. Or maybe she just didn't know how to be known. Over pizza last week, she'd told us that she didn't like getting together with Laurie because she hated having to answer lots of personal questions. Getting to know Melissa without asking questions was going to be work.

We had learned a couple of other things about Melissa during our first visit: she mentioned at our first meeting that she liked Gummi bears, and she missed eating steak. So as she got into the car, Terry handed her a bag of Gummi bears. The gesture was meant to indicate that we'd been paying attention during our first meeting, and that we wanted to be, you know, pals. Melissa looked at the bag, then at Terry.

"They're Gummi bears," Terry said, "you said you liked them."

"You didn't have to get me Gummi bears."

She wasn't hostile; it was a statement of fact. We *didn't* have to get her Gummi bears; that was true. Getting closer to Melissa was going to be harder work than we'd thought.

As Terry pulled out into the street, I asked Melissa if she was hungry—she wasn't—and if she wanted to maybe go have steak later. At least this time I didn't ask her *where* she wanted to have steak, just whether she wanted to go *somewhere* for steaks.

"I don't care."

We didn't know what to make of "I don't care" in this context. Was Melissa being polite? If someone offered me a lunch I couldn't afford to buy myself, I wouldn't want to seem too eager to spend their money. Should we insist? Or was she just not in the mood for steak? We didn't want to force steak on her, but we had made plans to get together for lunch, and she had said she missed steak—just as she'd said she liked Gummi bears. Suddenly, our second meeting was like a bad blind date.

We parked the car and walked around downtown, Melissa pointing out the gutter-punk landmarks. She showed us where to buy drugs, which gangways were safe to sleep in, and what businesses would let you use their bathrooms, and she taught us the secrets of spare-changin'. Melissa talked about spare-changin' like it was her job. With a friend, sit or stand on a corner, asking "Spare change?" of everyone who passes by. Never spare-change alone. When there's two or three of you, folks are less likely to yell at you to get a job or take a bath.

"And they seem less scared of you if you're with someone," Melissa said. "But you can't be with, like, more than two other people, because then you look like a gang or something."

With anyone over thirty or well-dressed, say you need the money for food. Under thirty or hip-looking, say you need the money for beer or pot. People who say no don't piss Melissa off, it's the people that pretend not to hear her as they walk by.

"That's when I'm like, 'Hello, I exist.' That's when we'll follow you down the block."

I looked at Terry. At home, I always made a point of looking the gutter punks on Broadway in the eye and saying, "Not today." Terry would pretend not to hear them and walk by. Walking around talking about spare-changin' seemed as good a time as any to see if she remembered us. She knew we lived in Seattle, so I explained to her that Terry and I walked up Broadway almost every day. She looked at us and . . . she . . . smiled.

"No shit?" Melissa said and laughed. "I spare-changed Broadway all last summer. I must have spare-changed you guys, like, a hundred times."

How many times had I looked at Melissa last summer, before she got pregnant, and said, "Not today, sorry"? It was in Seattle that she got pregnant, and it's possible that she spare-changed me or Terry or both of us with the baby we were hoping to adopt already growing inside her. I looked at Melissa, and tried to picture her less pregnant and on Broadway, asking me for change. Nothing. Even if I looked 'em in the eye, I didn't really see the gutter punks any more clearly than Terry did.

We walked past an antiques store with an enormous terra-cotta bust of Pope Pious XII in the window. Before the tactlessness of spending a lot of money on something so useless in front of Melissa occurred to me, we were in the store, pricing it. The bust was cool, but it wasn't a thousand dollars' worth of cool. We poked around the store, trailed by a salesclerk. Terry ran out to put some more money in the parking meter, leaving me alone with Melissa and the clerk. Here among the high-priced tchotchkes seemed an appropriate place to address the gay issue, so I asked Melissa if it mattered to her that we were gay. I'm not sure what I expected or even wanted to hear, but what it might mean for her son to grow up with two gay dads must have crossed her mind. Why gay men?

"I don't know. I didn't think about the gay stuff. You just weren't like the others."

Carol and Jack were right. In the crowd of straight, white, Christian couples, Terry and I stood out.

"Why would anyone spend so much money on all this old crap?" Melissa asked no one in particular.

Terry was back, and I tried to ask Melissa the gay question in another way.

"It's something we've thought about. He'll have different experiences growing up with gay dads than kids who grow up with with straight parents. There are places we won't be able to go as a family, and times in his life he might catch shit for it. Do you worry about that?"

"No," said Melissa. "I didn't really think about that."

Terry was looking at me with his jaw hanging open. He mouthed, "Stop," and shook his head.

"Did you pick us because you wanted to be the only mom in your kid's life?"

"No."

"Do you worry about other kids picking on him?"

"Everyone gets picked on for something."

Melissa wandered up to the front of the store, the clerk trailing her, leaving me and Terry alone with the Pope.

"Would you shut up," Terry hissed. "Don't ask her about the kid getting picked on! Are you insane? Do you want her to change her mind? Drop it!"

Melissa was eyeing the store clerk, who was eyeing her, and we made our way up to the front of the store to prevent a scene. Outside, it was getting cold and starting to rain. We couldn't walk around anymore, so I suggested we go eat somewhere.

"You wanna have a steak?" Terry asked Melissa.

"I don't care." Melissa shrugged.

"Well, I care and I want a steak," I said.

There was a steakhouse on the same block as the antiques store, and Terry asked Melissa if it would be all right with her if we went and ate there. She didn't have to eat, but she could get off her feet.

"I don't care."

We walked into the steakhouse—white tablecloths, dark paneling, over-made-up hostess—and asked for a table near the window. The hostess looked at us as if we'd asked her to drink a cup of piss. She didn't know what to make of us: Terry and me looking like a couple of urban fags/frat boys (jeans, T-shirts, baseball hats), and Melissa looking like a gutter punk (filthy clothes, dirty face, body odor).

It was about three o'clock, and the place was practically deserted. A few late lunchers were scattered at tables around the dining room. I asked again for a table, locking eyes with the hostess, doing my best rendition of one of my mother's looks: I was smiling, but don't-fuck-with-me waves emanated from me. One look and our hostess knew there'd be an ugly scene if she tried to stick us in a table at the rear or tell us the kitchen was closed.

We were shown to a booth in the window, and as we sat down the hostess gave me a nod. She was standing behind Melissa, facing me and Terry, and now it was her turn to lock eyes. My look said "Don't fuck with us," and her look said, "I sat you in a good table, I'll see that your waitress is here in a heartbeat, and I'll make sure your food flies out of the kitchen." She'd keep up her end of the deal, but she didn't want us in her window all afternoon. I nodded. It was a deal. We understood each other.

Looking at the menu, Melissa's eyes went wide. The steaks were twenty dollars and up—way, way up—outrageously steep if you make your living a quarter at a time. Melissa thought it was stupid to spend so much money on lunch. We could buy steak at the supermarket around the corner for five or six bucks; why would anyone pay twenty dollars for one in a restaurant? Melissa hadn't found an apartment yet, I pointed out, so even if we did buy steak at the supermarket, we didn't have anywhere to cook it or anything to eat it with. Since I didn't want to sit on the sidewalk and eat raw steak with my bare hands, we'd have to pay more for lunch than we should.

Our waitress arrived, clearly forewarned, and demanded to know if we were ready to order. I ordered a Coke, Terry ordered a beer. Melissa didn't order anything. The waitress left to get our drinks.

"This is too expensive," Melissa said after the waitress left to get our drinks. "I don't want to waste your money."

Terry looked at me, raised his eyebrows, and tilted his head toward Melissa. My serve.

"If we can afford to adopt a kid, we can afford to take you out for steak. Order what you want, it's not a problem."

Melissa knew Terry worked in a bookstore; now she asked me what I did for a living. I wasn't a writer she'd heard of.

"It's not like you're Anne Rice or Stephen King," Melissa said, "you can't have all that much money."

"I write a column that runs in a bunch of different papers," I explained. "I write one column a week and I get paid for it twenty times. I'm not Anne Rice, but I have enough money that I can afford to buy you a steak."

Melissa looked back at her menu, but didn't seem convinced.

"I don't have a problem spending Dan's money," Terry said. "I'm going to have a steak, and if you don't order one for yourself, I'll order one for you. And if you don't eat it, I'll take it home and have it for dinner."

The waitress was back with our drinks, anxious for us to order, eat, and get the hell out of her steakhouse. I'm not a big steak eater, but I did what I had to do: I ordered myself the most expensive steak on the menu: twenty-nine goddamn dollars. Terry ordered the same steak. Melissa looked at us blankly, looked back down at her menu, and slowly nodded her head. Then she ordered herself a steak just a little less expensive than the steaks her hosts had ordered for themselves: precisely what Miss Manners would have told her to do in a situation like this.

"How would you like that done?" the waitress asked Melissa.

"Extra, extra well done," Melissa answered, to our waitress's dismay. The longer it took that steak to cook, the longer we'd be sitting in the window. When the waitress left, practically running to the kitchen with our order, Melissa looked around the room. Maybe it was rude to take Melissa to a place like this, a restaurant where she probably felt uncomfortable. But Terry and I aren't all that comfortable in steak-and-martini places, either. When we go out to nice places without gutter punks, we still usually get bad, out-of-the-way tables, because of my slovenly appearance and Terry's carefully put together seventies male hustler look.

"You see them?" she asked, pointing at two impossibly thin women a few tables over, picking at salads in a steakhouse. "I spare-changed them. They walked right by me."

We had plenty of time to kill while Melissa's steak was cremated, and Terry asked Melissa a few questions about her family while we waited. Something clicked, and Melissa opened up. Her parents owned a house on about an acre of property, where they raised goats and chickens. She had one sister close to her own age, and a younger brother that she "pretty much" raised all by herself. Her mother wasn't much of a mom, Melissa said, and pushed

a lot of the housecleaning, cooking, and child-rearing responsi-
bilities onto Melissa. When she was eighteen, Melissa came home
one night and had a blowout with her mother over bullshit. Her
mother told her to get out, Melissa packed a bag, said good-bye
to her brother, and walked out the door.

"That was almost two years ago."

Melissa hadn't seen her mother or siblings since the fight over
bullshit. She had a car, but had to leave it at home because it didn't
run. She worried that her family might sell her car, but mostly
she worried about her little brother.

"I was basically his mom. Now he doesn't have a mom, really. I
hope my mother doesn't mess him up like she messed me up."

Melissa could go home and check on her younger brother, but
she didn't want to deal with her mother.

"If my mother cared about me, she'd come and find me. They
know I'm downtown. Portland is a small town; they could find
me if they wanted."

Melissa did see her father once a year. He was folk music fan,
hosted a radio program on a community station in Portland and
traveled around Oregon and Washington attending folk music
festivals. She went up to Seattle every year for the summer to see
her father at the Folklife Festival at Seattle Center.

"My father knows everyone who's anybody in folk music. I go
to Folklife and he's always there."

Listening to Melissa talk about her father, it was clear she ad-
mired him. Listening to her talk about her mother, it was clear
she despised her. Maybe Melissa picked us for her baby *because* we
were both men, and that's what appealed to her. That we were
gay didn't matter, but maybe subconsciosly, she wanted to spare
her kid the thing that made her miserable all her life: a mom.

When our food came, Melissa ate her potato first, then her
carrots, then her steak. Melissa eats very slowly. Terry and I were
finished before Melissa was done with her carrots.

We'd been together four hours or so, and we'd done very little
talking about the baby. At our first meeting, Laurie asked an ice-
breaker question about naming the baby, and Melissa shrugged
and said she didn't care if we changed his name after we adopted

him. While we ate, Melissa talked more about her family. Like a lot of people estranged from their families, when Melissa wasn't complaining about how she'd been mistreated, she talked about her family with pride. The boy she was carrying would be the first of his generation, and there weren't many boys in her extended family. She wanted to give the baby her last name, Pierce, even if he only got to keep it until the adoption was finalized.

In closed adoptions, the birth mom names her baby when he's born, and the names she picks out appear on the child's original birth certificate. When the child is adopted, a new birth certificate is issued and the original is sealed. The adopting couple changes the child's names, and the new birth certificate lists the adopting couple as mother and father. In most states, adoptees can get a copy of their original birth certificate after they turn twenty-one, learning not only the names of their biological parents, but their "real" name as well. Many adult adoptees will then change their names back to their original names, the names their adoptive parents "took away" from them.

In open adoption, many birth mothers and adoptive couples agree on one set of names, which then appear on both birth certificates.

"What are you thinking of for names?" Terry asked Melissa.

"I don't know. Maybe after his father."

"Bacchus?" I asked.

"No, not Bacchus," said Melissa, rolling her eyes. "That's not his father's real name. His name is Kevin. I wouldn't call a kid 'Bacchus.' "

We wanted to avoid having two sets of names, if possible, but we also had already picked out first and middle names. Terry told Melissa that he had wanted to name the baby we adopted after his father, Daryl, who died at the hospital where Melissa's baby was going to be born.

"You guys can change his name when you adopt him, Laurie told me that's what happens, and that's fine, I don't care."

Terry looked at me.

"We're kinda nervous about the kid having two sets of names," I said, "the names you give him and the ones we give him. We don't want him to get mad at us when he's grown about 'taking away' the name his mother gave him."

"Kids look for things to get mad at their parents about when they're teenagers," Terry said to the girl living on the streets because of a fight she had with her mother over "bullshit." "It seems like an obvious thing for him to get upset about. 'You took my name away from me! You had no right!' Maybe we could pick his first name, and you could pick his middle name?"

Melissa didn't respond. She didn't seem upset; she chewed her steak and looked like she was thinking it over.

"Dan kinda wanted to name the baby after his mother, too," Terry said. "We were thinking Daryl for my father, Jude for Dan's mother. D.J."

Melissa pushed her plate away and sighed.

"I want to name him. You can change his name later on, I don't care. But I want to give him his names and my family's last name; it's important to me. When you adopt him, you can do what you want."

Pool Parents

When Jack had called to invite us to the pool parents' support-group meeting, we were in the pool. Nine days later, driving to the meeting in our fourth rental car in four weeks, we'd been picked, discovered that we both have FAS, met with our birth mom twice, said yes, learned the baby was a boy, and picked out a name. Back at Lloyd Center, Carol and Jack had predicted we would be the first couple from our seminar to be picked. Tonight we were going to tell them just how right they were.

We were twenty minutes late for the meeting, and by the time we slipped into two empty folding chairs in the meeting room off the lobby, we'd missed the group introductions. Some of the people sitting in the room looked at us uncomfortably. We didn't appear to belong. Not only were we two guys, but today we were both looking particularly scruffy: I hadn't shaved in a week, and Terry's shoulder-length hair was fashionably greasy, with a crooked center part. For all anyone could tell, we were a couple of thugs from the bowling alley across the street who had come to crash the support group and make fun of the infertile people.

Carol and Jack nodded, and seeing that someone in the room knew us set the five other couples at ease. Everyone was sitting in chairs arranged in regulation support-group formation—a squared circle; besides Carol and Jack, no one was there from our seminar back in May. One couple looked close to our age, another looked closer to my mother and stepfather's age. Everyone else was in their late thirties or early forties. One couple had a baby, and they were telling their story.

Until last week, the couple with the baby were members of the support group. Carol and Jack told us later that every meeting began with a couple who recently adopted sharing their story. These new-parent visits boosted the morale of couples who were still waiting. And the boost was needed: some of the couples in the support group had been waiting a year or more. Seeing former members of the support group with their new babies reassured the languishing that they would get a baby, too, if they hung in there.

Tonight's baby was only a week old and had a dark pelt of hair on her head. The baby was Hispanic, her adoptive mom was white, and her adoptive dad was black. When we came in, the couple was telling their story. They'd been in mediation with a different birth mom, but they "experienced a disruption" before that baby was born.

"Our first birth mother was like a dream birth mother," the woman said, pulling a bottle of formula out of their baby bag. "She was seventeen, she'd been accepted at Stanford, she hadn't touched drugs or alcohol during her pregnancy, and she wanted to do an adoption because she wanted to go to college." At the last minute, the girl and her boyfriend decided to get married and raise their baby themselves."

"The disruption was quite a blow," the adoptive dad said. "We were really disappointed."

They jumped back in the pool, and a few months later they were picked again. The birth mom this time was not a dream. There were *issues:* she had done drugs during her pregnancy, and she drank.

"We thought about saying no, because of FAS—" said Mom.

"—but we took a chance," said Dad. "And she's perfect."

"Perfectly healthy," said Mom. "Not a thing wrong with her. Now, looking at her, we feel like all this was supposed to happen, that this is the baby we were supposed to adopt."

The new mom and dad rose to leave. Marilyn, the agency counselor running the meeting, thanked them for coming in, and as they gathered up their bags and blankets and baby and walked out of the room, all eyes followed them. The yearning in the room was palpable. A newborn baby at an adoptive-parents support group is like a five-pound bag of heroin at Narcotics Anonymous. Everyone was staring at the couple carrying the smack out of the room, and there were a lot of brave faces slapped over a deep and nearly desperate desire to have what they had. Everyone wanted to be the couple with the smack, and some were losing hope that they'd ever get their hands on any.

Carol and Jack had been attending pool support-group meetings religiously since before they were even in the pool. Carol was a businesswoman, Jack an industrial engineer, and they were applying to adoption the drive and determination that made them successful in their careers. They came to these meetings because they believed in doing their homework.

Terry and I don't believe in homework. Even if we did, the support group meets once a month and we weren't in the pool long enough to make it to a single meeting. The only reason we'd come to the meeting tonight was to see Carol and Jack, and to tell them in person that we'd been picked.

Not that we came to gloat. Naturally, I felt guilty about being picked before they were. By all rights, they should have gotten a kid first. They'd been trying to start a family for a lot longer, and they'd been through a lot more hell than we had. Their infertility story was a long and harrowing one. After years of trying to make a bio-kid—sex, fertility drugs, surgery, in vitro fertilization—Carol and Jack finally started to investigate adoption. They looked into closed, open, international, and state adoptions before finally choosing open adoption. If this was a contest, Carol and Jack deserved to win. They had earned that "You're pregnant" call; we hadn't. We'd lucked out.

Once Baby left the building, Marilyn paused to allow some oxygen to enter the room before introducing this month's speaker, a gaunt lawyer who specialized in finalizing adoptions. He was here to answer any questions we might have about adoption law in Washington State.

At the seminar, everyone was pretty shy. Not tonight: these couples had gotten to know one another, and they fired questions at him. Since this was the Seattle support group, all the couples expected to do a Washington state adoption, not an Oregon adoption; consequently, everyone seemed most concerned about the rights of birth fathers—and how to terminate them. The gaunt lawyer had a dry sense of humor, and managed to make us all laugh as he explained this unfunny business. Everyone in the room had seen the news clip of a screaming three-year-old being removed from the arms of the only mother he'd ever known.

In Oregon, of course, the birth father couldn't jump out of the woodwork and claim the baby. If he wasn't offering emotional and financial support during the pregnancy, he had no rights. But in Washington, couples adopting babies from women who couldn't find the birth father have to make a good-faith effort to locate the guy.

"If you have a name, you go to the phone book or the DMV and look him up. If you don't have a name, you take out ads in papers in the city where you think the birth father resides. In many cases, you have no information about the birth father at all. We try and find those missing-in-action birth fathers. The temptation is not to try too hard," the lawyer said, and a few of us chuckled, "but if you think there's any chance your birth father may turn up at a later date, you should do your damnedest to find him. You don't want to adopt the child of a birth father who may want his kid, or adopt from a birth mother you think may be lying about who or where the birth father is. If he pops up three or four years after the adoption, and can prove that you didn't make a good-faith effort to find him, or that the birth mother concealed the pregnancy from him, he can sue and gain custody of his child."

No one was chuckling now.

"That's a rare occurrence, however. In most cases, birth fathers are happy to sign whatever they need to sign to make us go away. A guy who knocks a woman up and disappears isn't usually interested in being a father. He's usually very young or already married. Most birth fathers who refuse to consent do decide to raise the baby themselves, which often results in the paternal birth grandparents raising it. That's the father's right. But most who deny consent don't want custody. They're just trying to punish the woman they got pregnant. You can go to court and have their rights terminated, but that can take years and isn't always successful."

The younger couple asked whether a birth mother could get around the birth father by having her baby in Oregon.

"Nope, you can't just run the birth mother over the border

when her contractions start. Adoptions have to be done in the state the birth mother resides in. Family courts frown on fraud, and hold birth mothers and adoptive families to different residency standards than, say, the Department of Motor Vehicles."

"If we have a situation with a birth father, what's our best hope?" asked the older couple.

"Your best hope," the lawyer said, "is getting picked by a birth mother who lives in Oregon."

Marilyn cut in, pointing out that in forty percent of the adoptions our agency did, the birth mothers lived in Washington state.

"Birth mothers do open adoptions so they can have contact with their children," she explained. "And they're likelier to pick a family that lives in the same state they do. So all of you are likely to be picked by birth mothers in Washington, and you should think about what it will mean if you adopt a baby whose birth father is unknown."

Terry nudged me. "Melissa got pregnant in Washington," he whispered.

I raised my hand.

"What if a birth mother lives in Oregon, but was in Washington for a few months at the time she got pregnant?" I asked. Carol and Jack both looked over at us. "What about the birth father then? What state's laws would the adoption be done under?"

"If she was only visiting Washington—if she hadn't done anything to imply her residency here was permanent, like register to vote or buy a house—it would be an Oregon adoption."

Whew.

After the meeting, we followed Carol and Jack to a Chinese restaurant in a strip mall a few blocks away.

Before the food came, Carol took their birthparent letter out of her bag and passed it to Terry. Since we forgot to hold back a few copies of our birthparent letter, we brought our anti–birthparent letter for show-and-tell. Soon we were stuffing our faces, swapping stories about home studies (Ann did their home study, too), background checks, paperwork, and medical exams. Carol and Jack had the same problems writing their birthparent letter we did, and they went into the pool at about the same time. We were all a little breathless after telling our stories.

"So, are you guys jumping every time the phone rings?" Carol asked.

A slight pause.

"Yeah," I said, "we got jumpy when we went in." When I looked up, Carol and Jack were staring at me.

"You guys got picked, didn't you?" Jack asked.

Terry and I smiled, and slowly nodded.

Jack, like any good engineer, was thrilled his calculations were correct.

"Ha! Didn't we tell you! We told you guys you'd be the first couple picked!" He slapped the table.

"We knew it when you asked the lawyer that question during the support-group meeting," said Carol. " 'What if the birth mother lives in Oregon, but the baby was conceived in Washington?' That was just a *little* too specific to be a hypothetical. I thought, *That's it, they were picked!*"

We filled them in: Melissa finding our home study sitting on a stack in the office, our first meeting, the FAS scare, Melissa's Seattle connection, our second meeting, the name problem, and Bacchus our absent birth father.

"We feel awful about being picked before you guys," I said. "You really should have been picked before we were, you've been trying for so much longer."

"That's not the way it works," Carol said, shrugging. "If we get picked, we get picked. What matters right now is that *you* got picked, and that's just so wonderful."

"So what happens after the baby comes?" Jack asked. "Who's going to stay home?"

When and if we got a baby, we explained, Terry would cut back to two days a week at the bookstore, and I would do more writing at home; Terry was going to be the stay-at-home mom.

"What about you?" I asked.

Jack's work had taken him all over the world, so when he and Carol got a baby he wanted to be the stay-at-home mom. Carol was running huge parts of her company, and was moving up the ladder, so she would be the bread-winning dad. In hopes of something panning out with a birth mother, Jack had just turned down a job that would've taken him out of the country for a year. He would do consulting work in the meantime, but if they weren't picked after a year in the pool, Carol and Jack planned to take that as a sign that they weren't supposed to have kids.

"If open adoption doesn't work for us, we're done," Jack said. "We've been trying for a long time, and this is our last attempt. We figure if we don't get picked, we're not supposed to have kids."

"You guys will get picked," Terry said. "If we got picked, you will, too."

"We'll see," said Carol. "But we're not going to die if we don't."

Carol and Jack had made up their minds to wait only a year. The older couple at the meeting tonight, Jack told us, had been in the pool for almost two years.

"They come to the meetings every month," Jack said, "and watch couples that got in the pool a long time after they did get picked and get babies. They've both been made a little crazy by the experience. Every meeting begins with someone dragging in a baby that could've been theirs. After a while, that's gotta hurt."

Two years. The couple knew that dozens of birth mothers had seen their letter, looked at their picture, and turned the page. Since the "Dear Birthparent . . ." letter was about the only thing adoptive couples had any control over, the agency allowed them to rewrite their letters and get new pictures taken as often as they liked; the longer a couple was in the pool, the more they tended to tinker.

"I think they've changed their letter three or four times already," Jack said. "So far, nothing works. We're not going to put ourselves through that."

Oh my God, I thought, listening to Jack, *what is that straight couple going to say when they hear that the homos at tonight's meeting got picked after two weeks?*

"You know," I said, "I was feeling guilty about getting picked before *you.* What would I say to *them?*"

"We are not showing up at that meeting once we get the baby, no way," said Terry. "Their heads would explode."

Worst-Case Scenarios

Two weeks after our first meeting with Melissa, we headed back down to Portland for our third getting-to-know-the-birth-mom visit. We'd be tagging along on one of Melissa's pre-natal care appointments at OHSU. We had been calling the baby D.J. ever since we picked his names, but after our last visit with Melissa we'd stopped. Somehow, calling him D.J. when we knew Melissa would give him another name at birth felt disrespectful. Melissa had made it clear that the baby wasn't ours to name until after we adopted him, and that she didn't even want to discuss coming to an agreement about a name. She wanted to name him first. She didn't tell us what his name would be, only that it wouldn't be Bacchus. We wanted to respect Melissa's rights, including her right to change her mind and keep the baby, and somehow calling him D.J. felt like jumping the gun. Until he was ours he wasn't D.J. He was . . . the kid.

I also stopped using "D.J." around certain of our leftist friends after offending one at a party. With a beer in me, I called the mass of tissue lolling about in Melissa's womb "Daryl" twice and "the baby" three times in one run-on sentence, which earned me a cold look from my friend. Until delivery, my friend pointed out, that was no baby in Melissa's womb, but merely a fetus.

"Unless you're an Operation Rescue fanatic, fetuses don't have names," my friend said. "Calling a fetus that hasn't yet been born 'Daryl' or the 'the baby' humanizes it."

This, of course, placed the rights of women to control their own reproductive systems in grave danger. As a result of my careless rhetoric, women and abortion service providers would surely die.

I'd previously had a falling out with this same friend over late-term abortions, something I will admit to having some ambivalence about. Call me Randall Terry, but it seems to me that if you can't get it together and have an abortion sometime before month number seven, you might as well have the damn baby (provided, of course, that the mother's—oops, excuse me—provided the *woman's* health is not at risk). I said so when the subject of partial-birth abortions came up, most of which *are* performed to save the life of the mother. My friend informed me that I wasn't a woman, which I knew, and as I wasn't a woman and would never face this decision I really had no right to an opinion. Not being a woman didn't stop him—yes, my friend was another man—from having very strong opinions about abortion, I pointed out. As we stood and fought about abortion rights and rhetoric, the seven or eight real women in the kitchen got as far away from us as they could. It's a picture that pretty neatly sums up the abortion debate: two men who will never need or cause anyone else to need an abortion arguing semantics and driving everyone in earshot out of the room.

Anyway, by the time we were headed back to Portland, I wasn't calling our designated fetus anything at all. We were only planning on staying for the afternoon this time, though Terry would rather have stayed overnight. He had to do all the driving, and seven-hour round-trips were hard on him. Seven hours of Björk and Fatboy Slim, the only "artists" he was currently willing to drive to, were hard on me, too, so we were both going to suffer. I wouldn't have minded staying overnight, but the amount of money we were spending on rental cars and hotel rooms was starting to concern me.

The Mallory had become our home away from home, and they'd started to recognize us, I think: we were getting better rooms on higher floors with each successive visit. But we couldn't afford to blow a hundred dollars on a hotel room every week for the next six weeks. The agency was taking ever larger bites out of our checking account as we approached the adoption finish line, and on top of that we had just started paying $400 a month for an apartment for Melissa.

Finding an apartment that would have Melissa took some time—not that we had to do the finding. The agency encourages

birth moms to be as independent as possible, and so it was up to
homeless, pregnant Melissa to find herself a place to live. We sent
a check to the agency so that money would be on hand when she
found a place, but even with Laurie promising various landlords
that the agency would take responsibility for the condition of the
apartment, Melissa was turned away by a half a dozen apartment
managers. On paper, Melissa was not any landlord's idea of a dream
tenant. Kinda dirty, unemployed, homeless, very pregnant twenty-
year-old street punks don't appeal to most landlords. And, of
course, there were her animals.

When Laurie called to tell us Melissa found an apartment,
Terry wanted some reassurance that it wouldn't become a crash
pad for Melissa's street punk pals.

"We're paying for a place for Melissa to rest," he told Laurie,
"not for a place for her friends to crash or do drugs."

Laurie gently explained to us that while we were paying the
rent, we needed to respect the fact that it was Melissa's apartment
and not ours. It would be up to Melissa who came to her apartment, how long they could stay, and what they did there.

"It's an understandable impulse, wanting to control the apartment," Laurie said. "But you can't control who comes and goes
from her apartment without controlling Melissa. Not only isn't
that possible, but it wouldn't be healthy for Melissa, for you, or
for your relationship. You'll have to reconcile yourselves to letting
Melissa control her own space."

We reconciled ourselves.

The place Melissa finally found turned out to be the best of all
possible apartments. It was a studio right across the freeway from
Outside In. The apartment manager, Mary, was nervous about
renting to Melissa, but Laurie worked on Mary and she came
around in a big way. Mary scrounged up some furniture, loaned
Melissa pots and pans, and even managed to score a TV.

The day before this trip we had a close call.

Since Terry got the call from the agency while he was at work,
everyone there knew that we'd been picked. Most of our friends
knew people whom Terry worked with, so they found out what
was going on, and soon after that people we barely knew were
stopping us on street corners to say congratulations. But our fami-

lies didn't know anything yet, and we weren't ready to tell them. While the baby was due in five short weeks, we'd only just met Melissa, and we didn't dare take anything for granted. We didn't want to jinx this kid. And if things fell through, the way they had for that other gay couple, we didn't want to have to explain to everyone; we just wanted to slip back quietly into the pool.

Tracey, one of Terry's coworkers, called me at home the day before we left, wanting my help getting Terry to a surprise baby shower at the bookstore.

"We don't want a shower!" I about shouted into the phone.

"Okaaaay . . ." said Tracey, sounding hurt.

I explained to Tracey that we were concerned about jinxing things. This fetus wasn't ours yet and we didn't want to make any fate-tempting mistakes. After our first meeting with Melissa, "Babies are born dead"/"Birth mothers change their minds" had become our daily mantra. It was a little cumbersome as mantras go, and we shortened it to "BBD/BCM." Whenever either of us felt we were getting carried away—if we went on too long talking about how great it was going to be, or if we stayed too long in a Baby Gap—we would look at each other and say, "BBD/BCM." Tracey agreed that jinxing was a bad thing, and said she'd throw us a shower after the baby came.

Contemplating the baby's death on a daily basis sounds awful, but obsessively dwelling on the worst-case scenarios has always been my way of coping with stress. If I'm flying somewhere, I imagine my awful death in a plane crash and picture Terry's stunned face when he realizes that I never made a will. At this writing, none of the planes I've been on has crashed, which I credit to my overworked, underpaid, and unsettling imagination. I'm convinced that the day I get on a plane without first forming a clear mental picture of it bursting into flames and falling to earth will be the day I'm on a plane that crashes.

It's not just plane crashes that I picture. I also see car wrecks, train crashes, muggings, earthquakes, gay-bashings, waiters licking my silverware, and my mother walking in while I'm masturbating. Contemplating worst possible outcomes is my insurance that they won't come to pass. Once I've imagined the worst possible outcome I can generally let it go, sit back, and enjoy the flight/drive/ride/straight boys/meal/wank/etc. I know it works because none of the planes I've been on has ever crashed, I've never been in a car wreck, and my mother has never walked in on me masturbating (so far as I know, and if I'm wrong, Mom, I DON'T WANT TO KNOW). When I hear or witness a worst-possible-outcome scenario that I wouldn't have foreseen, I get very upset. For instance, there's a moment in *Titanic* when the ship is sinking, and people are jumping into the water. Suddenly, the ship breaks in two and the *Titanic* falls on the heads of hundreds of people bobbing in the water beneath it, killing them. The *Titanic*, of course, was the largest moving thing ever built by the hand of man (LMTEBBTHOM). Had I been on the LMTEBBTHOM's maiden voyage, I would've run the worst possible outcomes through my head. LMTEBBTHOM might sink and I'd drown; or a fire might break out on board and I'd burn to death; or some bad food might be served on the LMTEBBTHOM and I'd die of food poisoning. But I would never in a million years have imagined the LMTEBBTHOM could be lifted into the air and dropped on my head. I had to leave the theater.

I believe I inherited this kind of morbid Irish superstition from my mother, and I know where it leads. One day, I will *be* my mother, worrying whenever my children are out of sight, convinced they're dead when they're out five minutes later than they said they would be. My mother has always insisted that we let her know where we are at all times so that she doesn't have to worry, but she worries nonetheless. Only when we were home, as kids, or when she gets us on the phone, as adults, would she stop imagining worst possible outcomes for us, be they car crashes, falls out of trees, or collisions with trains. But you know what? My mother has lived in terror of some tragedy befalling her children all her life, and so far no tragedies have befallen us. Coincidence? I don't think so. Clearly this system of my mother's works.

So despite the fact that we were heading down for our third meeting and every indication was that we'd be coming back from one of these trips to Portland with a baby, we weren't allowing ourselves to get excited about Melissa or her fetus for fear that we might "experience a disruption." We behaved with everyone as if a disruption were the likeliest outcome. That meant no showers, no gifts, no announcements to family or friends. And no shopping. If our house filled up with diapers and pacifiers and baby wipes, and the adoption fell through, we'd be tortured by the sight of it all. So we hadn't said anything about Melissa to our families.

And we hadn't forgotten what we'd been told at the seminar: everything we needed for the first few weeks could be picked up on the way home from the hospital. There would be time for showers, presents, and shopping sprees after the kid was ours. Privately, we were excited, but publicly, we weren't letting on. Until that fetus was signed, sealed, and delivered, we weren't going to tempt fate.

Returning to OHSU for the first time since his father had died four years earlier was going to be traumatic for Terry, so I decided to indulge him. We couldn't afford to stay overnight, so I let him listen to whatever music he wanted to in the car. I let him play the CDs of his choice for as long as I could stand it.

Which was about fifteen minutes.

Our conversations on these drives to and from Portland had become routines, parodies of themselves and of our relationship. We should have taped one and played it every time we got in the car, saving ourselves the trouble of having the same argument over and over again. I complained about the music; he complained about my complaints. I pointed out that my complaints would stop when the music did. He pointed out that I don't have a driver's license, and invited me to shut up or walk to Portland. I pointed out that we'd both be walking to Portland if it weren't for my credit card. Then, around the halfway point, just outside Chehalis, Washington, Terry snapped off the music and we drove the rest of the way in silence.

As we drove, I thought about the time we'd spent with Melissa so far. In our previous visits, we'd covered a lot of ground but neither of us had said anything to her about how excited we were about becoming dads or how happy we were that she had picked us. In our effort not to get too carried away about the kid in public we'd made the mistake of not letting ourselves get carried away with Melissa in private. We hadn't even thanked her for picking us. Her drinking gave us a scare, but we liked our birth mom-to-be, and the three spooky coincidences—the Seattle conception, the likelihood that Melissa had spare-changed us on Broadway, and the fact that the kid would be born at OHSU— made our coming together seem somehow preordained.

But Melissa didn't invite mushy talk or touchy-feely any- thing. In addition to what we hadn't said, we also hadn't hugged, laughed much, or cried at all, which were all things we'd been told adoptive couples and birth moms did together during pre- birth meetings. We'd never even shaken Melissa's hand.

We knew we'd be talking with a social worker on this visit— not Laurie, but Melissa's social worker at the hospital. Melissa had told us the day we met that she hated meeting with Laurie be- cause Laurie asked her questions about how she felt. But today, with the help of her hospital social worker, I decided I would try to tell Melissa how we felt.

We were supposed to pick up Melissa in front of Outside In, not at her apartment—her idea. When we pulled up, Melissa walked over to the car, said she'd be a minute, and disappeared into the building. People over twenty-one are not allowed in Outside In except on official business, like our first meeting with Melissa and Laurie. Now that our calls on Melissa were social, we had to wait outside with the rest of the grown-ups. While we stood on the sidewalk, three homeless kids came out of the build- ing and stood on the porch. They were checking us out.

We smiled and nodded like a couple of squares. Two went back into the building, but a large girl with pink hair and a ring through her nose lit a cigarette and came down to get a closer look.

"You're the guys?" she asked. It wasn't a question, but an as- sessment. Terry confirmed that, yes, we were the guys.

"Melissa likes you. She's cool, totally my favorite person. I think this is great, you know, this whole thing you three are doing. It's really radical."

We hadn't sought their approval, but it was nice to know Port- land's homeless youth approved of gay adoption. What appealed to the girl with the pink hair and the nose ring wasn't Terry and me becoming parents, though, but how "radical" it was for gay men to adopt a homeless girl's baby. She and Melissa were out- siders—literally—and gay people are outsiders too. If Melissa was going to give her kid away, the girl with the nose ring said it was only right the kid should go to other outsiders. That was "radical."

Melissa came out of the house, tied her dog up on the porch, and walked straight up to us. She didn't look at the girl with the pink hair, who turned and walked back into the house. We exchanged heys.

"Your friend approves," I said. "She thinks this is radical."

Melissa shrugged. "She's not my friend."

We had about an hour to kill before Melissa's appointment, and Terry asked if she wanted to get something to eat.

Melissa looked away, shrugged, and said, "I don't care."

By now I was beginning to suspect that in Melissa-speak, "I don't care" meant yes, and "I don't know" meant no. So I insisted we go get some food. Ten minutes later we were sitting in Hamburger Mary's, an antiques- and tchotchke-filled burger joint that had definitely seen hipper (and cleaner) days. Melissa, another week bigger, had trouble squeezing into the booth, and while we waited for our food to come, Terry asked her how things were going.

Melissa had been caught sitting in a park the police had banned her from for three months. The same cop had caught her sleeping there a couple of times and warned her that if he found her in the park again, asleep or awake, he'd arrest her, she'd have to spend a night in jail, and she'd be fined.

"They think that's supposed to scare us," Melissa said. " 'You'll have to spend the night in jail.' You sleep in a bed, they feed you, and you walk out. It's better than sleeping in the rain."

What worried Melissa was the $200 fine, which she had ninety days to pay.

"I told the judge I couldn't pay it, that it wasn't like I had any money. I mean, that's *why* I was sleeping in the park. But he didn't give a shit."

If Melissa didn't pay the fine in ninety days, a warrant would be issued for her arrest. If she was stopped for anything by any cop—and gutter punks are always getting stopped by the police—she'd have to spend a couple of months in jail.

"It doesn't really matter for me," Melissa said, "but who would take care of my animals?"

It occurred to me that we didn't know the names of Melissa's dog and cat.

I wasn't sure Melissa had even told us their names. We'd seen her dog twice, and Melissa didn't introduce us, and we'd never seen her cat, which was always inside Outside In. Melissa took pride in how well she cared for her animals despite living on the street. She didn't like to be separated from them even for the hour or two she had to spend with us or at the doctors. But when she talked about them it didn't seem as if she enjoyed them much. They were a burden; she had trouble finding people she could trust to watch them when she had to be away, and she had a hard time traveling with them.

"No one will pick up a hitchhiker with two animals," she explained, "so that rules out cars." Melissa rode the rails instead, jumping on box cars in train yards and hoping they were going in the direction she wanted to go. Listening to her talk about jumping trains, I asked how she managed when carrying two animals.

"My cat goes in my pack," she said, looking at me as if I were the dumbest person she'd ever met, "and I don't have to carry my dog. Dogs can jump, you know. Anyway, getting on trains is the easy part," said Melissa. "It's getting off that can be hard."

She pointed to the scar above her eye. She was riding the rails with another kid late last summer, pregnant at the time though she didn't know it. The train was pulling through the town they were headed to in Montana, and it started picking up speed.

"Right after this town there's, like, a seven-mile-long tunnel. The tunnel fills up with the engine's exhaust and you can suffocate in it." They stayed on the train as long as they could, hoping it would slow down. It didn't. The train started into the tunnel.

"We had to get off so we jumped."

"With the dog and cat?" Terry asked.

"Yep."

She hit the ground hard, and smashed her head against a rock, ripping open her forehead.

"It was a pretty deep cut," she said. "But I was just glad my animals didn't get hurt." Her friend was hurt too, and probably they both should've seen a doctor. "But we didn't have any money and we didn't have anyone to leave the animals with."

"Are you going to pay the fine?" Terry asked, steering the conversation back to Melissa's run-in with the law.

"No. Anyway, in ninety days, I won't be pregnant anymore and I won't be in Portland anymore. I'm going up to Seattle, and then I'm heading to New York. It's not like they're going to come and get me."

Paying Melissa's fine occurred to me, but two things worked against the idea. First, birth-mother expenses were handled by the agency—we wrote a check to the agency for Melissa's rent; the agency wrote her landlord a check—to keep any money from changing hands between birth mothers and adoptive couples. Second, getting Melissa out of this jam could establish a very dangerous precedent. While we could afford to buy Melissa a steak when she wanted it, we probably couldn't afford to get her out of every jam the gutter-punk lifestyle can get a girl into.

Instead of offering to pay her fine, I brought up my arrest record. At three different ACT-UP demonstrations in the early nineties, I was hauled away in handcuffs, once from the rotunda of the U.S. Capitol. Along with two hundred others, I was arrested, held for ten hours in a room with no food, water, or toilets, and ordered to appear in court two weeks later. Two days later, though, I was back at home, with no intention of returning to Washington, D.C., until I'd been elected to Congress.

Melissa listened to my stories of being booked and sitting in holding cells. She nodded at me, and I could feel the beginnings of a bond. Terry liked the same music she did, and I'd been arrested. Melissa and I were fugitives, running from the law. Finally we shared something.

With Melissa in the back of our rental car, Terry drove us up the winding road to OHSU. Why would anyone put a hospital on top of a hill? I wondered. How do ambulances make it up in time to save anyone's life? We turned off the main road and drove past an emergency room I hope I never have to get to in a hurry. OHSU is a collection of buildings from the twenties, fifties, and seventies clumped together over three or four acres; the place feels more like a college campus than a hospital complex.

By the time we found the parking lot and made our way to the prenatal care clinic, we were late for Melissa's appointment. She signed in, and the three of us—two fags and a gutter punk—sat reading *Parenting* magazine while we waited for Melissa's name to be called. The first part of the appointment included a physical, and we weren't invited. When the nurse called her name, Melissa disappeared down the hall, leaving Terry and me alone in the waiting room.

"You okay?" I asked.

"I'm fine." Terry shrugged. "I thought I'd be upset, but I'm not. I'm okay."

I'd seen Terry get upset about his dad. His family learned the day before Thanksgiving that his father's second liver had failed and that the cancer had spread. He died five weeks later, two days after Christmas. A couple of years afterward, we were at my place getting ready to go to a friend's house on Thanksgiving when Terry walked into the bedroom and told me he missed his father. I didn't even look up.

"Really," I said, "hand me my shoe."

I didn't understand why he was bringing his father up; we were late for the party. He had told me his father died around the holidays, but he hadn't told me the dates, or if he had I wasn't paying attention. Anyway, we were late for dinner, I thought, what's with this dad stuff? Terry sat on the bed and started to sob. I dropped my shoe, held Terry, and apologized for being the World's Worst Boyfriend. Having seen what Thanksgiving can do to Terry, I assumed that being back at OHSU would be hard on him. But he seemed fine, and when the nurse told us Melissa's physical would take about twenty minutes, I suggested we go get something to drink in the cafeteria. We walked through a skyramp into another building, made our way to the elevators, and went down to the cafeteria. I got tea, Terry got coffee, we paid, we sat down in the dining room.

And it hit.

The ward where Terry's father had died was in another building. But this cafeteria was where bad news was passed from mother to sons, as they sat staring at food they couldn't make themselves eat. Terry didn't break down; he just needed to get the hell out of there. We took our drinks and headed back for the elevators.

"This is just so weird, being back here," he said. "God, I hate Portland."

★   ★   ★

When we returned to the prenatal care clinic, Melissa was looking for us. Her checkup had gone well. If we wanted to meet her hospital social worker, Melissa said, rolling her eyes, we'd need to go and sit in a counseling room with her and wait.

The room was small, windowless, and stuffy, and the three of us waited in silence for the social worker to show up. Despite having access to a shower and laundry room, Melissa still smelled like a homeless person. So far as we could tell, she hadn't bathed since we met her, or washed her clothes. On the street or in restaurants we didn't notice, but in a tiny room or a car, we could tell Melissa didn't do soap. She didn't smell filthy—she didn't reek—but her scent was strong and, in enclosed spaces, not very pleasant. I could only imagine what the doctor who did her physical thought.

The door opened and a less glamorous version of Laurie walked into the room, carrying a clipboard. Nancy was bright and cheerful, delighted to meet Terry and me, and she chirped "Hello" at Melissa, who faked a half-smile. She led us through a conversation about the birth; what Melissa needed to do when labor started, what floor she'd be on, how long Melissa could stay at the hospital after the birth. Nancy asked if she could make a note in Melissa's chart about a gay couple adopting her baby.

"That way, no confusion or misunderstanding, 'kay?" Nancy said. " 'Kay."

As long as she was making notes, Melissa asked Nancy to make a note about drugs. When she went into labor, Melissa wanted drugs and lots of them. She didn't want to be in pain at all during this birth, and she wanted the drugs to come early and often. Nancy explained that there were only certain times during labor when drugs could be administered; Melissa needed to come to the hospital as soon as she went into labor to ensure that she got all the drugs she had coming. She made a note in Melissa's chart about her concerns.

Nancy asked us if there were any other issues, and I said yes. I explained to Nancy that we'd been playing it cool with our friends about Melissa picking us, in case she changed her mind about us or about adoption.

"We realized that we've been playing it cool with Melissa too," I said, "and we probably shouldn't. We want her to know that we're excited about being dads and we're happy she picked us," I continued, looking at Nancy and talking about Melissa as if she weren't sitting in the room with us. "But we want to respect Melissa's right to change her mind, and keep the baby if that's what she wants to do. I think we maybe were worried that acting too excited would make Melissa feel like she had to give the baby up. I think not letting ourselves get carried away was a way to respect her rights."

Melissa and Terry were looking at me as if I were insane.

"I mean, do you feel pressure not to change your mind?" I asked.

"I don't feel any pressure," Melissa said, shrugging. "If I change my mind, someone else will pick you."

She said it matter-of-factly, and she meant to be comforting, but Melissa really spooked us. After we dropped her off at Outside In, Terry and I talked about what had seemed a hypothetical—Melissa changing her mind—now seeming like a very real possibility. What if Melissa was the only birth mother on earth who would see our picture and think, "That's them"? There might not be another "Susan" out there, we worried, and if we went back into the pool, there might not be someone else that would pick us.

Good News Will Come by Phone

I couldn't keep the news from my mother any longer; I was choking on guilt. Telling Mom would invite some jinx-y energy into our lives, but not telling her was becoming more difficult. Whenever we talked on the phone, she asked if we'd heard anything from the agency. Before we went into the pool, I'd explained that the average wait was a year. Whenever she asked what was up, I reminded her that we'd only just jumped into the pool.

"Well, I've got my fingers crossed. I'm rooting for you."

"It's not a race, Mom. And, anyway, no one gets picked in the first month. It's going to be a while."

"Well, I'll keep you guys in my thoughts."

That's code: when my mother says she'll keep us "in her thoughts" what she means is "in her prayers," but she defers to my delicate atheistic sensibilities and doesn't mention prayer.

By this point, of course, we had been picked. Most of our friends and coworkers knew about Melissa, and we'd told them that barring "BBD/BCM," Terry and I would be dads in a few weeks. But our parents didn't have a clue. Since my mother and her husband live outside Chicago, and Terry's mom and stepdad live at the other end of Washington state, keeping the news from them was easier than keeping it from our friends and coworkers. We had to get time off work to go to Portland, and when friends were over we were constantly on the phone with the agency and generally acting like dorks. Our friends demanded answers. But our parents? All they knew was that lately we were a little harder to get hold of.

Even if our parents had been in town we wouldn't have told

them about Melissa right away. Our friends could keep calm, and they understood why we weren't letting ourselves get excited. We could say "BBD/BCM" to our friends. When we begged off the baby shower, Terry's coworkers understood. But our parents? By which I mean, But my mother? My mother treats every occasion—every trip to the corner store, every birthday, every holiday—like the invasion of Normandy. Every contingency must be planned for, every worst possible outcome must be imagined and prepared for, and everything and anything that might be needed must be packed in.

For example, when I was suddenly making grown-up money for the first time in my life, I made good on a promise I'd given my mother when I was a child: I took her to Europe for New Year's Eve. When we were getting ready to leave for the airport, I took a long look at my mother's suitcase. I was the sherpa who'd be lugging her bag from Zurich to Vienna to Munich and back to Chicago, and I had a stake in just how heavy it was. The bag she'd packed was a little bigger than, oh, the state of Vermont, though it weighed more. I opened it up to see what was in there, and what did I find among the ten pairs of shoes, the rolls of toilet paper, and the case of Tic Tacs? Chocolate. My mother was taking a two-pound bag of crappy American chocolate on a trip to *Switzerland*. I pulled the chocolate out and begged my mother to leave it behind, assuring her that, yes, we could get all the chocolate we might need on our trip to Switzerland *in* Switzerland.

"But we might need some on the plane or at night in the hotel," Mom insisted, shoving the bag of M&Ms back into her bag. "And it's not that heavy."

Okay. Why three pairs of boots? Why toilet paper? Why Tic Tacs?

"My feet hurt if I don't wear different shoes every day, and we're going to be doing a lot of walking. Phyllis from work went to Europe once and there wasn't any toilet paper in her hotel room. And I like Tic Tacs."

I was willing to concede (and carry) everything else, but I insisted she leave the chocolate behind. My mother responded that she needed everything she'd packed, and that if the chocolate wasn't coming, she wasn't coming. She was a grown woman, and who was I to tell her what she couldn't bring on this trip?

We fought long and loud, as is our family custom, before I fi-

nally gave up. And I carried that two-pound bag of Peanut
M&Ms from Chicago to Zurich to Vienna to Munich and back
to Chicago. We never opened it, never touched the stuff, and
what chocolate we ate on our trip was purchased en route. When
I pointed this out to my mother once we'd arrived safely back in
Chicago, she said she "felt better" knowing she had chocolate in
her bag, "just in case."

Just in case of what?

"Just in case we wanted chocolate."

My mother being the kind of woman who carries chocolate to
Switzerland "just in case," we had a good idea what to expect
once we told her we'd been picked: baby stuff, tons of it, in the
mail, every day, and three or four of everything "just in case." I
imagined a typical conversation:

"Mom, why did you send us three car seats?"

"A woman from work, her daughter had an ultrasound, and
the doctor said she was having one baby, just one. She goes into
the hospital and comes home with three. Triplets, Danny! If
Melissa has just one baby, you can return the other two car seats,
but I thought, you know, just in case."

"But we already bought a car seat, Mom."

"Well, then pick the one you like the best and get rid of the
other three. I won't be hurt if you don't use any of the car seats I
sent."

Also, we were making a conscious effort not to fill our house
with baby stuff for fear of, well, of our apartment filling up with
baby stuff. If anything went wrong, we didn't want to wind up
sitting in a house full of baby stuff with no baby. Since the call
came, we'd allowed ourselves to buy exactly one thing for the
baby: that flannel shirt from Baby Gap. That was it. Three weeks
to go, and we had no crib, no diapers, no bottles, no car seats, no
bibs, no rattles, no onesies—no nothing. In case this adoption fell
through—BBD/BCM—we weren't going to be tormented by
empty car seats and unused diapers. We weren't going make the
same mistake that other gay couple made—no, we were going to
make new mistakes.

To keep the news from my mother, we had to keep it from
Terry's mother too. Our mothers had joined the information age.
They were e-mailing each other daily, and anything we told

Claudia would be shared with Judy in five minutes flat. On the other hand, while we feared an overexcited shop-happy grandma reaction from my mother, we dreaded the opposite from Terry's mom.

Not that Claudia had a problem with Terry being a homo; she didn't. She had a picture of us hanging on a wall in her living room. But the Christmas letter that covered every aspect of her straight son's life while neglecting to mention that her gay son was, for all intents and purposes, pregnant had given us some indication of his mother's feelings. Terry dreaded telling her about Melissa—and her first grandchild!—because he expected an underwhelmed response. Terry's mother wasn't the most expressive person to begin with, and it was sometimes hard to tell when she was excited or pleased. We might not be able to tell the difference between her usual unflappable demeanor and disapproval, and we might overscrutinize her reaction to the news and misread it. Maybe she thought what we were doing was great. Or maybe she didn't mind having a gay son but gay adoption crossed the line for her. We were about to find out.

My stepfather, Jerry, answered the phone when I called to lay the news on them. We spoke for a few minutes, discussing the things men and their stepfathers discuss, and said good-bye when my mother clicked on the line. I let her have it:

"Mom, we got picked. Her name is Melissa, the baby is due March twenty-second, and it looks like it's going to happen."

"Oh, my God! That's wonderful! When did you get the call?"

I was afraid she'd ask me that. Telling my mom that she was among the last to hear the news was something I dreaded. My mom and I are close, and she likes to be the first to know when anything important happens in my life.

"Three weeks ago."

"Ahhhhhhh! Jerry! They got the call three weeks ago! What day? What day?"

"On a Saturday."

"I KNEW IT!"

I could hear my mother jumping up and down.

On the day the call came, she and Jerry were eating at the Chinese restaurant they went to on their first date: "We've been eating in Chinese restaurants for ten years, Danny, and this has never happened before. We never got the same fortune in our cookies before, not once. And what was our fortune three weeks ago? 'Good news will come by phone.' In both our cookies! I looked at Jerry and said, 'Dan and Terry got picked.' I knew it! Aha! I KNEW IT!"

Mom saved the fortunes, "for the baby book," and would bring them out when she came to see the baby. We talked about Melissa for a long time, and just when I thought I was in the clear my mother asked why on earth we'd waited three weeks to tell her.

"Because babies are born dead, and birth mothers change their minds."

"Danny!"

"This could still fall through, Mom. They call it a disruption. And we didn't want to do anything that might jinx things, like blabbing about the baby or Melissa to our friends and family. Acting like the baby is ours before he really is would jinx things."

I told her about the other gay couple and their house full of baby stuff, and told her we weren't buying anything.

"And we don't want you sending crates of stuff either," I explained. "Are you listening to me? No shopping. Don't buy things for a baby that isn't really ours yet, okay?"

There was a short, stunned silence. And then, the deluge.

We had to shop! We had to prepare! With a tone in her voice I'd never heard her use before, she warned me that if we didn't start shopping we would be bad parents. There was another person in the picture—her second grandson—and he had to be provided for. There was a life at stake.

"There's going to be this little person in your life who's dependent on you guys for everything," Mom said, "and when you get him home and he needs a blanket or he has a fever and you need a thermometer, you can't say, 'Sorry, little person, we'd have everything we need to take care of you in our house but we didn't want to jinx things!' You're going to be parents in a few weeks! You have to get ready!"

Mom had a point.

She wanted to start shopping that afternoon, but she didn't want to feel guilty about it. She wanted my blessing, but I wasn't budging. I explained again about the other gay couple: they had showers, they sent out announcements, their house was full of baby stuff, and then . . . no baby.

"It ruined their relationship, Mom. They broke up from the stress. We don't want that to happen to us. Babies are born dead—"

"Stop being morbid!"

"—birth mothers change their minds. It's not just the jinx we're worried about. If this falls through, we don't want to be basket cases. A house full of bibs and diapers and toys will turn us into basket cases. Do *not* send presents."

"But if it doesn't fall through, your baby will freeze to death! Danny!"

"The agency told us that we could get everything we need for the first week on the way home from the hospital. You are *not* to send anything until we get home with the baby, and that's final. You have the rest of his life to buy things for him, but until he's ours any packages from you go straight in the trash."

There was a pause as my mother searched for a way out.

"Okay, I won't *send* anything. I'm not saying I won't shop. But I promise I won't send anything until you say I can, okay?"

"All right."

Mom sounded very oppressed. To cheer her up, I told her that we'd chosen Daryl Jude for a name, for Terry's father and for her.

"Oh, Danny. I am so honored," she said. I could hear her starting to tear up, and to avoid a scene, I changed the subject back to shopping.

"You're not the only one we're oppressing with a no-shopping order. Terry's friends from the bookstore tried to throw us a shower and we wouldn't let them."

"How come they knew before me?"

"Because Terry got the call at work. You're the first person we told on purpose, Mom. I swear."

"You're more Catholic than you know, Danny," my mother said, and told me a family story I hadn't heard before:

When my mother was pregnant with my oldest brother, some of her girlfriends decided to throw her a baby shower. My mother, thrilled, invited her mother—my grandmother—and all of her aunts. They refused to attend.

"Good Irish Catholics didn't have baby showers then," Mom

said, "because to have or attend a shower was to presume God would let your baby live, and you don't presume upon God."

According to my grandmother and great-aunts, having a baby shower was tempting fate. If our Heavenly Father got wind of your presumptiousness, He might kill your baby out of spite.

"The time to celebrate, your grandmother told me, was after you had the baby and it was healthy. You could have a shower and accept gifts after God blessed you with a healthy baby, not before, never before."

My grandmother, like a lot of Irish Catholics in her time, believed the Lord her God to be something of a psychopath-cum-hit man. If He found out you had a baby shower, He'd send an angel down to wrap the umbilical cord around your baby's neck, or trip you at the top of a long flight of stairs. If you were just considering having a baby shower, maybe an angel would come down and put a horse head in your bed. Nice guy, our Irish Catholic God. My mother went ahead and had a shower over her mother's objections. Billy was born prematurely, and for a few days it looked as if he might die. My grandmother—who was not a well woman—informed my worried mother that the premature birth was her fault: she'd gone ahead and had a baby shower, and now God was going to kill her baby.

A priest rushed to the hospital to baptize premature Billy; this was before Vatican II, and if little Billy died unbaptized, he wouldn't have gone to heaven. But God, all merciful, took pity on my shower-havin' mother and let Billy live, much to my grandmother's dismay.

This story makes my grandmother sound like an ogre. While she was a suicidal alcoholic who took out her anger at the world on her oldest child, my mother, *my* memories of Grandmother Hollahan are sweet. But I didn't spend my high school years pulling her head out of the oven, and she didn't wear black to my wedding. Until I was ten years old, my family lived in the same two-flat apartment building my mother had grown up in. My grandparents and a couple of my mother's siblings lived downstairs; we lived upstairs. We were multigenerational in a way that seemed perfectly natural then—we weren't the only family on the block sharing a two-flat. All I remember is a sweet old lady with syrupy breath who used to pop her dentures out of her mouth to scare us, and handed candy out the back door to the kids in the neighborhood after school. When I was in the first grade, my grandmother died in her sleep.

"You're resurrecting a fine old tradition, Danny, not having a baby shower. Your grandmother would be proud."

The same day I told my mother, Terry told his.

Terry gets annoyed when I describe his mother as cold. She isn't cold, he insists, just a little standoffish, and not so gabby as certain members of my family. While Terry's mom doesn't believe in asking intrusive questions, like "How are you?" she's still a warm and loving mom; just quiet and undemonstrative.

But she isn't cold. Nonetheless, when he picked up the phone he feared a cold reaction most. He told Claudia we'd been picked, told her the due date, told her the baby was a boy, and told her we were naming him after Terry's father and Claudia's late husband, Daryl. Terry's mother said, "Wow, that was really fast. You didn't have to wait long, did you?"

And that was all she said. She changed the subject, she and Terry talked for a few more minutes about other things: a trip she and Dennis, Terry's stepfather, would be taking to Alaska; her garden; Terry's absolutely fascinating older brother. Then they hung up.

A minute passed, and the phone rang.

"Do you want us to bring the crib over?"

The crib is a family heirloom: Terry's grandmother bought it in a Montana junk store in the forties, and no one knows for sure how old it is. It was Terry's mother's when she was a baby, then his older brother Tom's, then Terry's. It hadn't been used in twenty-five years, and was sitting in his grandmother's basement.

"When you went into the pool, I went over to Grandma's to see if it was still there, and to see what kind of shape it was in," Claudia said. "It looks good. And the mattress you used is still in there, and smells fine. No mold or anything. I thought it might be nice for your son to have your, and my, crib. You want us to bring it over?"

Terry said yes, he'd like that very much.

"Dennis has a meeting in Seattle in two weeks"—the day before the baby was due—"and we'll bring over the crib then. Okay?"

Okay.

Before she hung up, Claudia asked Terry what my mother wanted to be called: Grandma Judy? Grandmother? Gramma Judy?

My mother had been signing letters to us "Grandma" since we went to the seminar six months ago.

"We're pretty sure she want to be Grandma Judy," Terry said.

"Good. I want to be Grammy. Grammy Claudia, okay?"

Okay.

She asked if she could relay the news to Tom, and Terry told her that would be fine.

When he was about to hang up, Terry said, "Bye, Mom."

"Oh, no. Call me Grammy. I have to get used to it."

Apparently, Claudia was warming up to the idea.

When we let our families know, I forgot to tell my father. Not only didn't he know we'd been picked, he didn't even know we were adopting. He called me the day after I told my mother; he and his wife Joellen were coming up for a couple of days. Could we get together for dinner?

My parents divorced when I was sixteen years old, more than half my life ago. When my father moved out, in the summer of '81; he left my mother with four teenagers, no money, and no property. But the spookiest thing about his leaving was what little impact it seemed to have on our physical home. His desk disappeared, my mother was destroyed, and were it not for the generosity of our next-door neighbors and landlords, Kathy and Denis Paulach, who never raised our rent again, we would've been homeless. But everything else was right where it had been the day before. It was as if my father had never been there at all.

I'd been planning to come out to my mother that summer, but I couldn't bring myself to tell the weeping divorced lady that— surprise!—one of her kids was gay, too. I put off coming out to her for two more years.

My mother tells me that early in our lives my father was very involved, much more than other fathers were at the time, and that he was a great dad. My early memories of him are colored by the strain my sexuality put on our relationship and by the pain of the divorce. Quack therapists who claim they can "repair" gay men believe poor relationships between father and son are the root cause of homosexuality. If only I'd bonded properly with my father in childhood, they argue, I wouldn't spend so much time fantasizing about bondage with Matt Damon today.

These quacks fail to take the obvious into consideration: gay boys sometimes have strained relationships with their fathers *because* they're gay. My homosexuality damaged my relationship with my father; my damaged relationship with my father did not create my homosexuality. Of his three sons, I was the only one who hated sports, baked cakes, and listened to musical comedy. Something about me just wasn't right in his eyes, and while I know in my heart he loved me, I was painfully aware that he didn't understand me and that I embarrassed him. By the time I was old enough to realize what my thing for musical comedy meant, my dad had figured it out a long time ago.

And, of course, by that time much of the damage was already done. One of my most painful childhood memories is of my father explaining to my mother why Anita Bryant was right about "the gays." I was in the backseat of our green Chevy Nova, wedged among my three oblivious siblings. "The gays are a threat to society economically because they don't fall in love, get married, settle down, and have kids. They don't buy cars or washing machines or lawn mowers. So gay rights will mean fewer jobs for people who make cars, washing machines, and lawn mowers. Gays should be tolerated, but they couldn't be trusted with kids."

He spoke out of ignorance, not malice. But I didn't know that at the time, and his comments hurt me. The irony is that of my father's four children, only the homo has fallen in love and settled down. I'm the only who can afford to buy a washing machine right now.

It didn't help that my dad was a Chicago homicide detective whose beat included Chicago's gay neighborhood. In the seventies, gay neighborhoods were not filled with trendy restaurants, pricey condos, and rainbow geegaws. They were filled with sleazy bars, male hustlers, and violent predators. Before I came out to my father, most of the gay men he'd met were murderers.

When my parents' marriage began to fall apart, I was fourteen years old. I knew I was queer and no longer felt welcome at the neighbor boys' reindeer games. So, I spent a lot of time hiding in the attic, up a tree in the backyard, or lying under the dining room table listening to musical comedy on eight-track tape. I was home a lot during the two years when my father was pulling away from my mother. My siblings were not around, so they missed out on most of the fights. My dad would storm out, and I would find my mother sobbing in her bedroom. There were fights where things were thrown and broken, usually by my father, and the things broken were usually very important to my mother, tchotchkes that had belonged to her grandmother. Once, after they had separated, my dad came over. He and my mother went for a walk while I lay under the dining room table listening to *Camelot*. They walked back in the front door just as Robert Goulet started singing, "If ever I would leave you . . ." My mother burst into tears; my father looked at me and sighed, and then walked back out of the house.

As things fell apart with his wife, my dad made a lot of promises to his four kids, all of which he seemed to break. He promised he wouldn't move out. He did. He promised he wouldn't divorce my mother. He did. He promised there was no one else. There was. He promised he wouldn't marry Joellen. He did. He promised he wouldn't move away. He moved to California.

On a visit home years later, my father took my brothers and me out for drinks. Out of nowhere, he announced that he and Joellen weren't going to have any children. He wanted us to know that. It was a promise. When he got up and went to the bathroom, my brothers and I looked at one another in stunned silence.

Finally, I said, "Joellen must be in labor."

"With twins," said Eddie.

"Conjoined, I hope," said Billy.

As a result of the lies and the pain I believed he'd caused, for years I refused to speak to my father. I wouldn't see him at Christmas, or talk with him on the phone. If we walked in the front door, I walked out the back. By the time I was willing to talk to him again, I was almost twenty. By that point, I'd pretty much forgotten how to talk to him.

That was when he married Joellen.

Joellen is a very nice person, she's good for my father, and the time I've spent with her over the last decade has been very pleasant. She knows, I think, that the divorce was very hard on me and all these years later she still tiptoes around me. But the day my father married her was among the most painful of my life. It ripped open and rubbed salt into every one of my mother's wounds, and put my relationship with my father back on ice for five years.

My dad married Joellen on Mother's Day, 1983.

Billy and I often argue about that. I don't know if the choice of Mother's Day was intentional, but it was a terrible thing to do. If my father or Joellen picked the date on purpose, it's unforgivable. If they picked it by accident, they should have changed it the minute they realized. They didn't, and early in the morning on Mother's Day, 1983, my mother helped dress her four children in formal wear and waved good-bye as we headed out to her husband's second wedding. On Mother's Day.

Why did I go? Why didn't I stay home? The divorce left my mother with fears of abandonment that will last the rest of her life. And we abandoned her on Mother's Day, left her alone in an empty house. My father asked Billy and Eddie and me to usher, and at least I refused to do that. But I wish I'd stayed home. My father had the bad taste to select that love-never-dies, love-never-alters passage from Psalms or Corinthians or somewhere, and as it was read, I started sobbing. The video camera recording the service was set up right behind the pew I was in, and all you can hear on the video is me crying.

My father and I have a perfectly cordial relationship these days. He's come to Seattle to visit, and he's met Terry. A hesitation and tentativeness linger over our relationship, though. Sometimes I get the sense that my father still worries that I'm angry. I'm not, not really. The wedding was a long time ago. But we were alienated from each other for so long, from the time I was about nine years old, that I'm not sure we'll ever have the kind of relationship that he has with his other children.

When I have news to share with my family, it never occurs to me to call my father in California. So Terry and I were two weeks away from getting a baby when I told him we were adopting, and even then it was only because he came to town. It wasn't even until we were standing on a sidewalk outside a restaurant in Seattle, waiting for a table, that I realized I hadn't told my father we were going to be dads.

My father was also the last to know I was gay. I waited until I was twenty-one and away at college to tell him, afraid he would react badly. He drove down with my sibs and my mom to see me in a play, and while the rest of the family waited inside the Courier Café, my father and I stood on the sidewalk out front and I told him what he already knew. He was upset, but not about me being gay.

He was upset that I didn't tell him sooner.

Spelling Out Melissa's Rights

For the first time since we met Melissa at Outside In six weeks ago, the three of us were going to get together with Laurie. Melissa was hugely pregnant now. When we picked her up in front of her apartment, she had trouble getting in the car. The last time we saw her, Melissa had a kid-induced barrel chest, but now the baby had "dropped," and she was carrying him lower to the ground. She was having trouble sleeping, sitting, standing, and walking.

She told us she was anxious to get this whole thing over with. She was sick and tired of being pregnant, being counseled, and being housed. I got the feeling that Melissa was sick and tired of our weekly getting-to-know-you meetings, too, but she was too polite to say so. She was looking forward to not having to talk with Laurie about her feelings anymore, and she was happy she wouldn't be living in an apartment for much longer. She wanted to get back out on the streets with her friends, and she wanted to travel with her animals. But while Melissa was looking forward to not being pregnant, she dreaded giving birth.

"I hate pain," she said flatly. She was worried the doctors wouldn't give her pain meds in the hospital because she was a street punk. "They might think I don't need the drugs, that I just, you know, want to get high or something."

We'd come to Portland to hammer out our Open Adoption Agreement. This was the last piece of paper we had to sign before the birth, spelling out Melissa's rights: how many visits per year, how many phone calls, how many times per year we'd send photos. The numbers are floors, not ceilings. If we wanted to get together more, we could. If there was any conflict down the road, the agency would mediate, using the Open Adoption Agreement as a guide. The birth mother's visits could be terminated only if she was abusive, or became a danger to the child.

When we arrived at the office, Laurie was in the waiting room. She wanted to speak privately with Melissa for a few minutes. We plopped down on the couch; Terry picked up a *People* magazine and I flipped through the world's most depressing publication: a newsletter published by the state of Oregon profiling adorable-looking but hard-to-place children. DG kids. Three years' worth of newsletters were in a binder, and I flipped through them as we waited. Under each photo of a smiling child, three paragraphs detailed the "tremendous progress" little Susie/Mikey/Jenny/Andy had made since being placed in foster care. Next, the horrendous abuse that got little Susie/Mikey/Jenny/Andy taken away from his or her biological parents and placed in foster care was detailed. Reading about these DG kids sandpapered every guilt nerve in my body, which is to say *every* nerve in my body. That we were adopting—or hoping to adopt—a healthy baby boy when there were abused children out there who needed homes made me feel . . . rotten.

I showed the newsletters to Terry and told him that reading these kids' stories made me want to adopt a DG kid. He rolled his eyes and advised me to stop reading the newsletters. Terry was unashamed of his desire to adopt a healthy baby, and refused to feel guilty about it or any of the other things I wasted hours every day feeling guilty about. I felt guilty about having enough money to rent cars and buy children, but besides overtipping whenever we ate out, I didn't do anything about other people's poverty. I felt guilty about the decimated rain forests, but I shopped at Ikea.

When Laurie called us into her office, Melissa was sitting against one wall, staring at the floor. Terry and I sat down on a low couch against the opposite wall. Laurie sat at her desk. Laurie asked us how our meetings were going. Terry and I did almost all the talking, telling Laurie that things were fine—we went out to eat; we attended Melissa's prenatal appointment last week at OHSU. . . . Laurie listened and nodded.

"It sounds like things have been going very well," Laurie said. "Would you say that, Melissa?"

"Yeah." Melissa shrugged.

Laurie asked whether Melissa had given any thought to how many visits she wanted per year. Melissa stared at the floor and mumbled, "I don't care." For Melissa, this should have been enough—she didn't care, end of discussion. But Laurie pressed her, calmly laying out all her options and encouraging her to make a decision. Melissa was in hell. "I haven't really thought about it," she said, sinking into her chair, miserable.

Laurie turned to us. Had we given visitation any thought?

I gave a little speech about how we wanted the baby to know his mother. One of the reasons open adoption appealed to us, I explained to Melissa while looking at Laurie, was that we wanted our kid to have a relationship with his mom. Some couples were threatened by the presence of an "extra" mom: they might want to limit the number of visits, so the adoptive mother could feel like the "real" one.

"We welcome," I heard myself say in perfect agency-speak, "a high level of contact. We wrote that in our birthparent letter, and we meant it. We're not threatened by the baby having a relationship with Melissa." Finally, I turned and looked at Melissa. "We want him to know you. So as far as we're concerned, Laurie can put any number of visits on that form. She can write down three hundred and sixty-five visits per year. You can see the baby as much as you want."

Laurie intervened.

"Why don't we write down four visits per year?" She looked from me and Terry to Melissa. "If you want to get together more, that's fine. But most couples and birth moms set four as the minimum. Does four sound good?"

We nodded; Melissa said, "I guess," and Laurie wrote down, "Four."

"Remember," Laurie said, "that this is the *minimum* number of visits. You can get together as much as you care to, if you're all willing. But Dan and Terry can't give you less than four visits per year." Laurie had clearly pulled this maneuver before. Overly Solicitous Adoptive Couple makes unrealistic offer of daily visits to Birth Mother. Counselor steps in, brings the couple back to reality, writes down a workable number, and saves Adoptive Couple from the logistical nightmare of legally enforceable daily visits from Birth Mother.

"How many photo exchanges?"

Melissa asked for two sets of photos per year, except in the first.

"Kids grow a lot in the first year," she informed us all. "So more photos during the first year would be good."

Laurie wrote down four sets of photos during year one, and two sets per year thereafter. Since Melissa didn't have an address, we agreed to send the photos to the agency, which would keep them in Melissa's file.

Phone calls? We put down one a month, though we told Melissa she could call as much as she wanted.

"I'll have to call collect, you know."

"That's fine," Terry said.

All these numbers we were tossing around—four visits, two sets of photos, one phone call per month—bound only Terry and me. Melissa wasn't compelled to call every month, nor did she have to come for her four yearly visits. The amount of contact Melissa had with the baby would be up to Melissa. The day after the placement, the birth mom was free to disappear, if that was what she wanted, and we were told at the seminar that some did just that. The adoptive couple was not free to disappear. Until the baby was eighteen years old, we had to make sure the agency had our current address and phone number.

Before our session ended, Laurie told us Melissa had one special request that she wanted written into the open adoption agreement. If she ever patched things up with her family, she wanted us to let the baby meet her mother, father, and siblings.

"Is that acceptable to you guys?" Laurie asked. Before we could answer, Melissa broke in. "This baby is their first grandchild, you know, and they'll probably want to meet him at some point," she said. "And my little brother might want to know he's an uncle."

Holding her pen over the form, Laurie looked up at Terry and me. Birth grandparents have no rights in Oregon, nor do birth uncles, and we didn't have to agree to this request. All we were required to do was allow Melissa to visit the baby in our presence, but we had no obligation to Melissa's extended family.

"Is one mandatory visit with the birth grandparents acceptable to you guys?"

I looked at Terry, who shrugged the question back into my lap. "Of course."

We left the agency's offices and headed over to Lloyd Center. With the baby due in two weeks, Terry and I had decided that it was time to buy a few things we'd need right away. Like a car seat. The hospital, Laurie told us, wouldn't let us leave with the baby unless he was strapped into a car seat. Laurie also told us that shopping for a car seat was a good thing for birth moms and adoptive couples to do together: "It makes the birth mother feel like she's doing her part to get the baby home safe from the hospital."

We wound up at the Toys "R" Toxic that Terry and I had wandered through when we got lost on our way to the seminar back in May. In the aisle with the car seats, we had our first encounter with hot-plastic injection-molded products. Maybe one of the reasons I'd been putting off shopping, and letting others shop for the baby, was to temporarily stave off the onslaught of plastic products that would fill every last bit of our house once the baby did arrive. Plastic baby carriages, play stands, car seats, walkers, high chairs, toys, baby baths—how did people raise kids before plastic came along? "Everything for Baby," said the sign over the aisle we were in. It should have said, "Everything for Baby Is Made from Molded Plastic in Ugly Primary Colors."

Terry, always prepared, pulled *Consumer Reports* ratings for car seats out of his wallet and began to search for the top-rated model—the only one that would do. Melissa and I sat down on the floor and watched Terry do what Terry does best: shop. Melissa and I were equally uncomfortable and out of place in Toys "R" Toxic. Once Terry found the car seat, we made our way to the "newborn" aisle. Some boldly patterned red-and-black toys hanging on one wall caught our eyes. We read the packages and were all shocked—shocked!—to discover that babies needed to be exposed to red, black, and white colors, in bold patterns, or else their brains would turn to poo and dribble out their ears. How did any of us survive the light pastel shades and fuzzy edges that decorated everything for baby when we were newborns?

While Terry waited in line to pay for our pastel plastic car seat and a couple of red-and-black toys ("Just in case . . ."), Melissa and I sat down on the floor again, this time by a jungle gym display near the doors. Melissa was enjoying our shopping mall field trip about as much as she enjoyed walking into that steakhouse. Two blond girls walked by, staring at Melissa's dirty clothes and knee-high Doc Martens boots. Once they'd passed us, they started giggling, looking back at the freaky pregnant girl and her . . . what am I? Her brother? A security guard? Her parole officer? Melissa's eyes narrowed and followed the girls as they left the store.

"That's everyone I went to school with."

We ate dinner in a fifties-nostalgia diner off Lloyd Center's food court, and talked about David, a friend of Melissa's who was staying in the apartment with her.

"He eats the food I cook and doesn't help clean," Melissa said, shaking her head. "You would think that if you cooked for someone they would at least offer to, like, do the dishes."

Terry kicked me under the table. Terry cooked for me, but I resented having to do dishes. As I saw it, Terry liked cooking—he enjoyed it, he told me so. Well, I didn't enjoy washing dishes—I hated it, and I'd told him so—and didn't see why I should have to do something I hated after he got to do something he liked. I mean, that wasn't fair, was it?

While we ate our hamburgers and BLTs, a family sat down in the booth next to ours. Their little boy started playing peekaboo with me, popping his head over the booth. I played along, wiggling my ears, raising my eyebrows, making faces. This, naturally, drove the boy wild. He was jumping all over, shrieking, and his mother couldn't get him to calm down—I was just too amusing. Finally, I got caught making faces: the little boy's mother turned to me and said, "Would you stop."

Melissa laughed her low, quiet laugh. "Just wait," she said, "people are going to do that to you when you're out with the kid, and you're going to be the grouchy parent. Just wait."

On the way back to Outside In, Terry and Melissa made plans to hook up next Monday, as I couldn't come down next week. When we dropped Melissa off, her inconsiderate roommate

David, looking every inch the crystal addict, was waiting on the porch with Melissa's dog and cat.

Melissa said good-bye, got out of the car, and made her way up to the porch. She took her dog's leash and turned and waved at us. Terry shouted, "See you Monday!" from inside the car, and Melissa nodded. As we drove off, I turned and looked back. Melissa was sitting on the porch, petting her dog and talking with David.

It was the last time we saw her pregnant.

Birth

David Kevin

When we got home with one plastic car seat and red-and-black toys, I had a small panic attack. Besides what we bought in Portland with Melissa, and the flannel shirt we'd allowed ourselves to buy at Baby Gap, we had nothing we needed for the kid. No crib, no diapers, no bottles, no formula, no changing table. Nothing. This was our own fault, of course. Actually, it was my fault, since my fear of jinxing things led to the shopping ban. But with Melissa's due date only two weeks off, we had more bondage stuff in the house than baby stuff.

With the religious right threatening to go after the gay adoptions, I probably shouldn't mention the bondage stuff in our basement. Gay men with bondage stuff adopting little baby boys will give Pat Robertson and Jerry Falwell screaming nightmares. I don't want to play into hands of my mortal enemies, but I shouldn't have to lie. In a corner of our basement, there was a box filled with nylon rope, some leather restraints, a paddle, and a blindfold. Some of these were gifts: when a sex-advice columnist has a birthday, he gets sex toys and you can't return sex toys. While bondage wasn't something Terry and I did—which is why the bondage stuff was in a box in the basement and not in our bedroom, where it was with my last boyfriend—I'm not going to lie and say I haven't done it. Or dug it.

Like a lot of people—Madonna comes to mind—I've been tied up with erotic intent, and I've tied others up. Bondage and SM aren't the depraved nightmare stuff the religious right fantasizes about; they're cops and robbers for grown-ups, with full frontal nudity and orgasms. And anyway, even if I wanted to deny ever having been tied up, I couldn't. I've been writing about sex—and my sex life—for too long to cover it up effectively. (And there are those awful Polaroids floating around out there somewhere.) If having been tied up and fucked disqualifies people from having kids, how come no one wants to take Lourdes away from Madonna? In *Sex*, Madonna's pictured all tied up with lesbian SMers, male strippers, and Vanilla Ice, for Christ's sake. No one has suggested Madonna's an unfit parent—not because of *Sex*, anyway.

During our interviews with the agency, we were never questioned about our sex practices by any of the counselors. None of the straight couples I know who've adopted were asked about their sex practices either. The assumption is, I think, that if you're an adult without a criminal record or a North American Man/Boy Love Association membership you're capable of making a distinction between your sex partners and your children. I assume that Pat Robertson enjoys missionary position sex with his wife, but not with his daughters (if he has any). Like Pat, I am capable of making a distinction between my spouse and my kids. My straight mom didn't sleep with my straight brothers, my father never slept with his daughter, I've never made a pass at my brothers. Incest isn't something we Savages do.

Some straight people worry gay people aren't capable of making distinctions between appropriate and inappropriate sex partners. Since we reject the taboo against same-sex sex, the "reasoning" and the far-right fund-raising appeals go, we're necessarily inclined toward rejecting taboos against incest, necrophilia, and gerbils. There are sexual taboos that I am comfortable with, and have not only observed all my life but also done my best to shore up. I come down very hard on incest in my sex-advice column, and will continue to do so as long as I can crawl to my computer and type. But how can I convince someone who believes being gay means I want to sleep with all men, any man, alive or dead, any species, whatever his relation to me, that I've never been interested in having sex with my brothers? Or my father? And that I will never be interested in having sex with my son?

The religious right maintains that gay men who want to teach or lead a Boy Scout troop or be Big Brothers are somehow a threat to children. The implication is that gay men who want to be near children, or adopt children, must want to fuck them. Forgive me if that's indelicately put, but it's the truth. This is the fear that led two states to outlaw gay men and lesbians adopting children (though one, New Hampshire, recently overturned its anti-gay adoption law) and made it nearly impossible for gays and lesbians to adopt even in states where it was technically legal. Like most gay men, I have a sense of humor about the lies told about my life.

What's funny about the whole evil disco-dancin' gay baby-rapist nightmare is that the truth of why gay men want to be dads is so much *more* disturbing. When I fantasized about becoming a dad, I didn't picture myself having sex with my children. No, in my dad fantasies, I saw myself going to work, making money, and coming home to Terry and the kid. I help the baby learn to walk and talk. Years later, I help him with his homework while I half-listen to Terry tell me about a PTA meeting. I wanted to be a dad so I could take my kid to ball games and McDonald's and on camping trips.

What the religious right fears most about gay adoption is not that we'll be bad parents, or that we'll have sex with our kids, or that we'll try to make them gay. What they fear is that we'll be pretty good parents. I've done drag. I did Barbie drag, dominatrix drag, nun drag, and glamour drag. Now I'm going to do dad drag. I pulled Barbie off pretty well, and I was gonna be good at this dad stuff, too. And that's what worried Pat Robertson. The more gay men and lesbians raise children, the harder it's going to become for the right to convince people that we're monsters. Once straights have seen boring gay parents at a PTA meeting bitching about class size and school uniforms (I'm in favor smaller formers and mandatory latters), we're not going to seem so scary anymore, even if (like a lot of straights) we do have old bondage equipment in our basements.

Terry got on the phone with his mother. She'd been planning to bring the crib over the day before the baby was due. They were coming to Seattle for an antitobacco meeting, and because the heirloom crib couldn't be disassembled, she and Dennis were planning on driving over the mountains in their six-blocks-to-the-gallon motor home. For the crib to arrive the day before the baby was due was cutting things a little too close, in, uh, my opinion, so Terry asked Claudia if they could bring the crib over sooner.

The next day, Claudia and Dennis pulled up in their motor home and carried in the heirloom crib. The crib I'd heard so much about was . . . pretty ugly. I'd been imagining something tasteful, something we might discover was worth a lot of money when the *Antiques Roadshow* came to town. Terry's family crib looked like something built from scrap during the Depression. It was covered with a thick layer of cracking white paint—you could smell the lead—and had large forties decals of pastel rabbits on the head and baseboard.

Terry's mom handed us a bag full of baby clothes she "just couldn't resist." We had some tea. Claudia took our picture standing in front of the crib, and then she and Dennis climbed back in their motor home for the six-hour drive back to Spokane. Terry promised me the crib would look fabulous, "once we clean it up," but even in the hour it had been in the house the crib had already started to grow on me, maybe because it was Terry's. When I pictured him in the crib, weighing seven pounds, and fourteen inches long, my heart melted. The crib was clunky and the decals were peeling, but who cared? The crib's history was its charm. We'd just have to get another one before the baby could roll over and chew the lead paint off the bars, but Terry's son would spend his first couple of months in the same crib Terry did.

I started picking through the clothes, and when I looked up at Terry he was standing over his crib, looking as if he might cry.

"My mom drove all the way to Seattle and back to Spokane in one day, so that her grandchild could have this crib. She's okay with this."

And so she was, and so apparently was Dennis, who actually did the driving. My family loves to talk, but in Terry's family actions speak louder than words. This action—an expensive twelve-hour round-trip in a motor home on one day's notice—spoke very loudly.

Later that afternoon, I opened our front door and found a box the size of a washing machine sitting on the step. Inside was a note from my mother. She'd sent "a few things" she picked up for the baby. Each gift was wrapped in tissue paper, and we didn't have to open any of them until after the baby came.

"That way, you won't jinx anything," my mother's note read. "Set the box aside and unwrap the contents after you get home with the baby. This way, there won't be any jinx, and I'll sleep better knowing that my grandson isn't coming home to a completely unprepared house."

"What do you want to do?" Terry asked.

"Set it aside and open everything when we bring the baby home."

Terry pouted. Jinx or no jinx he didn't want to wait.

"We've got a crib in the house," he argued. "There can't be anything in that box your mother sent more jinx-y than a crib."

I relented.

We dragged my mother's box into the living room, and we dumped the baby stuff on the floor. There were bottles, onesies, baby clothes, blankets, pacifiers, and bibs. A day earlier, we were panicking because we had nothing we needed. Today, thanks to my mother and Terry's, we were totally set up.

My mom had sent four bibs. Two were a boxed set of matching "I Love Grandma" and "I Love Grandpa" bibs. The other two bibs were also from boxed sets. My mom had bought two sets, opened them, pulled out one bib from each, and packaged them back up. There was a note:

"I wanted to send you a matching set of 'I Love Daddy' bibs to go with the grandma and grandpa bibs (which I expect my grandson to wear at every meal!), but there weren't any 'I Love Daddy' sets. So I had to make one."

The phone rang.

It was Saturday morning; Terry was at work and I was in bed reading the paper. I didn't get out of bed, but let the phone ring until our voice mail picked up. Whoever was calling would just have to wait. The Bill and Monica thang was unfolding, and as a sex writer I had a solemn duty to keep up with every salacious detail. *The New York Times* was using words the editors of the raunchy "alternative" papers I write for won't allow me to use. When I finished the paper, I headed for the bathroom, grabbing

the portable phone on the way. Boop, boop, boop; there was a
message. When I heard Laurie's voice my heart and bowel movement both dropped. Melissa was at the hospital; Terry and I had
to go to Portland right away.

Holy shit.

I called Terry at the bookstore.

"Oh, my God!" he screamed. "Oh, my God."

We make a plan: Terry would call Michael, his manager, who
had agreed in advance to cover for him if the "You're in labor"
call came when Terry was at work. As soon as Michael arrived,
Terry would run downtown and rent a car. In the meantime, I'd
pack our clothes. We hung up, and I called Laurie. Melissa had
been at the hospital since early that morning. She could give birth
at any moment.

"You never know how it's going to go. It could happen right
now, it could happen twelve hours from now. When can you get
here?"

I told Laurie that we'd be at least three hours.

"I'll tell Melissa, but you should hurry."

"We're on our way," I said, "and since we're not there to do it
for her, tell Melissa to demand all the drugs she's got coming."

I called the Mallory in Portland and reserved a room, then left
messages for Bob and Kate and Carol and Jack.

Ten minutes later, with a bag of clothes packed, I was sitting
on the couch, waiting for Terry to drive up. Our place was a
wreck. We'd sold our condo three weeks earlier, and then pretty
much stopped keeping house. We had to be out of the place in
four weeks, so we were not only going to be dads, we were going
to be homeless dads. The pressing problem, though, was the
mess. We're not neat freaks to begin with, and neither of us could
see the point in keeping the place up after we sold it. We'd only
be tearing it apart when we moved, so why bother? Now the
mess mocked me, seeming to say, "You're not fit parents—just
look at this place! You can't bring a baby home to live in this
pigsty! It's a disaster area!" The mess's voice sounded a whole lot
like my mom's.

But a messy home was better than no home—which was also a
problem. We live in the land of the Microsoft Millionaires; once
we sold our condo we couldn't find another place we could af-

ford. Every house or condo we looked at was bought out from under us by some Microshithead paying cash and bidding thousands of dollars over the asking price. By the time we did find something, it was too late: we had to be out of our old place a month before we could move into the new one. In a few days— barring BBD/BCM—we'd be bringing a baby home to a messy house that wouldn't be ours for long. This was not the plan. We were supposed to go into the pool, sell the condo, find a new place, and *then* get a baby! We'd expected to be in the pool at least a year, and we were going to be in a new place by then, settled and ready! No one said anything about getting a baby in eight weeks!

Emily and Rich, friends of mine from work, had offered us their basement for our homeless month, so we wouldn't be on the streets. And we did have a crib covered in lead paint, a car seat, two "I Love Daddy" bibs, six bottles, and the four-foot-high pile of baby clothes that our mothers, thankfully flouting the no-shopping order, "couldn't resist."

Forty-five minutes into my panic attack, with my mother's voice still screaming in my head—"The bathroom! Look at the mildew on that shower curtain! Oh, my God, the sink! The baby will have malaria by the end of the week!"—Terry finally pulled up. It was Saturday morning, and the only car Budget had left was an enormous white van. It seated nine. We could have driven to Portland and adopted a Little League team. Terry stood in the living room, looked at the mess, and said, "We're not ready." Then he picked up a camera and started taking pictures. He wanted the kid to see what we lived like before we brought him home. We tossed the car seat, our bag, a blanket, and some baby clothes in the back, and drove off.

Today our lives would change forever, and all I could think while Terry sped down I-5 in the van was . . . *I look like shit.* Terry was presentable; he'd cleaned himself up for work this morning, but even if he hadn't, Terry's one of those people who could look good falling down stairs. I, on the other hand, looked like a mob hit. I'd been up late the night before, I hadn't shaved or showered, and in the rush to get our stuff together and get down to Portland, I forgot to brush my teeth or pack any toiletries. We had nothing to fight over on the drive down, as there was no CD or tape player in our maxivan, only an AM radio, so we fought over stopping in Olympia to buy toothbrushes, toothpaste, soap, razors, and shaving cream. Terry wanted to get to Portland, but I didn't think the voice in my head—"Look at you! You're filthy!"—would allow me to walk into the maternity ward at OHSU without at least stopping to shave and brush my teeth.

On our way up the hill to OHSU, we got lost and had to double back. Finally we found the entrance and parked. The building with the maternity ward was built into the side of the hill, and the ground-level entrance from the parking lot side was on the ninth floor. Melissa was on the fourteenth. Still worried that no hospital would let someone as grubby as me near a newborn, I insisted we stop in a bathroom so I could clean up. While Terry waited beside me and Melissa pushed five floors up—I washed my face, shaved, flossed, and brushed my teeth. Terry looked at his watch: twenty-five after two. Almost four hours had passed between Laurie's phone call and our walking through the hospital door.

On the fourteenth floor, we weren't sure where to go. When we finally found the doors to the maternity wing, we stopped. What should we do? Knock? Just stroll in? Were boys even allowed? There was a small window in each of the swinging doors, but we couldn't see anyone through them. Nor could we see a nurses' station, and we hadn't passed an information desk since the ninth-floor entrance.

"What do we do?" I asked Terry. "Go back downstairs?"

"We don't have time." Terry pushed open the door. "If we're not supposed to be in here, someone will tell us."

The hallway was long, dark, and deserted. We walked past four empty birthing suites, rounded a corner, and found ourselves standing in front of a nurses' station.

"Can we help you?"

We hadn't braced ourselves for this moment, or this question. Laurie wasn't here to "facilitate our initial contact" with the maternity ward nurses; I guess we'd assumed someone from the agency would be here holding our hands, walking us through this step just as we'd been walked through every other. Apparently, this time we were on our own.

Terry looked at me. I looked at the nurses. They looked at me. Terry nudged me.

"Um, we're the guys adopting Melissa Pierce's baby," I said. "We just got here."

The nurses all smiled as if they'd been expecting us—Nancy, Melissa's social worker, *did* make a note on her chart. One picked up a clipboard.

"Melissa had her baby a few minutes ago," she said, "at two-twenty-six P.M. Melissa and the baby are doing fine." She showed us to a waiting area; we'd be able to see Melissa in a few minutes. The waiting area was by the elevators; I wasn't sure how we'd managed to miss it. It had an information desk, several couches, and a couple of television sets tuned to the Saturday afternoon sports programs. Golf. The nurse told us the doctor would be out in a few minutes, pointed to a pot of coffee and told us to make ourselves comfortable. We plopped down on a couch. It was now 2:36. At the moment the baby was born, Terry and I were in a bathroom, Terry watching me shave. Not that it made any difference where we were, since Melissa hadn't wanted us in the birthing room. We had to be somewhere, so why not a bathroom? We'd spent our first moments alone together in the bathroom of a gay bar.

We were sitting close together on our couch. Terry started to say something about the hospital, the baby, his father—then he stopped. I looked around. There were some thugs on the other side of the room, all from one family if I could judge by their shared fashion sense. I risked it: I put my arm around Terry and kissed him on the forehead. He leaned into me. The thugs didn't rush us; they didn't seem to notice or care that homos were cuddling in the maternity ward's waiting room. Wives and girlfriends were pushing out pups down the hall; thugs or not, these guys had more important things to worry about.

A short woman who couldn't have been more than fourteen walked into the waiting area and called our names—an aide or a hospital volunteer coming to take us to Melissa, I assumed, expecting her to turn and walk us back into the maternity ward. She didn't budge, and only then do I take her in. She was wearing scrubs, with little paper booties on her feet. She introduced herself as Melissa's doctor, and told us the baby was healthy, and that we could see him and Melissa just as soon as Melissa "passes the afterbirth."

"And if she flunks it?" I asked.

Not funny, but I was delirious. The polite little doctor laughed a polite little laugh, gave me the fish-eye—clearly she'd heard that one before—and said we should be able to see Melissa in about ten minutes.

Melissa was sitting up in bed with the kid in her arms. He was wrapped up like a burrito, with a tiny knit hat on his cone-shaped head. Melissa was wearing a hospital gown, her long hair was pulled back into a knot, and she looked . . . clean. She smiled at us and nodded toward the baby, as if to say, "Look what I did." She wasn't glowing or beaming or gushing or crying. Melissa was as composed as she always was—and her baby was pretty composed, too. He was awake, but not crying. He was looking up at Melissa, blinking and looking bewildered, as if he were trying to figure out what the hell happened. No one said anything. The nurse who showed us in left, closing the door, and the four of us were alone. We said hey; Melissa said hey. Terry and I crossed to one side of the bed, stepping over a small puddle of something or other. Terry sat on a chair; I leaned against the windowsill.

"You okay?" Terry asked.

"I'm fine," said Melissa. "It wasn't like a surprise."

She looked down at the baby.

"He's healthy," she said. It wasn't clear who she was talking to—the baby, us, or herself. That her baby was healthy must have felt like a victory for Melissa. Two couples had rejected her for fear that he had been damaged by her drinking and drug use. They were wrong. He was healthy.

"They give you your drugs?" I asked.

She nodded. "It still hurt like hell, though."

The baby yawned, blinked his huge blue eyes, and stared up at Melissa.

From everything we'd heard and read, these first moments—the adoptive couple and the birth mother checking out the baby together—were supposed to be profoundly moving, full of pathos, cementing the bond between birth mothers and adoptive families. Not today. We took our cues from Melissa, and Melissa was underplaying this moment. Subtle. No weeping, no hugs. Just the facts: Here's the baby. He's healthy. It hurt.

Terry and I made no sudden moves. We didn't ask to hold the baby, and we didn't approach the bed. Neither of us wanted to appear too anxious to snatch the kid away from Melissa. If she didn't change her mind, Melissa would be signing away her rights to the baby tomorrow. We'd have plenty of time to hold him; legally, we were going to be dads forever, but Melissa was only going to be a mom for the next twenty-four hours. In olde-tyme closed adoptions, birth mothers weren't allowed to hold their babies, and often weren't told the baby's sex or whether the baby was healthy. They were supposed to pretend nothing had happened, to make believe they didn't give birth. Keeping the baby away from the birth mom helped prevent her from bonding, and was supposed to make the "Baby? What baby?" pretense easier. We didn't want to prevent Melissa from bonding, or from basking. She'd given up booze and drugs, found an agency, found us, gotten off the streets, and taken care of herself. A healthy infant was her goal, and she'd pulled it off. She had a right to be proud of what she'd done, and she had a right to bond, so we hung back. Way back.

I told Melissa that at the moment the kid was born, we were in a bathroom on the ninth floor. When I told her why—I thought I was too dirty to be allowed in the maternity ward—she laughed.

"They let *me* in," she said. "You had nothing to worry about."

Melissa named the baby David Kevin Pierce; David for her current roommate, Kevin for his biological father (a.k.a. Bacchus), and Pierce, Melissa's family name. Melissa asked if we'd like to hold the baby. We nodded. She passed him to me—I was closer, and the moment he was in my arms I felt . . . nothing. Terry gave me his chair; I sat down and he knelt next to me. The baby was all of twenty minutes old, and weighed all of seven pounds. I slipped one finger into his hand, and as he gripped, I felt . . . nothing.

What the hell is wrong with me? The kid was doing his part: his huge blue eyes were open and he was looking up at me, blinking. His little hand was strong and warm, his fingernails were large and surprisingly sharp, and he kept gripping my little finger. He had a pushed-up nose, and some blondish hair poked out from under his blue hat. The baby yawned, let go of my finger, and closed his eyes. Terry put his arm around my waist, and sighed. Clearly, Terry was feeling something; I could practically see him bonding. What was wrong with me?

Now that the baby was in my arms, I didn't have to hang back anymore. I told Melissa he was beautiful, that she'd bred well, and I smiled down at the squishy little face looking back up at me. But no rush of feeling swamped me. I ordered myself to bond, dammit, but no "This is my son" epiphany took place. Terry took my picture with the baby; as I smiled for the camera, I wondered why I was having to will myself to feel something.

I passed the baby to Terry; he walked over to Melissa's bed and sat down on the corner. I took a picture of Terry and Melissa with the baby, and then sat down on the other corner of the bed.

"He's so beautiful, Melissa," Terry repeated over and over, "so beautiful." Terry looked as if he might burst, he was so happy. Even Melissa was smiling.

And I felt nothing.

We'd been working toward this moment for years. We'd been to seminars, read baby books, written stacks of progressively larger checks, and opened our bank accounts, police records, and skulls for inspection. We'd been talking about this moment—the moment we would become dads—for so long that maybe it had come to seem like so much talk. One big abstraction. Maybe I was numb. Maybe I had a spinning ball of rock and ice where my heart was supposed to be.

Terry was about to pass the baby back to Melissa when a nurse came in to take some tubes out of her back, from the epidural anesthetic. The nurse asked us to step into the hallway, and told us to take the baby with us. We both looked at Melissa, and she shrugged. It was okay with her.

In the hallway with the baby, the first time the three of us were alone, I looked at Terry, he looked at me. We looked at the baby. We looked at each other again.

"What have we done?" I said, half joking.

"He's so beautiful!" Terry said.

The hallway was dark, and the place was deserted. Only two of OHSU's twenty birthing suites seemed to be occupied. Terry leaned against the wall, the baby in his arms, and I slid an arm around him, afraid he might sink to the floor.

The door to Melissa's room opened, the nurse came out, and we walked back in. We hung out, taking pictures and passing the baby around. Melissa told us that she'd gone into labor early in the morning, and taken a cab to the hospital a couple of hours later. We told her the story of our drive down. The nurse who'd removed the tubes from Melissa's back returned, weighed the baby, put him in a diaper and a tiny cotton shirt, and wrapped him back up. She then shook and opened a two-ounce bottle of baby formula, and asked which one of us wanted to do the first feeding.

"I've done enough work today," Melissa said, leaning back in bed. "You guys do it."

Terry took the bottle from the nurse, and Melissa handed him the baby. The formula was in a tiny glass bottle, with a yellow label and a little brown nipple. Terry gently touched the nipple to the baby's upper lip, and his tiny lips parted. He sucked in the nipple, and as he pulled on the bottle he gripped Terry's little finger. Terry looked up at me, and then at Melissa.

"He's so beautiful," Terry said again. "He's so beautiful."

"We know, we know," said Melissa, rolling her eyes. "You told us that already."

The nice nurse left the room, and a different nurse came in. She wanted to know long Melissa was thinking about staying.

"By law, you're entitled to stay forty-eight hours," the nurse explained. "But if you're feeling all right, you can be discharged sooner." She then pursed her lips and asked Melissa, a little too brightly, how she was feeling. There was a smile on her face, but there was also a tone in her voice. She didn't say so, but she was letting us all know that Melissa, uninsured and having had a relatively easy birth, shouldn't take advantage of Oregon's taxpayers by lying around for two days.

Melissa stared at the nurse, and said nothing.

"You can check out tonight, if you're feeling up to it. Or tomorrow morning."

"Forty-eight hours is two days, right?" Melissa asked, turning to me. I nodded. Melissa stared straight ahead, the way she did in Laurie's office when we were trying to decide on the number of visits per year. Melissa, the girl who jumped off trains, was probably well enough to leave tonight or tomorrow, but if she went through with the adoption, the time she spent in the hospital with the baby would be her only time as a full-time mom. I wanted to explain that to the nurse, standing by the door with her clipboard, but this decision was Melissa's to make.

There was a long pause. The nurse was no longer smiling. She looked hard at Melissa, and said, "That's right, forty-eight hours is two days, and by law you can stay two days. But you did have a relatively easy—"

"Two days means I can stay until Monday, right?" Melissa asked, looking down at her bed.

"Yes, but—"

"So I'm staying until Monday."

When they moved Melissa and the baby down one floor to the recovery suites, Terry and I slipped out of the building and down to the van. Terry needed some more film for the camera, and I needed a walk.

When we found Melissa's new room, she was alone. The baby was in the nursery at the end of the hall. The nurses on the floor—all smiles and reassuringly officious—knew Melissa was doing an adoption and were keeping him in the nursery to prevent her from bonding "too much." Olde-tyme habits die hard. In the nursery, a nurse showed us how to bathe a newborn and clean his umbilical cord. He wasn't ours yet, but all the nurses were deferring to us as if he was. We explained that it was okay with us for Melissa to see the baby, and they let us wheel him in his crib down the hall to her room.

Melissa's recovery room was pretty swank, apparently designed to attract moms who have private health insurance to pay for their two-day stay. Her regulation hospital bed had a maple headboard; there were a matching table and chairs, a cushioned window seat, a TV, a VCR, a private bathroom, and a large picture window with a view of the Willamette River. There were real light fixtures—lamps, wall sconces—with real lightbulbs (instead of fluorescent lights) on dimmer switches. The baby's rolling crib was as tall as Melissa's hospital bed, made of the same maple as the headboard, though the sides of the crib were Plexiglas. When

Melissa didn't want to hold the baby, she could set him in his crib and lie right next to him, nose-to-nose, watching him sleep.

Terry and I dashed around the room, getting Melissa and the baby whatever they needed and taking pictures. Melissa gave the baby his second bottle, and I had the honor of changing the first poopy diaper, filled with what looked like Hershey's Syrup. I wiped his butt carefully, then ripped open an alcohol wipe to clean his umbilical cord. As Terry and Melissa watched me fumble, I began to feel . . . something. Not quite a bond yet, but definitely more than I was feeling earlier in the birthing suite.

The nurse who'd showed us how to bathe the baby came into the room with a case of bottled formula and a video. She popped the video into the VCR, and we watched an ethnically diverse crowd of new moms and dads care for their newborn babies, as a soothing male voice explained the importance of regular feedings, cleaning the umbilical cord, and relying on friends and family for support during "those important first weeks."

Melissa said, "Well, duh," over and over. "Don't forget to feed it, don't forget not to drop it on its head, don't forget to change its diapers." She turned off the video. "We know this, right?"

Melissa wanted to nap, so Terry and I left her in bed with the baby. She asked us to turn off the lights as we went; she lay on her side, facing the windows, the baby in her arms. Leaving was hard, and as we walked down to the van, Terry admitted he was afraid that Melissa might change her mind and decide to keep the baby. We'd find out the next day, when Laurie came to the hospital with the papers. We drove down the hill and over to the Mallory, checked in, and took a nap ourselves. Before we headed back up to the hospital, we stopped at a video store and picked up some *Simpsons* tapes—something else Melissa and I shared.

Back at the hospital that night, the lengths all three of us were going to to avoid calling the baby by name became comic. None of us was using the names Melissa gave him at birth, David Kevin, or the names Terry and I intend to give him, Daryl Jude. Melissa called the baby "little guy," and Terry and I called him "kid." Melissa asked the baby over and over, "How you doin', little guy?" When it was time to pass the baby around, Terry or I said, "Gimme the kid." We had hoped to revisit the name issue in the two weeks before Melissa's due date, but now that the baby had come early, we'd never come to an agreement on one set of names. I couldn't help but think that little David Kevin/Daryl Jude would be discussing this with a shrink someday.

When Melissa's dinner came, she passed the baby off to Terry. She complained about the hospital food—there wasn't enough meat on her plate, and the chocolate cake didn't taste like anything—so I offered to run down to the cafeteria and get her something else.

"Too late," Melissa said, shrugging. "The food wasn't any good, but I already ate it."

At about eight o'clock, a nurse came in to check on us and the baby. She listened to the baby's heart, and said, "Hmm . . ." We were all a little troubled by the sound of that "hmm." The baby had a heart murmur. She told us not to worry—too much: many babies are born with slight heart murmurs, and most disappear in twenty-four hours. But this was a particularly loud murmur, so she thought a pediatric cardiologist should drop by. She didn't want to panic us, she said, she just wanted an infant heart specialist to come and "give this a listen." The fact that she didn't want to panic us naturally put all of us in a panic.

Three hours, two EKGs, and one chest X ray later—all this work done in Melissa's room—a pediatric cardiologist was standing at the foot of Melissa's bed, explaining that we should be concerned, but not worried. The doc was another young woman, as tall as Melissa's obstetrician was short. Her rap was reassuring—"We have to wait and see; we should know better by morning. Some heart murmurs are louder than others. But right now, we shouldn't worry, not too much"—but the look on her face connected every dot. There was something potentially wrong with this baby's heart. A heart murmur this loud could mean a hole in the heart, and that could mean . . . this infant would need surgery, and that would mean . . . this infant might die.

I was holding the baby while we listened to the pediatric cardiologist. I looked down at his tiny face, his head tucked into his little knit cap, and I watched his eyes open and close. Terry was sitting next to me, and the baby was holding on to one of my fingers. The kid yawned, blinked, and went to sleep. And I thought to myself, *Do NOT bond. This baby might die, so let's not waste time and emotional energy bonding with it.* This option—the freedom to shift gears like this—was available to me because I was not the baby's biological father. This was not my baby. This was not flesh of my flesh, blood of my blood. This was flesh of my paperwork, blood of my checkbook. And since the paperwork wasn't done, we weren't related—not yet.

If this baby died, Terry and I wouldn't have lost a child, not really. We would've lost a baby that was *almost* ours, and this adoption we almost did with Melissa would have been simply—disrupted. We would go back into the pool, and adopt some other baby, and name him D.J., and we would love that baby so much that . . . we couldn't imagine things working out any other way. All this was running through my head as I listened to the doc. I would be upset if this baby died, but I wouldn't be devastated. After all, it wasn't my baby yet, and I wasn't the father. This was David Kevin I was holding, not Daryl Jude—not yet.

But in the eight hours we'd spent at the hospital, Terry had bonded, and he had no distance. As we left the hospital, Melissa and the baby sleeping together in her bed, he was visibly upset. He was in love with that baby, he said, and he was worried. I put an arm around Terry's shoulder in the elevator and swore the baby would be fine, even as I silently wondered whether we could go right back into the pool or whether we'd have to do all the paperwork all over again.

Back at the Mallory, we ordered dinner from room service: pork chops, baked potatoes, and tomato salad. We like heavy, old-fashioned hotel food, but we couldn't bring ourselves to eat. Terry was distraught about the baby, and I was distraught about having a lump of rock and ice where my heart should be. We wound up back at the Eagle, watching porn and playing pinball, and pulling for that kid up at OHSU. In Pioneer Square, we saw a pack of gutter punks sitting on the ground, passing around a space bag. I looked at the boys, wondering if one could be Bacchus. Probably not. If Bacchus had been in Portland, he would've heard about Melissa's pregnancy from the other street kids, and probably have turned up at the hospital. But if that baby at OHSU lived and we adopted him, neither of us would be able to walk past a boy gutter punk again without wondering, "Is that him? Is that Bacchus? Is that our baby's birth father?"

Daryl Jude

Early the next morning, we were up, out of the hotel, and back at the hospital. Any rational couple would have dashed up to the maternity ward, anxious for news: Were we going to be parents or were we going back into the pool? But no couple adopting or birthing is entirely rational, so instead of heading upstairs, we headed for the cafeteria. Terry needed coffee, I required tea, and we both needed something to settle our stomachs before we got the news. We'd been uncharacteristically quiet as we dressed that morning, and we drove the hospital in relative silence. We were pretty quiet on our way down to the cafeteria, too. Neither of us had much to say—to each other or anyone else—until I walked over to the bagels.

Bagels are ring-shaped rolls with a tough, chewy texture, made from plain yeast dough that is dropped briefly into nearly boiling water and then baked. After hanging out in a hospital for the last twenty-four hours, worrying about little David Kevin/Daryl Jude's heart, I was naturally in a health-conscious frame of mind when we strolled into the cafeteria. So I ignored the doughnuts and Danish and baked eggs, and bellied up to the bagel bins instead. I was saddened to note that such things as butter-pecan and cinnamon-sugar bagels existed.

While I was trying to decide between a chocolate-chip bagel or a blueberry bagel, one of the cafeteria workers came out and filled an empty bin with . . . bacon bagels. Butter-pecan bagels saddened me, but bacon bagels gave me fits. First, while bacon is delicious, this was a hospital cafeteria. One would think hospitals would take a hard line on bacon, similar to the line they take on cigarettes. All hospitals are smoke-free, because smoking is bad for you—really, really bad for you. Well, bacon is really, really bad for you too: more people die of heart disease than of lung cancer. Why the double standard? If you're gonna serve bacon in the cafeteria, why not let people chain-smoke in the maternity ward?

When you're worried about one thing—say, a dead baby—sometimes an unrelated and comparatively unimportant thing sets you off. Perhaps I was more bonded to that baby upstairs than I'd realized. Shrinks call it transference or projecting or something, and at OHSU's hospital, I was suddenly transferring in a very big way. All the anxiety I was feeling about David Kevin/Daryl Jude flipped onto that bin of bacon bagels. I was suddenly very, very angry. It's not that the bagels were crap; they were, but living in Goyland, a.k.a. the Pacific Northwest, means getting used to crap bagels. No, my problem was the adding-insult-to-injury-ness of it all. In transforming this basically good-for-you food product into yet another grease 'n' gristle delivery system, a line had been crossed. Was this how we intended to thank the Jews for the bagel? By filling it with food products that—however delicious—God specifically instructed his Chosen People to refrain from eating? I'm not Jewish, and like most of my Jewish friends, I wouldn't keep kosher if I were, but there was a principle at stake. American mass culture co-opts and regurgitates just about anything—I'm old enough to remember when we stole croissants from the French—but bagels observant Jews can't eat?

I asked the cashier if I could see the manager. It was Sunday morning, she told me, and the manager didn't come in on Sundays. I pointed out to the woman at the cash register that bacon bagels were an insult to Jews, and that it didn't make much sense for a hospital to be serving bacon regardless. The cashier looked at me as if I were nuts, which I was, and invited me to fill out a comment card. Before I could fill out the comment card, Terry dragged me out of the cafeteria and into the hall. But! But! But! The bagels! The Jews! The bagels!

"Fuck the bagels!" Terry barked at me, pulling me toward the elevator. "That baby might be dying upstairs and you're down here screaming about bagels! Who cares!"

★ ★ ★

When we got to the maternity ward, the EKG, the pediatric cardiologist, the heart murmur, and the gloom were gone. We had just stepped through the big swinging doors when one of the nurses brightly informed us that our baby—little David Kevin/ Daryl Jude—was perfectly healthy: "It was just one of those murmurs that goes away." Terry and I just stood there, almost unable to speak.

She asked if we had a nice night; we lied and said we did, and then she commented on the wonderful weather. We smiled, and observed that, yes, it was unseasonably warm. Awfully warm for early March, the nurse agreed, and told us the baby was with Melissa in her room.

This reads like something of an anticlimax—something of an enormous anticlimax, considering the buildup. Well, it *was* an anticlimax. We hadn't been able to sleep; we'd stayed up all night playing pinball and watching shaved-buttcrack porn stars get fisted; I went Golem in the cafeteria, blowing up about bacon bagels; Terry was near tears in the elevator on the way up, and then . . . nothing. Baby fine, drama over, nice weather we're having. I had imagined we'd get the news, good or bad, gathered around Melissa's bed, one of us holding the kid, all of us crying tears of grief or relief. Instead, the news—hey, your baby is gonna live!—was just dropped into how-was-your-day chitchat.

Melissa was sitting up, her picked-over breakfast tray next to her bed. She was holding the baby, feeding him, and she smiled. We exchange heys.

"He's healthy," Melissa said flatly, just the way she said it the day before.

We told her we'd heard, and she passed the baby to Terry. I sat on the window seat, and watched Terry hold the baby, and thought to myself, *Okay, bond.*

Laurie was coming to the hospital in a few hours, Melissa told us, bringing papers for everyone to sign. The hospital food sucked, and Melissa was upset that none of her friends—including David, the guy she named the baby after, the guy who was staying in her apartment—had come to visit. She was sure they'd be around today—they probably thought she couldn't have visitors yesterday, you know, the day the baby was born. We told her about our sleepless night, and going to the Eagle to blow off steam. She told us that the sidewalk in front of the Eagle was a good place to spare-change. We took more pictures: me with the baby; Melissa with the baby; Terry with the baby. No one talked about the future—about tomorrow, when Melissa would check out; about the papers we'd all be signing today—and no one called the baby by name. Any name.

Changing a diaper, I got nailed. I tried to dodge, but ducked the wrong way and got hit again, this time in the opposite direction. The baby pissed a big X onto my chest. Melissa laughed, and Terry took a picture.

"So, it's going to be like this, is it?" I asked the baby, passing him to Terry. Melissa told me to get used to it, and as I stepped into the bathroom to change my T-shirt, I looked back at her and said, "Usually guys who want to do that buy you a drink first."

When he was awake, the baby looked around, blinking slowly. He had long eyebrows, and a round face, like Melissa. Unlike Melissa's, his eyes were blue, and his hair was blondish. Bacchus was lighter than Melissa, with blue eyes, so maybe he'd keep the eye and hair color. Terry and I, a couple who didn't care about the baby being white or male or perfect, were on the verge of adopting a blond-haired, blue-eyed, white male infant, the adoption industry's holy grail.

The baby didn't cry at all. The only time we'd heard him cry was while a nurse bathed him in the sink. Last night, we'd speculated that maybe he wasn't crying because his heart was weak. Maybe he was too ill for healthy, robust yowling.

Nurses came in and out, bringing us little cases of bottles, more diapers, wipes, hats, and T-shirts, and checking on Melissa and the baby. We asked why he wasn't crying—was something else wrong?

"Some babies just don't cry that much. It doesn't mean anything, except that his parents are going to get more sleep then other parents," the nurse replied. "If it keeps up like this, count yourselves lucky!"

Laurie arrived, beaming her empath beam. She listened as we described last night's drama; she held the baby and pronounced him "beautiful." Her presence was comforting, but it brought us down to earth. She'd been at Melissa's side every step of the way, and she'd brought the three of us together. I'd expected her to be at the hospital yesterday, when Melissa was in labor, but yesterday was about this baby and his parents, she explained, birthparent and adoptive parents. Laurie was about paperwork and placement, and we didn't need to think about any of that yesterday. We needed to bond with the baby and one another. But with the baby a day old, and Melissa checking out of the hospital the next day, it was paperwork time.

Up to this point, the three of us had been sitting around Melissa's room—taking care of the baby, watching videos, eating, and talking—as if it would always be thus, as if we were going to stay here at the hospital for the next twenty years and bring up this baby together. Laurie's arrival reminded us that tomorrow, like yesterday, would also be a day of drama. If Melissa signed the papers Laurie had brought, Terry and I would be taking this baby back to the Mallory with us, and Melissa would be leaving the hospital alone, returning to her apartment alone, and going back to the streets a few weeks later. Laurie asked Terry and me to step out into the hallway with her. It would take her about thirty minutes to go over the paperwork with Melissa; why didn't we go have some lunch in the cafeteria and come back around one? Laurie didn't mention it, but she didn't have to: this was Melissa's final opportunity to change her mind. Once she signed the papers, she was no longer David Kevin/Daryl Jude's legal parent. If she wanted to keep this baby, she had to say so now.

Laurie went into Melissa's room and shut the door. We stood in the hallway for a minute, staring at the closed door, and then slowly turned and walked out of the maternity ward and to the elevator. Terry asked if I'd be all right in the cafeteria.

"Can you remain calm at the sight of bacon bagels, or will I have to drag you out of there again?"

Walking through the cafeteria—bacon bagels now in their proper perspective—I remembered my conversation many months ago with the gay man whose adoption fell through at the last possible moment. When I told him we were doing an adoption because it offered us more autonomy, he laughed.

"What you don't understand is that you have less, much less, doing an open adoption," he told me. "At least coparenting, or if you're having a baby with lesbians, or if you're doing a closed adoption you're dealing with adults. Doing an open adoption, your fate is in the hands of some teenage girl who may not be thinking very clearly right after she gives birth. You have no autonomy in that situation, believe me. You have none."

Terry was suddenly nervous, more nervous now than he was that morning. What if the heart scare bonded Melissa to the baby, and she couldn't give him up now?

"She could be explaining to Laurie right now why she can't sign those papers," Terry said, as we stood in line to pay for our cinnamon-sugar bagels. "What will we do if she changes her mind?"

"We'll go home, stay sane, and go back in the pool."

"I want that baby," Terry responded. "He's Daryl. He's the baby we're meant to have."

"Maybe. But if she keeps him, then he wasn't the baby we were meant to have. We have to be rational, Terry. We're 'meant to have' the baby we wind up getting, and no other."

"You have no heart," Terry said.

"I do have one, Terry. But I'm not going to volunteer to have it stomped on. That baby isn't ours until he's ours."

We were both too nervous to eat our bagels, so we took our drinks and headed back up to the maternity ward. Melissa's room was near the end of a long hallway, and about fifteen feet past her door was a window seat with a tremendous view of Portland and the Willamette River. We sat, drank our Cokes, and waited. And waited. One o'clock came and went. Laurie said the signing would take a half an hour, and soon ninety minutes had passed.

"She changed her mind," Terry said.

We talked about what we'd say to Melissa if she decided to keep the baby. Would we even be allowed to see her and the baby to say good-bye? We wouldn't argue with her, or attempt to change her mind, but we would want to say good-bye.

Laurie came out of Melissa's room, closed the door, and waved us over. With a gesture, she indicated that she'd rather not talk in the hall. Terry looked as if he were going to drop, and as soon as Laurie turned her back to us, he grabbed my hand and shook his head. We walked up the hall, away from Melissa's door, and into an empty room identical to hers.

"Well," Laurie said, "Melissa signed the papers. . . ." We

exhaled, and Terry groaned his relief. "Were you worried?" Laurie asked. Yes, Terry explained, since Laurie took three times as long to come out of Melissa's room as she'd predicted. Had Melissa had doubts?

"Well, you know Melissa. We talked about a lot of other things before we got down to looking at the papers. But, no, she didn't have doubts. She seemed very sure of herself and her decision to do an adoption."

Technically, the agency now had custody of the baby, and would be David Kevin's legal guardian until the adoption was finalized. Laurie took out some papers for us to sign. These indicated that the agency was placing the baby in our care; all she needed was our signatures—and the name we intended to give the baby, if it was different from the name Melissa gave him.

We told Laurie that Daryl Jude would be the baby's new first and middle names. She wrote those names down, and then she looked up. "Have you decided on a last name?"

For most of the drive down to Portland, we'd argued about that. Savage? Miller? A hyphenate: Savage-Miller? Miller-Savage? Hyphenated names were so twenty years ago. Terry said we should give the baby my last name.

"We shouldn't give him my last name," I said.

"Then let's give him Miller."

But he shouldn't have Terry's last name either. I'd feel like the odd man out if there were two Millers in the house and only one Savage. We knew a lesbian couple with two kids; rather than choosing one name, or hyphenating both, they gave their daughter an old family name. So all three—mom, mom, son, and daughter— had different last names. Maybe we could do the same? There was a great name in my family—Hollahan—that was dying out; why not name him Daryl Jude Hollahan? Terry liked the ring of that, so it was settled: D. J. Hollahan.

But half an hour later, this scenario popped into my head:

"D. J. Hollahan? You must be Irish."

"No. I'm French and Scottish and German."

"But your last name, Hollahan, that's Irish, isn't it?"

"Yes."

"But you're not Irish?"

"No."

"Then how come—"

"I was adopted by a gay couple, and one of my fathers is Irish, and his grandmother's name was Hollahan, so rather than choose one of their last names, or give me both, they gave me an old family name of one of my dads, Hollahan, which is Irish, like my dad. But I'm not Irish."

"Why would they do that? Didn't they want you to have one of their names?"

"LOOK, I DON'T KNOW. OKAY? YOU WANT TO KNOW SO BAD, CALL THEM AND ASK!"

Considering how often people in America inquire about the ethnic backgrounds of people they've just met, and considering that a kiss-me-I'm-Irish name like Hollahan invites the question, D.J. would have conversations like this over and over again all his adult life. He would come to hate us for giving him such a green-beer-and-shamrocks last name. There were a couple of other family-name possibilities—Keenan, my middle name and also my other grandmother's maiden name; and Bunbaker, Terry's mother's maiden name. But Keenan presented the same "So you must be Irish" problem as Hollahan, and a name like Bunbaker could get a kid beaten up on the playground daily through grade school. With two gay dads and the name "D. J. Bunbaker," he would never get out of junior high alive. We might was well name him Liberace.

I don't remember whose idea it was, mine or Terry's, but at some point, one of us tossed out another idea: give the baby Melissa's last name, Pierce. We wouldn't even have to give it to him; he'd already have it, we just had to leave him with it. When anyone asked about his last name, he could say, "It's my mother's name." And if in adolescence, he got his panties in a bunch about his gay dads "taking away" the first and middle names his mother gave him—which I worried he would—we'd be able to point to his last name and say, "We left you with the most important name your mother gave you: the name you share with her."

Terry nudged me; Laurie was waiting.

"We want him to have Melissa's last name."

Laurie looked touched.

"Oh, that's really sweet, you guys," she said. "We'll have to check with Melissa to make sure it's okay, but I'm sure it will be. I think that will mean a lot to her."

"We figure he'll have a name I gave him—Daryl, for my dad, a name Dan gave him—Jude, for Dan's mom, and a name his mom gave him," Terry said.

Laurie wrote down the name—Daryl Jude Pierce—and we signed the papers.

"Melissa wants to be alone with the baby in the morning," Laurie said. "She has to check out by two, so if you guys came in around one o'clock that would be good." Laurie would be available to Melissa all morning, in case she needed to talk, but otherwise Melissa would be alone with the baby.

"Adoptive parents usually present the birth mother with a small gift—a locket, a bracelet—and if you guys wanted to go out in the morning and get some pictures developed, presenting the birth mother with a small photo album of hospital pictures is always a nice gesture."

Laurie suggested we bring in a few going-home outfits.

"Let Melissa pick the outfit and dress Daryl." Hearing the baby called Daryl startled me. "And don't forget to bring your car seat up, because the hospital won't let you check out without one. At about one-thirty, we'll have a little placement ceremony."

"A placement ceremony?" Terry asked.

We're not big on touchy-feely stuff. We're not huggers, and neither was Melissa. Even after all we'd been through in the last six weeks, we hadn't hugged Melissa, and she hadn't hugged us. Looking dubious, I asked Laurie what exactly a "placement ceremony" would consist of. Was it like a baptism? And who officiated?

"No, no. The ceremony is just what the adoptive parents and the birth mother want it to be. Maybe you'll say a few words, give Melissa her photos and a placement gift; maybe she'll want to say something to the baby," Laurie explained. "It's a special moment, when the baby is given by the birth mother to the adoptive parents. Marking it, pausing to let the moment sink in, is good for everyone."

We walked into the hall and down to Melissa's door. Laurie knocked as she opened the door, and Melissa was lying in bed, TV off, looking at the baby sleeping in his crib. He was no longer David Kevin, he was Daryl Jude. The baby was asleep on his side, Melissa was on her side, facing him, their faces separated by eights inches of air and a quarter of an inch of clear plastic. He was wrapped up, his little face poking out from under his knit hat. Melissa looked up at us as we filed in, then looked back at the baby.

Laurie sat on the side of the bed, and asked if she was all right. Melissa nodded, and sat up.

"Terry and Dan signed everything, so we're all set for tomorrow," Laurie said gently. "They gave him your last name, Melissa. I wanted to make sure that was okay."

Melissa look up at Terry, then at me.

"Really?"

We nodded.

"That's cool," she said, smiling at Daryl. "That's cool."

We left the hospital to run some errands and get a nap in back at our hotel. Before we left, we promised Melissa we'd bring her some decent chow for dinner—which meant steak. Since Melissa likes her steak well-done, the hotel restaurant was the obvious choice. There isn't a restaurant in the lobby of the Mallory Hotel, just a dining room, and everything from the food served to the decor reminded me of my dead grandmother's apartment. When we told them we wanted to take dinner to a friend at the hospital who'd just had a baby, the Mallory went that extra mile. The Mallory dining room doesn't do to-go orders, the manager explained, but for our friend, the new mother, they would make an exception. We ordered three steaks, and three pieces of chocolate cake. When we came down, not only had they boxed up three steak dinners, but also salad, rolls, butter, silverware, real plates, salt and pepper shakers, a tablecloth, cloth napkins, chocolate cake, and flowers.

We overtipped.

Melissa laughed when we came into her room carrying a box with flowers sticking out of the top, and when we pushed a table up to Melissa's bed and started pulling napkins and flowers out of box, setting the table for dinner, Melissa sat shaking her head. She would've been happy with some hamburgers, she said, but we had to make a big production out of dinner. We weren't the ones

who made a big production out of dinner, I told her, the restaurant manager was.

The baby slept while we ate, and the chocolate cake met with
Melissa's approval. We watched TV, passed the baby around, took
some more pictures, and didn't say one word about tomorrow. We were still behaving as if things would go on like this forever, the three of us living at the hospital and taking care of the
baby, with no one calling him by name.

When we'd come in with dinner, Melissa said she was worried
that David would show up and there wouldn't be enough food to
go around. She was sure he'd come tonight. When eleven o'clock
came and went, and David still hadn't shown up, Melissa's mood
got darker. Melissa and David weren't involved, nothing roman-
tic; she had taken him in, and spoke of him with the same weary
affection with which she spoke of her other animals. Like the dog
and the cat, David was her responsibility. Melissa had updated us
on him whenever we visited: he had a job, he'd lost a job, he was
on crystal, he was off crystal. Melissa had never introduced us to
him, but we got a look at him when we dropped Melissa off after
our visits: he was a skinny kid, good-looking, with intense blue
eyes. He'd been living with Melissa since she moved into the
apartment, eating her food, and she couldn't understand why
David—or any of her other friends—would fail to come see her
and the baby. Did her friends get busted? Were her animals okay?

The gutter-punk ethos is all honor and loyalty; the only real
and the only dependable people on the street are other punks.
Melissa romanticized street life. Her network of friends and fellow punks were her "real" family, she told us, and they were always there for her—unlike her biological family. They were the
people she could count on, the ones who looked after her animals when she got busted or sick, the ones she spare-changed
with and shared beer with. So where were they?

They were, I thought, drinking out of space bags, and they
were used to people disappearing, whether they got busted, or
decided to leave town on a moment's notice. Melissa was out of
sight, and quickly out of mind.

I asked Melissa if we could stop by her apartment on our way
back to the hotel, and see if David was okay. She looked at me for
a moment, and gave us her apartment number.

When we left the hospital, we drove past places Melissa told us David hung out: Pioneer Square, Outside In, the downtown Safeway. The Mallory was only two blocks from Melissa's apartment, so the apartment was our last stop. We parked, and walked up to the door. I rang the doorbell, and a few seconds later a stoned-sounding voice said, "Yeah?"

"Is this David?" I asked.

"Yeah, who's this?"

"It's Dan and Terry, the guys adopting Melissa's baby. Can we come up and talk to you for a minute?"

There was a long pause.

"I'll come down."

While we waited—in the rain—I got pissed. Why hadn't he come to see Melissa at the hospital? She'd named the baby after him, for Christ's sake; he was living in her apartment—which we were paying for—and he couldn't get his ass to the hospital?

When David came to the door, he looked a little surprised to see us. He wasn't wearing shoes, and either he was stoned or we'd awakened him.

"Remember Melissa?" I asked.

He knew it was a trick question. He smiled a stoned smile—his eyes were very big and his pupils very black—and told us that, yeah, he remembered Melissa.

"She's upset that you haven't come to see her at the hospital. She wants you to meet the baby."

David looked down at the ground.

"Oh, yeah, I was planning on going up to see her, but I got real busy, I'll go up tomorrow."

"She has to be out tomorrow at two, so you better go up early," Terry said.

He nodded, but I wasn't sure he'd even remember this conversation in the morning.

"Tell you what," I said, "we'll come over at nine, pick you up, and drive you there. Be outside."

"Okay, thanks, that would be great," David said, as we turned to leave. "Hey, what did she name the baby?"

"I think Melissa wants to tell you the baby's name," I said.

"Okay, cool. See you in the morning."

The Logic of Open Adoption

When we drove up to Melissa's apartment building in the morning, David was waiting outside, saving us the trouble of kicking down the door and dragging him out to the car by his neck. He was appropriately sheepish, and thanked us for reminding him to visit Melissa, which made it hard to stay angry. We headed up to the hospital, David telling us about his new job—landscaping—and us filling David in on the birth and the last couple of days.

After we dropped David off, we had three hours to kill before meeting Laurie and Melissa for the hand-off. We needed to get photos developed, and find a gift for Melissa—which wasn't gonna be easy. What do you get for the woman who has, and wants, nothing? We didn't think Laurie's suggestion, a locket, would go over well: it might work for your average birth mom, but it was a little girly for Melissa. We knew Melissa needed a new backpack, but something practical didn't seem right either, given the occasion. We needed a keepsake, something slightly sentimental, but Melissa wasn't—or tried not to be—a sentimental person. Somewhere in the vastness of Lloyd Center we hoped to find something we could present to her with straight faces, something that said, "Hey, thanks for the kid," without too much mush.

Walking into the mall, I was seized by a sentimental impulse, which was very unlike me: I'm not a terribly sentimental person either. But whatever else we did this morning, I wanted to skate.

Terry wasn't interested in skating; there was too much shopping to do. We had to get photos! Blankets! Something to eat! A gift for Melissa! I put my foot down: we didn't have to spend all

morning on the ice; just a couple of spins. And since skating had
brought us good luck at the seminar, maybe skating on the day
we were bringing the baby home would bring us good luck all his
life. Skating might prevent him from ever falling off a swing and
cracking his head open, running with the wrong crowd, becoming a Christian, or taking a gun to school and shooting his home-
room teacher. But when we got to the rink, thirty little girls in
flouncy outfits were learning to skate, and the rink wouldn't be
open to the general public until one, the same time we were supposed to arrive at the hospital for the hand-off.

We dropped our film off at the one-hour photo place; mean-
while we checked out the jewelry stores, hoping there might be
such a thing as a butch locket. No one had a locket we could
picture on Melissa, but we spotted something else that was perfect: a man's ID bracelet. Heavy silver, it would go perfectly with
Melissa's other chunky-punky jewelry. We had "David Kevin
Pierce: 3/14/98" inscribed on the bracelet, ate BLTs, and
shopped a little, and before we knew it, the three hours we had to
kill were dead.

Feeling dazed, we headed out to the van with our baby blankets, a couple of outfits from Baby Gap, and some more black-
and-red toys we picked up at Toys "R" Toxic. Still feeling
superstitious, I insisted we head to the car by way of the skywalk,
which took us past the conference rooms where we grieved our
infertility so many months ago with the infertile straight people.
We'd left that seminar convinced that no birth mother would ever
select us, and that we were wasting our time even considering
adoption.

Laurie was waiting for us at the nurses' station when we
walked into the maternity ward. She told us Melissa was doing
okay; she'd spent the morning with the baby, and she was "really
touched" that, as promised, we'd dragged David's ass up to the
hospital that morning.

"Melissa said you guys always do what you tell her you're going
to," Laurie said, "and that's really important for building a trusting
relationship with your birth mother. I don't think Melissa's had
many people in her life who did what they told her they would."

Laurie asked where our car seat was. We'd left it in the van, assuming we would carry the baby out of the hospital in our arms,
like in the movies, and strap him into his car seat when we got to
the car. But the hospital's policy was not to discharge an infant
until he was strapped into his car seat. While Terry ran down to
the car, I asked about the hospital's policy concerning actual cars:
what if we didn't have a car to strap the car seat into? Could
pedestrians have babies?

"All we have to do is make sure the baby leaves in a car seat,"
the nurse said. "The assumption is made that if you have a baby
and a car seat, you have a car."

When Terry got back, we all walked down the hall to Melissa's
room, and Laurie softly knocked on her door. The shades were
drawn, the lights were off, and Melissa was lying on her side, the
baby asleep in her arms. We said our heys; Laurie sat on the edge
of the bed, and Terry and I retreated to separate corners of the
room, Terry in a chair next to the table, me on the window seat.
Once again, we were hanging back, not wanting to appear too
anxious to snatch the baby away.

It was one, and Melissa was supposed to check out at two
o'clock, so we had an hour. We sat chatting as if nothing special
was going to happen, telling Laurie stories about the last two
days: our mad dash down to Portland, the nurse who wanted
Melissa to leave right away, that first poopy diaper, getting peed
on, last night's steak dinner. Melissa made observations about the
baby's eating habits, criticized my diapering, and showed Terry
the right way to hold a bottle. We talked about the mall, our
hotel, and David's visit. We were all acting as if Laurie had come
to pay us a visit, and once she was gone the three of us would go
back to lying around, watching TV and taking care of little David
Kevin/Daryl Jude Pierce-Miller-Savage.

The first sign that things wouldn't go on like this forever came
when a nurse appeared with a case of formula, a few days' supply
of diapers, and a gift baby bag filled with diaper and formula
coupons. Melissa got up and changed into her street clothes—
boots, baggy shorts, sweatshirt, and Guinness T-shirt—and when
she came out of the bathroom her hair was down. She was trans-
formed: for the last two days, she'd been the picture of a young
mother, but now she was herself again, the Melissa we met six

weeks ago at Outside In. She smelled like her old self, too; her clothes were gutter-punk filthy when she arrived Saturday morning, and for three days they sat ripening in a plastic bag on a shelf under the TV. When she sat back down on the bed, Melissa asked the nurse for something to wear over her clothes. She didn't want to get the baby dirty.

Melissa told us some more about David's visit ("He figured out the baby's name when you guys wouldn't tell him what it was. He's not stupid, you know"), about her breakfast ("I couldn't eat it, it was terrible"), and about her last visit from her doctor ("She's cool"). Terry, Laurie, and I weren't saying anything now; we were just listening to Melissa, who sat on the bed with the baby in her lap, filling the time with her own voice, putting off the moment when Terry and I would leave with the baby. When Laurie met with Melissa yesterday, they discussed who would leave first. Some birth mothers prefer to leave the hospital first, leaving the adoptive couple in their room with the baby. Melissa wanted us to leave first with the baby; then she would leave with Laurie, who would drive her back to her apartment.

Two o'clock came, and at Laurie's prompting we gave Melissa her I.D. bracelet and a small photo album full of pictures. Laurie said a few words, but none of the rest of us rose to the bait. We were all very quiet. Melissa asked about baby pictures, the kind taken at the hospital immediately after a baby is born. Laurie explained that these cost money and that you had to request them; they weren't taken automatically. Melissa shrugged, disappointed.

"Well, we better get the little guy dressed," Laurie said, falling in with our avoidance of names, but she didn't say why we should get him dressed. Melissa changed the baby's diaper and, with Terry's help, dressed him in the going-home outfit the three of us picked out a month ago: a brown terrycloth jumper and a matching hat. Terry and I put our coats on and gathered up the diapers, bottles, and bag.

Melissa buckled the baby into the car seat the three of us picked out at Toys "R" Toxic, and the room got very quiet. Laurie sat down on the bed next to Melissa, and murmured, "It's time." Terry rose from the bed, put his hand on the car seat's handle, and looked down at Melissa. Melissa didn't look up at us; she looked at the baby, who was wide awake, blinking at the incomprehensible world, blissfully unaware of what was transpiring in front of and because of him. David Kevin squeezed his mom's finger, and Terry and I stood there, like fools, not sure what to do. Should Terry pick up the car seat and walk out? Should we wait for Melissa to draw back her hand? What should we say?

Time stopped, and we stood frozen, until Laurie put her hand on Melissa's shoulder, and Melissa pulled her finger out of David Kevin's hand. Laurie looked up at Terry, and nodded. Terry carefully picked up Daryl Jude, and Melissa's eyes followed her son as he was lifted off the bed. Laurie raised her eyebrows, indicating that this might be a good time to say something, anything.

"We'll see you soon, okay?" Terry said. We'd agreed yesterday to come back down with the baby in two weeks, so Melissa's friends at Outside In could meet him. "Bye, Melissa. Thank you so much," Terry said, and then he picked up the car seat, walked past me, and very tentatively stepped into the hallway with the baby. As soon as the baby was out the door, Melissa looked down at her bed and started to breathe in and out, trying to stay in control. Melissa didn't look up at me, and I wasn't sure what to do; was I supposed to say something now, too? Laurie nodded toward the door, and I started to go.

Melissa crumpled into a ball sobbing, I could see Terry standing in the hallway, waiting for me. I looked at Melissa, and stepped up to the bed. Not once in the last six weeks, not even over the last two days in the hospital, had Melissa and I touched each other. I walked over to the bed and placed a hand on her shoulder. She stopped sobbing, either from the shock of my touch or from the sudden realization that I was still in the room.

"We're not the hugging type, you and me," I heard myself saying. Melissa nodded. "But thank you, Melissa, thank you so much. You will be a part of this baby's life, he's going to know who his mother is. You'll get to see him, and you'll get to love him, and he'll love you. You'll always be his mom, his only mom."

Melissa's shoulders started to rise and fall. She didn't look up, but Laurie nodded at me, as if to say, "Nice try, amateur, now beat it." As I crossed to the door, Laurie gestured that she'd like me to close it on my way out.

As soon as the door was shut, Terry and I locked eyes for an instant and then looked away. We couldn't look at each other, or we'd both start to sob. We had to make it at least to the car before we let ourselves get sloppy, and there was a whole busy hospital to navigate. We stopped by the nurses' station to say good-bye and thank you. The nurses wished us the best of luck, and beamed at us in a way that made me uncomfortable. We smiled, but all we could think about was how Melissa was feeling in her room, alone with Laurie, waiting for us to leave. We walked out of the maternity ward and over to the elevators. When the doors closed, we were alone. We looked at each other again for a split second.

"That was so hard—" I said.

"Shut up, don't say anything."

The doors opened on another floor. We were doing all we could to hold ourselves together. We weren't alone on the elevator now.

We walked through the lobby, across the street, and over to the parking garage. Terry opened the van; we locked the car seat in place, shut the side door, and climbed into our seats. Then we both folded up, sobbing, heads in hands. No one warned us about the moment when you pick the baby up and walk out of the room, leaving the birth mom sobbing in her bed. We were unprepared for all the planning and check-writing and seminar-going to end in a moment of such blistering pain. Sitting in the van finally a family, we felt no joy at having become fathers.

"She looked so miserable," I choked out between sobs.

"I know, I know . . ." Terry sobbed in response.

Suddenly, it occurred to me that Laurie's car might be parked near our van, and that if Melissa came down and saw us sitting there, her pain would be compounded. I told Terry to drive, and slowly, sobbing, we made our way down the hill.

North Americans feel too much, latching on to grief that isn't our own, drooling over Princess Diana's all-star funeral or the televised memorial service for the dead in Oklahoma City or Littleton, Colorado. No one's allowed to grieve in private anymore, and pain has become one of the performing arts, one that the simpleminded and the talentless can excel at. We open up and let it all out for Oprah or Sally or Diane or Barbara, and private grief is public property. But to see Melissa's pain at the moment she gave up that baby, and to feel pain ourselves at that same moment, drove home the logic of open adoption, its absolute necessity.

In a closed adoption, we wouldn't have witnessed the moment our son's mother gave him up. That we saw what we did, however painful, is to the ultimate benefit of the kid in the car seat. The idea of starting off as his parents without experiencing what we did was suddenly unimaginable. One day, D.J. may worry that his mother didn't want him, that she didn't care about him, that she didn't love him. Because of open adoption, we'll be able to sit him down and tell him about this day; we'll be able to describe the moment Melissa gave him to us, and how it hard it was for her. We won't have to guess at what it was like, or tell him that we're sure his mother loved him. We know she loved him; we saw it.

And seeing how hard it was for Melissa to hand us her baby, and knowing that we would never have been a family if she didn't trust us with him, how could we even think of denying her the right to see her baby as he grows? Having seen what we did, how could we begrudge her visits, pictures, or phone calls? After what she'd just given us, how could we deny her anything?

Somehow we made it to the Mallory. Terry pulled into a parking space, his head down on the steering wheel, and wept. When we walked into the lobby, the clerk cooed and ah'ed over the baby.

"Whose is he?" she asked.

"He's ours," Terry told her, "we adopted him."

"Congratulations!"

From our room, we called Laurie's voice mail and left her a message asking her to call and let us know Melissa was all right. (Later, Laurie called: Melissa was fine; it was hard, but she was home, and David was with her.)

The baby's fingernails were long and sharp, and when he wasn't gripping our fingers or his blanket, he was scratching at his face. We didn't have a nail clipper with us, so I went out to buy one. On the way back to the hotel with the nail clipper, I passed the Eagle and if I couldn't skate at Lloyd Center for luck this morning, I thought, maybe I should duck into the Eagle for one last game of pinball. A youngish guy sitting on a bar stool next to my machine struck up a conversation. He asked me where I was from, and I told him Seattle.

"What are you doing in Portland?" he asked.

I told him I'd just adopted a baby, and he laughed.

"No, really, my boyfriend and I just adopted a baby. He weighs just under seven pounds, he cost us about fifteen thousand dollars, and we broke his mother's heart when we picked him up and carried him out of her hospital room this afternoon. The baby is back at the hotel, with my boyfriend, and they're waiting for me to bring back a fingernail clipper."

"Right."

I pulled the infant-sized fingernail clipper out of my pocket and showed it to him.

He still didn't believe me. He excused himself and walked off.

Afterbirth

Father Days

Two days after we brought D.J. to the Mallory Hotel in Port-land, the state of Oregon gave us permission to bring D.J. home to our messy condo in Seattle. We checked out, put the baby in his car seat, and drove up I-5.

During those first few weeks at home, we cleaned and packed. D.J. ate, slept, peed, and pooped. Brand-new babies are all about excrement: there's no crawling, no cooing, no smiling—no nothing—in those first few weeks, only poop. And since he wasn't a cryer, poop was the only feedback we were getting from D.J. on our parenting. Every bowel movement became a referendum. Terry and I were soon having long, involved conversations about the consistency, frequency, and hue of D.J.'s Gross Domestic Product. We each set aside diapers with suspiciously large GDPs for the other's inspection, as well as any diapers whose contents were oddly colored, too thin, too thick, or too stinky.

D.J. was devoid of personality in the first few weeks, and I'm going to resist the anthropomorphic urge and refrain from endowing our human infant with any human characteristics. The expression on his face changed occasionally, but only when he was taking a crap, cutting a fart, or preparing to throw up. He made cute gurgling noises now and again but rarely smiled. He looked angelic when he slept, and he couldn't move much on his own, so he was always right where we'd left him. Every once in a while he would open his eyes wide, give us an astonished look—"What the hell is going on? Where the hell am I? Who the hell are you?"—and then drop off to sleep.

We poured over several how-to-keep-your-baby-alive books,

consulting them daily at first, and then as we grew more comfortable, less and less. The best book was on the first year, with each month getting its very own chapter. Every four weeks or so, we pulled this book out and read the next month's chapter. It made parenthood seem like a college-level biology class, one with a lifelong lab, where to pass all you really needed to do was not fall too far behind on your reading.

Our mothers descended on us to share their "parenting expertise" and made sure we weren't doing anything that might imperil their grandson. But so much has changed in the thirty years since their kids were in diapers that their advice was, according to the books we were reading, a little dangerous. We had been told to put D.J. to sleep on his back, not his stomach, to prevent sudden infant death syndrome. Our mothers told us to put him to sleep on his stomach, not his back, to prevent sudden infant death. We'd been told not to put our baby in a playpen, or his brain would turn to mush. Our mothers pointed out that we'd spent time in playpens and our brains weren't mush. With both grandmas in the house, Terry and I slipped away for an hour. When we returned, D.J. was wearing a diaper backward. Terry picked him up, and it fell off. Neither of our mothers had ever encountered a high-tech, Velcro-tabbed disposable diaper before.

Terry took the baby to see Melissa two weeks after he was born, as promised. (My mother and I stayed in Seattle to pack.) Until May, Melissa could stay in the apartment the agency had arranged for her, but she met Terry at Outside In. (She was about to age out of the drop-in center; she would be turning twenty-one in June.) With Terry carrying the baby in his car seat, and Melissa carrying her cat and leading her dog, they walked down to Pioneer Square, and hooked up with a group of Melissa's friends.

After our mothers left, my sister came to visit. Thankfully, she had encountered disposable diapers, and proved to be a great help during our move from the condo to our friend's basement. After we moved, and my sister left, my dad came to meet his second grandson. When my dad left, my mom returned with Jerry and helped us move into our new house. When my mom and her husband left, Claudia and Dennis came to visit. Then my mom came back. Then Terry's mom came back. Then my sister called and asked if she could come back. We had no choice: Terry and I called a halt to family visits. We needed time alone with the baby, and while we couldn't forbid anyone from visiting Seattle, we forbade our mothers, fathers, brothers and sister from getting anywhere near *us* for two months.

A friend printed up some incredibly tasteful birth announcements for us, and my mother sent a list of addresses. When I got to my grandmother Savage's name and address, I hesitated. I hadn't spoken to my father's mother, my only living grandparent, since my grandfather's funeral ten years ago. She was not a pleasant person. When my parents divorced, my grandmother announced to her family that my siblings and I were no longer her grandchildren. We stopped getting cards from her at Christmas and on our birthdays, which was actually something of a relief. Being disowned by Grandma Savage was like losing a job you hated.

When I saw her name on the list, though, I thought, *Why not?* On the back of the card, I wrote, "Hi, Grandma. Just wanted to let you know that you've got another great-grandchild. Hope you're in good health. Love, Dan."

A week later, an envelope arrived for me with some vaguely familiar handwriting on it, but no return address. I looked at the postmark—Palatine, Illinois—and realized it was my grandmother's handwriting, handwriting I hadn't seen since my father left my mother eighteen years ago.

Inside the envelope was D.J.'s birth announcement. Grandma Savage had opened it, read it, gone to her desk, gotten a new envelope, written my address on it, put D.J.'s birth announcement back in its original envelope, placed it in the envelope she'd addressed to me, sealed it, put a stamp on it, and mailed it back. There was no note.

I called my mother, who loves to hear about what a cunt her former mother-in-law is. Then I called my brother Billy, who begged me not to blame this on Dad. Then I called my dad. My dad didn't want me to call up my ex-grandmother and scream at her, and I promised him I wouldn't.

"She's a sick old lady," my dad said. "What can I say?"

When I got off the phone, Terry and I sat with the card, wondering what could possess an old woman to be so . . . mean. D.J.'s other great-grandmother, Terry's grandma Audrey, was so excited to hold her great-grandchild that she looked as if she might explode. But my grandma? I found myself wishing we had given D.J. my middle name, Keenan, as his last name. Keenan is not only my middle name, it was my Grandma Savage's maiden name. That would've given her a stroke.

We saved the birth announcement my grandmother had mailed back, and we keep it in a safe place. Grandma Savage is an old lady, crazy and mean. When she dies, Terry, D.J., and I will attend her open-casket wake. And when no one is looking, I will slip D.J.'s birth announcement into her casket. She'll spend eternity with that birth announcement.

In the first few months of D.J.'s life, Terry and I deadlocked on just two issues: circumcision and baptism. I got my way on both.

Like most American males, Terry and I were circumcised as infants. And like most American homos, we prefer circumcised men as sex partners. I lived in Europe for a while, and came to appreciate uncut men. But given my druthers, I'd rather put a cut dick in my mouth than an uncut one. Cut cock just tastes better, and in a culture that's embraced oral sex as enthusiastically as ours has, gay and straight, taste counts for something. Discuss circumcision with new parents—hip ones, living in urban areas—and along with the standard pro-circumcision arguments ("We want him to look like his father"; "We don't want him made fun of in the locker room"; "It's easier to keep clean") you'll hear implicit and occasionally explicit concerns about how he's going to taste. Straight folks won't usually come right out and say, "We worry about his dick tasting awful"; instead, they communicate their concern with cryptic comments about what his sex partners will think, the smegma issue, and whether being uncut might limit his options sexually . . . and they trail off.

Unfortunately for oral sex, logic is on the side of the anticircumcision activists. Family resemblance? Not something we usually judge on the appearance of genitals. Teasing in the locker room? Half of all boys born in America today are not circumcised; if your son gets teased, he and the other uncut kids can form a gang and beat the shit out of the snip-dicks. Ease of cleaning? We don't cut off other body parts that are hard to keep clean.

With that kind of logic, the anticircumcision activists point out, we should have our teeth yanked out to save us the bother of flossing. But even with these arguments refuted, there's still the taste issue to worry about, and anyway, what does logic have to do with kids? Is there anyone less rational than a new parent?

Terry felt very strongly about circumcision: he was for it. I felt strongly about it too: I was opposed. Terry wanted his son's dick to look like his own, while I didn't foresee D.J. and me spending any of our quality time comparing dicks. As for taste, well, the slight possibility that D.J. would get a little less head than his cut friends bothered me less than the idea of taking a knife and lopping off the end of his dick.

At the hospital, Terry had asked Melissa how she felt, and Melissa shrugged. Interpreting this as a yes, Terry claimed it was two against one in favor of cutting D.J. I gave in. Terry could have D.J. circumcised, but I wasn't going to lift a finger to help. Terry made an appointment with a urologist, and then, having lifted a finger—literally, pushing the buttons on the phone all by himself—he decided it was my job to find us a ride to the hospital. I told him no, I meant it when I said I wasn't going to help. If he wanted D.J.'s foreskin cut off, he would have to do it all by himself.

Terry called my friend Dave and asked if he would drive him and the baby to a doctor's appointment. Dave and his boyfriend, Eric, are huge foreskin fans, so when Terry told me Dave would be taking D.J. in to the urologist, I couldn't believe it.

"Did you tell Dave what kind of appointment this is?"

"No. It's none of his business," said Terry, knowing full well that if he told Dave, Dave wouldn't be driving him to the doctor.

I lifted a finger and called Dave, filling him in on the nature and purpose of this doctor's appointment. Dave called Terry and told him he wouldn't be giving him a lift after all. Terry, furious, called the doctor and canceled D.J.'s appointment, then harrumphed around the house about how disrespectful I was being of *Melissa's* wishes.

"If D.J. grows up with a complex about not looking like us, or gets beat up in locker rooms, or can't find anyone who'll give him a blowjob," Terry warned me, "I'm going to tell him it's all your fault."

I assumed these risks, and D.J. remained intact. Barring infections, complications, or a conversion to Judaism, he'll remain uncut for life.

On the other contentious issue, baptism, I was pro and Terry was con.

My grandfather was baptized, wearing a white linen gown. My mother was baptized wearing the same gown. My brothers and sisters and I were all baptized wearing my grandfather's gown, as were all of my aunts, uncles, and cousins. Hundreds of members of my family have been baptized wearing my grandfather's gown, and I wanted to see D.J. baptized in that white linen gown too. I didn't want to raise D.J. Catholic, as I'm not a practicing Catholic myself. I waver between a cop-out agnosticism and principled atheism, and nothing about becoming a parent made me want to return to the Church, or any other church. But still, when anyone asks about my heritage, I describe myself as Irish Catholic. It's a cultural thing.

From the look on Terry's face when I told him about wanting to have D.J. baptized, you would have thought I wanted to take D.J. home and throw him in a wood chipper.

"You don't go to church," Terry said when I asked him to go to Chicago with me and have D.J. baptized. "You don't believe in anything."

But do you have to believe? Almost all of my Jewish friends are bright, atheistic pork eaters, and none would find anything objectionable about bacon bagels besides aesthetics. They don't believe in anything either, but they get together and celebrate Jewish holidays because doing so matters to them culturally. They're not wasting time waiting for the Messiah to come, but they do get together every once in a while and act like great big Jews. Why can't I do the same? Why can't I get together with my family and act like a great big Catholic?

"And it would be a nice thing to do for my mother and my great-aunts," I told Terry. "They go out of their way to be nice to us; why can't we go out of our way and do this small thing for them?" My family was great on the gay issue all year long; couldn't we be great on the Catholic issue just once? And if we wanted them to take our relationship seriously, and recognize D.J. as a member of the family, would it be too much for us to take him to Chicago, put him in the white linen gown, and let a priest sprinkle some water on his head?

"I'll get on a plane and go to Chicago," Terry said, "but I'm not going to lift a finger to help with the baptism."

My mother stepped in and saved me from having to lift any of my own fingers. She found us a church and a priest, ordered a cake, and had the linen gown cleaned and restored. Despite her numerous Catholic connections, though—the woman knows more priests than a Roman male prostitute—the arrangements were more difficult to make than we'd expected. In its tireless efforts to drive American Catholics into the arms of the Lutherans and Unitarians, the Catholic Church has become stingy with the sacraments over the last ten years. They don't want cultural Catholics showing up for the occasional baptisms, weddings, and funerals. The pastor at the church where I was baptized, my mother was baptized, my parents were married, and my grandparents were married, and which my great-grandparents helped build (there are stained-glass windows with our family names on them) refused to baptize D.J. He also refused let another priest baptize D.J. in "his" church. He told my mother it had nothing to do with her grandson's parents being homos, and my mother almost believed him.

Finally, my mother tracked down a priest, an old family friend, willing to baptize D.J. This man, one of the priests at my parish when I was growing up and the last to hear my confession, believed an expression of cultural Catholicism was better than no expression of Catholicism at all. And Mom found us another church, not one my family helped build but one where my great-aunt Katie volunteered, whose pastor was happy to let us come.

When we tried to board our flight to Chicago, the woman behind the ticket counter wanted to know why the baby didn't have the same last name as either of the adults he was traveling with. Who were we? Where was his mother? What was our relationship to each other? She was about to call security—she was worried we were kidnapping this baby!—when I started telling her the long story of how little adopted D.J. came to have a different last name than either of his dads. As I spoke, she put the phone down, looking at Terry and then back at me. Apparently, we looked enough like fags. She bought the story and gave us our boarding passes. (Now we carry as copy of D.J.'s birth certificate in our wallets, along with the adoption decree.)

On the plane, more problems presented themselves. The passengers in our row, the stewardesses, even the captain walked up and asked D.J. questions:

"Where's Mommy today?"

"Are you on your way to Mommy's house?"

"Are your baby-sitters taking good care of you for Mommy?"

"Did these two boys steal you from your Mommy?"

"Whose baby are you?"

These were questions, we realized on that flight to Chicago, that we'd be answering for the rest of our lives. Where's Mommy? Since we know where Melissa is, we can answer questions about Mommy truthfully. But answering "Whose baby are you?" will mean coming out over and over again, forever. Whose baby is he? He's our baby.

I hadn't been to a baptism in eighteen years, not since my cousin Amie was baptized and I stood as her godfather, and I'd forgotten about the Q&A. Most of the Catholic baptism rite consists of questions, with the priest grilling the parents and godparents about their beliefs. Whatever the priest asks, you're supposed to respond, "I do." Do you believe in the Virgin Birth? I do. Do you believe in the miracle of transubstantiation? I do. Do you believe the pope poops lilac water? I do.

Terry wasn't thrilled about having to profess his faith. He threatened to stand at the baptismal font with his mouth clamped shut, refusing to play along with my cultural Catholicism. But once we got to the church, where my mother dressed D.J. in the baptismal gown, Terry was swept away by the moment. With Amie standing as D.J.'s godmother, with Jerry standing as godfather, with my mother, my siblings, my nephew Mars, and forty of my other relatives standing around him, Terry felt compelled to say "I do" after each of the priest's questions, loud enough for all to hear. Under his breath, however, and only loud enough for me to hear, Terry whispered "not" after each "I do."

After the sprinkle and the "I dos" and before the picture taking, the priest welcomed D.J. into the Catholic community, and turned to me and Terry. He raised his hand and, in front of my great-aunts, my brothers and sister, my mom, and Christ on the cross, he blessed our relationship. I was stunned. This was above and beyond the call of duty, and more than we asked for or expected. The same church that blesses restaurants and race horses won't bless gay relationships, and our priest was taking some risk in blessing ours. He could be defrocked, I thought, as he blessed us. It was a wonderfully brave thing for him to do. And we did feel blessed. Then we left the church and headed to my sister's apartment, where D.J.'s baptism cake was set up on the dining room table. Mom had ordered it from the same bakery where she'd ordered all her kids' baptism and birthday and first communion and confirmation and graduation cakes. D.J.'s baptism cake was chocolate, with white icing, blue roses, and a yellow icing cross on top.

The next day, we baptized D.J. a second time. My brother Billy bought us all tickets to a Cubs game. In the bleachers at Wrigley Field, with my mother holding D.J., and my brother Eddie, sister Laura, nephew Mars, and cousins Tracey and Kevin serving as witnesses, Billy asked us if we believed in family, in the Cubs, and in beer.

"In that order?" Eddie asked.

"No," said Billy. "Normally, beer would come first, but Mom's here."

"You guys are awful!" Mom said, laughing. "My arms are getting tired, baptize this baby already!"

"Do you believe in beer, the Cubs, and family?" Billy asked again.

"I do," we all said, and Billy poured beer over D.J.'s forehead.

On the flight back home, newly baptized D.J. threw up all over Terry. We grabbed the baby bag and headed for the bathroom. The people waiting in line let us go ahead—parenthood has its perks—and we stepped into the tiny bathroom. At first, we left the door open while we struggled to get the baby out of his puke-soaked clothing. But the open door was in the way of one of the stewardesses, so she asked us to close it. Once the door was shut, I took over wiping up the baby so Terry could take his pukey shirt off. I was wearing a T-shirt and a button-down shirt; I started taking off my button-down so I could give it to Terry, and Terry took over wiping up the baby.

At this moment—Terry shirtless, me taking my shirt off—the bathroom door opened. A stewardess, a different one, looked in and saw Terry half naked and me fumbling to get my shirt off.

"Oh, my God!" she screamed. "You're disgusting! This is not what the bathrooms are for. Lock the door at least!"

We looked at each other, stunned. Then Terry threw open the door and—still shirtless—followed the stewardess into the aisle.

"We've got a sick fucking baby in here! I don't have a shirt on because I'm covered with vomit! We are *not* having sex in your fucking toilet!"

My hero.

A few weeks after D.J.'s baptism in Chicago, we were in Spokane for a wedding. Terry's older brother, Tom, was marrying a woman he'd met at a fundamentalist Christian church he'd recently started attending—very recently. Tom had known Pam only a few months when they decided to get married. Pam was a nice person, and they seemed like a good match, but why the rush to tie the knot? Why not have premarital sex first, shack up for a couple of years, and *then* get married, like all the other straight people? We disapproved.

Spokane, where Terry grew up, is crawling with serial killers and bomb-throwing white supremacists. All you need to know about this place is that you can stand in downtown Spokane and spit on Idaho. Before we left, I warned Terry that I was not above making a scene if there was any gay-bashing—overt or covert— at his brother's fundamentalist Christian wedding. A prayer for the preservation of marriage as a heterosexual institution, a reading from Leviticus or Romans, a dirty look from the pastor, and I would be noisily up, out of the pew, and out the door.

Terry's mom watched D.J. our first day in Spokane so we could attend Tom's fundamentalist Christian bachelor party. Tom's church frowns on alcohol and naked ladies, so there was no booze or strippers. Instead, we went mountain biking. Tom introduced me to his fundamentalist Christian friends as his brother's "friend." They'd arranged to borrow a couple of bikes for us, but only after driving to the top of Mount Spokane did they realize they'd forgotten bike helmets for Terry and his "friend." They were trying to kill us.

A lot of time at weddings, fundie or otherwise, is burned up with group introductions. The introductions at Tom and Pam's rehearsal dinner went something like this: "This is Jason, he's your Aunt Martha's oldest boy, and came all the way from California. Dennis is Claudia's husband, and Terry and Tom's stepdad. Walt, there, is Dennis's oldest boy. This is Susan, she's the best man's youngest sister, and she's a nurse. This is Chuck, he's Tom's best friend from high school. This is Chan, he's an exchange student staying with Aunt Millie's family, they came in from Vancouver this morning—Vancouver in Washington, not Canada. They had some car trouble, but they made it. And this is . . . this is Dan."

On Mount Spokane, I was my boyfriend's friend; at the rehearsal dinner, I was no one's friend. I'd dropped from the sky. And so had the baby: "And this is . . . this is the baby."

There may be a framed photograph of Terry and me in his mother's living room, but it was pretty clear that the sensibilities of Tom and Pam's fundamentalist Christian guests were being deferred to today. I was just Dan, not my boyfriends's boyfriend, and the baby was just Baby, and not *our* baby.

The service the next day was short and sweet, D.J. was good and quiet, and the photo-taking was long and hellish. There was no mention of homosexuality in the service, pro or con, and so no need for me to make a scene. There *was* some Operation Rescue literature on a table by the door, and a letter from the American Family Association tacked to a bulletin board. Another small-town high school cafeteria had been shot up by another teenage boy using his daddy's gun, and the American Family Association wanted Christians everywhere to stand up to those responsible: feminists and homosexuals.

I'd come to Tom and Pam's wedding prepared to go nuclear, but I couldn't get excited about the low-grade stuff we encountered. After being introduced as "This is . . . Dan" for the thousandth time, I started telling people I was the caterer. I let my guard down, and as I sat with my boyfriend's young cousins, D.J. was passed around the room. Everybody loves babies, and no one loves 'em quite so desperately as those fundamentalist Christians.

Everyone at the wedding wanted to hold D.J., just as everyone did at the shower Terry's coworkers held for us after we brought him home, and at the baptism we'd just been to in Chicago. Babies at parties get passed around, no big deal.

But when I looked around and couldn't see D.J. anywhere, I got a little panicky. Terry was at another table, talking with his uncle, but no baby. I remembered where we were: fundamentalist Christians, American Family Association, Operation Rescue literature . . . Oh, my God—what if someone had left with our baby? What if one of the other guests, some wacko fundy, couldn't stand the thought of this cute baby being raised by homos and decided to . . . rescue him? I stormed over to Terry, grabbed his arm, and whispered, "Where's the fucking baby?" loud enough for fundies praying two counties away to hear.

We found D.J. on the other side of the room, sitting on some fundy's lap, smiling. We retrieved him and didn't let him out of our sight or our arms again. Everyone at the wedding was nice, but this was the kind of church clinic bombers, doctor killers, and Buchanan voters are drawn from. After the scare we'd just had, however short it was, we weren't letting the pasta salad and bad dress sense lull us into lowering our defenses. D.J. stayed on my lap for the rest of the day.

Carol and Jack came over to check out our new place and see D.J. Jack had met him the day after we brought him home, but Carol's job had taken her out of town for months. When we all sat down, a smiling D.J. on Carol's lap, they told us they had news.

"You don't have to feel guilty anymore—" Jack said.

"You guys were picked!" Terry shouted.

Carol nodded, Jack laughed, and I could feel the guilt lift from my shoulders.

"We're going to Portland to meet our birth mom tomorrow." Carol said, "and I only hope we get a baby half as cute as yours."

In late July, a month after she turned twenty-one, Melissa came up to Seattle. We'd spoken with her a couple of times since Terry brought the baby down to Portland. When I asked when she was coming up, so we could make plans for a visit, she sighed and explained that it didn't work that way. She would get to Seattle when she could—she wanted to get up here for Folklife, the music festival her father attended every year—but she didn't have much luck hitchhiking with her animals. She would have to find a ride or jump a train, which meant she didn't have much control over when she got to town. Then one day a few weeks later, as I rode my bicycle down Broadway, I saw Melissa sitting on the ground outside a Jack in the Box, with her dog and her cat, spare-changin' with another gutter punk. I kept riding.

When I got home and told Terry I'd seen Melissa, he asked why I didn't stop and talk to her. I didn't know. It was good to see her, but somehow I'd felt that stopping and talking with her in front of her friends might be an invasion of her privacy. Did they know she'd given birth? Did they know she'd given the baby to fags? If not, what would she tell them about the big fag on the bike who rode up to say hello and asked her to come over for a visit?

Later that night, she called to say she was in town.

"Do you want to come see D.J.?" Terry asked.

"Yeah, I guess. Is that all right?"

"Of course. You want to come for dinner?"

"I don't know, whatever."

Terry went to pick Melissa up in a car Carol and Jack lent us, and I went to the store and bought some steaks.

As soon as Melissa was in the house, we stopped calling the baby D.J.; he was "the kid" again. Melissa didn't call him anything, either, and I felt like we were back at OHSU. We gave Melissa a tour, showing her the baby's room and, finally, the baby, asleep in his crib. It was time for a feeding, so we got him up, changed him, and warmed a bottle. While Terry cooked dinner, Melissa and I sat in the living room with the baby.

She'd arrived in Seattle five days earlier, after hopping a train with a friend, a kid she met in Portland after the baby was born. She spoke of this boy in the same tone we'd heard her use when she talked about David. He wasn't too bright, and hadn't been on the streets for very long. Without Melissa to look out for him, he wouldn't make it. She'd seen her father at the festival, but he didn't see her, and she didn't go up to say hello. She was planning on staying in Seattle for a few weeks; then she wanted to head east, out to New York, for the rest of the summer.

There were gutter punks in New York, of course, homeless young kids who begged for change. But New York is a meaner place than Seattle or Portland, and I warned Melissa that she might not find life on the streets there the same as life on the streets of Portland or Seattle.

"I'll be fine," she assured us, as she slowly ate her steak. "I've got a dog."

By the time Father's Day rolled around in June, I'd changed a lot of diapers, and spent a few long nights sitting up with the baby, but I didn't feel like a dad. I felt bonded, more than I had at the hospital, but I didn't feel like *Daddy*. Terry, on the other hand, was Superdad. Shortly after the baby came, he'd left his job. What bottles were washed, what diapers purchased, what formula was made was almost all thanks to Terry. He bitched and moaned about having to do "everything," and I countered by bitching and moaning about having to make the money to pay for "everything." If Terry was going to stay home with the baby, which was what he wanted to do, that didn't mean I could work less. It meant the opposite. I was working for three now.

While I got out of a lot of baby grunt work, I also missed out on the bonding that grunt work inspires. Terry was doing more daddying than I was, and naturally felt more a daddy than I did after three months. Biological parents are parents whether or not they lift a finger; they don't even have to be present. Their parent status is a genetic fact, as evidenced by the many adopted children who go out in search of their biological parents. Adoption is an act of will, and despite the placement papers we'd signed and the birth certificate we would get in the mail when the adoption was finalized (with Terry and me listed as "Mother" and "Father"), only the work of parenting would earn us the right to view ourselves, and be viewed by others, as D.J.'s fathers.

Most important, the work of parenthood would make D.J. see us as his parents. Sitting up with D.J. one night during a feeding, I realized that if I died the next day, D.J. wouldn't think of me as his father. I would be some guy who'd adopted him and had taken care of him for a short time. He wouldn't remember me, and no pictures of me holding him at the baptism, or at the wedding, would make him feel I was his father. So not only did I need to perform daily acts of parenthood to cement my daddy identity, enough time had to pass so that D.J. could recall these acts as an adult. I had to keep it up and stick around into D.J.'s living memory to earn my daddy identity.

When adoptive couples get nervous about who their kid's "real" parents are, or when strangers ask who the "real" parents are, the adoption books and the adoption counselors reassure us: the real parents are the people there in the middle of the night, the people taking care of the kid, and, most important, the people the kid calls Dad.

On our first Father's Day, D.J. was a little shy of three months; he wasn't calling us anything yet. I wasn't sure he could even tell us apart. But he did seem to know that the large, moving things that scooped him up usually did something that made him feel better—fed him, changed him, held him—and sometimes did things that made him feel worse—cleaned his umbilical cord stump with ice-cold alcohol wipes, sucked snot out of his nose with a blue bulb, gave him a bath. But on our first Father's Day, he wasn't sure what we were. He didn't know we were dads, or even what dads were.

He would soon, though. He'd understand that he had parents, two dads, and he'd know that we were the guys who were always there for him. And then he'd call me Dad. And that was when, I thought, I'd finally start to feel like one.

I hoped.

Bacchus

Melissa left Seattle in late July. She'd been to see the baby several more times, and on my way to work, I sometimes saw her sitting on Broadway, spare-changin' people. We didn't hear from her for a few weeks after she'd left; then, in mid-August, we got a call. She was in Lincoln, Nebraska, and the spare-changin' was easy; in fact, the money was so good that she and her animals would be working there for a couple of weeks before heading on to Minneapolis.

"I'll be in Minnesota for a month, probably," Melissa said, "before I go to New York."

"You want us to come over so you can see the baby?" I asked. "He's a lot more entertaining now that he's crawling around."

"Sure, if you want. I'd like to see D.J."

It was the first time Melissa had used the name we'd given her kid. She was apparently aware of the name game we'd all been playing, and decided it was time to call it off.

"Call us and let us know when you get to Minneapolis, and we'll make arrangements to come over."

"I'll call. Tell Terry I say hi, and D.J., too, not that he'll understand hi."

"I'll tell him anyway, practice for when he does understand."

August ended; September came and went; we didn't hear from Melissa. By the end of October, we were in a panic. Riding rails was dangerous, dog or no dog, and Melissa knew it. She was aware that white supremacist serial killers rode the rails—we'd seen them on *20/20*—picking off people and moving on. And if she fell between trains, she wouldn't be the first gutter punk killed that way. Terry knew a girl who'd lost both her legs riding the rails, and she hadn't been jumping on a moving train with a dog, a cat, and a pack. We had talked with Melissa about all this, but she told us we shouldn't pay attention to what the TV said about riding rails. She was the expert; she had the scar to prove it and considered riding the rails at least as safe as hitchhiking.

By mid-November, we were sure she was dead, and if that weren't nightmare enough, my worst-case-scenario software kicked in. The only personal papers Melissa carried were some I.D., D.J.'s original birth certificate, and the small photo album we'd given her at the hospital. If her body turned up somewhere, it would be returned to her parents, along with her personal effects. They would learn they had a grandchild from the birth certificate; they'd see Melissa and D.J. and me and Terry in the photo album. They could call OHSU, and that might lead them to the agency. While birth grandparents had no rights in Oregon, that didn't mean Melissa's parents couldn't sue for custody. They'd lose, but they could still sue. It would be grieving grandparents vs. dumb young fags, and it wasn't hard to figure out whose side *20/20, Dateline,* and *Hard Copy* would come down on.

We'd agreed during mediation to introduce D.J. to Melissa's parents once she reconciled with her family. We wanted to meet her parents one day, but not in court.

Then, one night in late December, the phone rang. Melissa was alive and well and living in New Orleans, by way of Minneapolis, Chicago, Cleveland, New York, Vermont, and Florida. She was sorry she hadn't called, but she'd been on the move since leaving Lincoln, and the piece of paper our phone number was on got wet and she couldn't read it. We weren't listed, and it wasn't until she got to New Orleans that she realized she could call the agency, get our number again, and call us.

"We thought you were dead! We were so worried!" I said, sounding like my mother.

"You don't have to worry about me," Melissa said. "I'm always fine."

Then she laughed, and it was different from her usual weary laugh. She sounded pleased. When we first met, Melissa had told us that her family knew she was on the streets in Portland and they never came looking for her. She would never say so, but I think it made her feel good to know that we worried, and that someone out there wanted to know where she was.

"You guys aren't my family," Melissa said. "You don't have to worry about me, you know."

"You're our kid's mom, and that makes you family," I said, echoing what we'd been told at the seminar. "And our moms ask how you're doing whenever they call, and that *really* makes you family."

"Worry about me, then," Melissa said, "if it makes you happy."

Melissa would be staying in New Orleans for a while. She had a new boyfriend, Ten Spot was his street name, and a friend had given them a van. It didn't run, but they were getting the money together to fix it. Like her animals, the van seemed to be more trouble than it was worth: the first time she and Ten Spot moved it, they got into an accident. Then, after weeks of pushing the van around town to avoid having it impounded, they finally found someone who'd let them park in their yard. They were living in the van, and would be in New Orleans at least two months. Ten Spot was doing some landscaping work, and Melissa was spare-changin'. Once they got the van running, they'd be leaving for California, but if we wanted to come see her, we could.

We ordered tickets and made hotel reservations for the last weekend in January.

A few days later, Terry was at home with the baby and got a collect call.

"Guess who I ran into," Melissa said. "Bacchus."

Before Terry could say anything, she passed the phone off.

"Hey, this is Bacchus, D.J.'s father."

Ten minutes later, Terry was on the phone with me, practically hysterical. He couldn't remember much they had talked about, only that Bacchus asked him to send pictures of "his" son, and kept telling Terry how excited he was to be a father.

"What did he sound like?" I asked.

"Like, I don't know, like Melissa. Like a stoner, or a street kid. What do you think he wants?"

"Well, whatever he wants, he can't have the kid—does he know that?"

"I don't know."

"What did Melissa tell him?"

"He knows we're coming to New Orleans in three weeks, and he wants to meet 'his son' when we come down. She also gave him our address and phone number. He knows everything, basically."

We were upset with Melissa—why had she given him our phone number? What was she thinking? We got more upset as calls from Bacchus continued to come in every night. It was December; we were gone most of the month, and weren't home when he called. With each message, he sounded more frustrated, as if he assumed we were avoiding or screening his calls. We weren't. We *did* want to talk to him: we wanted to tell him not to call us. Before we would see him, he needed to talk to the agency.

Melissa called to apologize. She ran into Bacchus in the street, and before she realized it might be a mistake, she'd given him our phone number.

Then Bacchus's father called.

"This is Kevin's father, D.J.'s grandfather. I just wanted to thank you guys for looking after D.J. It's a good thing you're all doin'," the stranger on the phone said, his tone a combination of sentiment and menace. "And I can't wait to meet the little guy. You two take care of my grandson until then."

Now we were really in a panic. Bacchus's father sounded drunk, and we didn't know where he lived. Was he in Seattle? Did he have our address?

We'd called Laurie, asking her to contact Bacchus. Our agency offers lifelong mediation with the birthparents, both of them, at no extra charge. Before we spoke with Bacchus again, we wanted him and his father to understand their legal rights to this child—i.e., their lack of any—and we didn't feel comfortable explaining this to Bacchus ourselves. Laurie suggested we write Bacchus a letter, and send it and a photo of D.J. to the agency. She wrote him a letter on agency letterhead, and sent everything off to Bacchus in New Orleans. In our letter, we assured Bacchus that we were open to his having contact with "our son," but told him he would have to speak with Laurie first.

"We feel strongly that the agency should be involved in our first meetings," I wrote, "just as they handled our first meetings with Melissa. We're glad you called, and we're looking forward to building a relationship with you, and we know that D.J. will want to know you as he gets older. But for right now, please don't call us at home, call the agency."

After calling us every day for two weeks, Bacchus suddenly stopped. He'd gotten our letter.

A few days before we were leaving for New Orleans, Laurie called. She'd spoken with Bacchus.

"He wants to have contact with D.J. While he has no legal rights, we believe birth fathers should have contact with their children, too, if possible, and we would encourage you and Terry to consider it," Laurie said. "He knows it's up to you guys."

Laurie filled us in: Bacchus was twenty, a year younger than Melissa. His mother lived in Arkansas, he had a sister Reno, and his father didn't live in Seattle as we had feared, but in Dallas, Texas. Bacchus would be living in New Orleans at least until May.

"He told me he thought Melissa made a good decision, and that he would have gone along with everything if he was with her at the time."

"Did he have anything to say about us being gay?"

"All he wanted to know was if you were good parents. His dad is supportive of the decision, and his mom is mad the whole thing happened—upset that he got someone pregnant—but not about the child being adopted by gay men. I explained that adoption is permanent, and that you guys are D.J.'s parents. I told him you chose an open adoption because you wanted D.J. to know his birthparents, but that no adoptive parent wants to invite dysfunction into their lives. I told him he would have contact with D.J., but at this stage it was too early to say what form that contact might take, or how frequent it would be."

"How did he sound about all of that?"

"He seemed pretty agreeable," Laurie said. "He was looking for direction more than anything. He's glad Melissa did an adoption, and he wanted to know how to work within this situation. I would encourage you guys to go ahead and meet with him."

I always swore I wouldn't be the kind of parent who drags yowling kids onto crowded flights. Flying is hard on kids, and it's harder still on adults seated near kids. But on our flight to Chicago for his baptism, D.J. didn't cry, he didn't squirm. Flying didn't seem to faze him at all. Oh, he puked on the flight back, but he does that at home, too.

After that first flight, work took me out of town often, and Terry and the baby came along for the ride. By the time we got on a plane to New Orleans to visit his birth mommy and birth daddy, D.J. was a frequent flyer, with trips to Chicago, Spokane, New York, L.A., Aspen, and Toronto under his belt. D.J. had been more places in his first nine months than I'd been in my first nineteen years.

The plane ride to New Orleans was tense, with the usual round of "Where's mommy?" questions directed at D.J., and both Terry and I too nervous about meeting Bacchus to lie convincingly. "She's in New Orleans," we told the stewardesses, the other passengers, and the pilots, "and we're going for a visit."

"Which one of you is the daddy?"

"We both are," Terry said, "we adopted him. We're his dads."

We'd sent Bacchus a letter telling him where we'd be staying, and told him to give us a call when we got there. We had a number for him where he lived, but it was a pay phone in the hallway and the line was always busy. Shortly after we got to our hotel—a real dump right off Bourbon Street—Bacchus called. He could come over on Saturday or Sunday morning for a few hours, whichever we preferred. Tomorrow, I told him, would be great, in the lobby at ten.

A few minutes later, Melissa called from around the corner. While Terry unpacked and fed the baby, I went down to the lobby and waited for her. Street kids aren't welcome in the lobbies of New Orleans tourist hotels, not even dumps like the one we were staying in, and I didn't want Melissa hassled by the management.

She looked the same, and was wearing the same clothes she was wearing when we saw her last in Seattle, not to mention the day she put D.J. in our arms, and the day we met her at Outside In: black boots, shorts cut off at the knee, Guinness T-shirt, black sweatshirt. Her black hair was a little longer, and she'd lost some weight, but all in all she looked good; traveling around the country agreed with her, apparently. As soon as she was in our room, D.J. crawled up to her and pulled himself to a standing position between her legs. Pulling himself up was D.J.'s newest trick.

"We did a pretty poor job of babyproofing our house," Terry said, "so D.J.'s finishing the job for us. Anything he can reach gets yanked down, knocked over, and broken—and he's reaching more things every day."

"D.J. has spent many happy hours doing what I've only allowed myself to dream about," I said, "throwing Terry's records and CDs on the floor and stomping all over them."

"D.J. looks a lot like Bacchus," Melissa said. "He doesn't look anything like me."

D.J. had Melissa's nose, and his eyes were shaped like hers. Melissa had been born with blue eyes and lightish hair, and at the hospital she'd predicted that D.J.'s eyes and hair would darken in a few months, just the way hers had. But his eyes had stayed blue, and his hair was still blond.

We went out to dinner at a place a few blocks from our hotel and, after dinner, walked around the French Quarter, D.J. riding on my back. Melissa explained the particular hardships of life on the streets in New Orleans. "The police here bust us for nothing," she said. "They're always nailing us for public drunkenness, but, like, that's such bullshit because *everybody* is drunk in New Orleans, all the time. They don't arrest tourists for being drunk, just us."

We woke up pretty early the next morning and moved to a different room. In chasing D.J. around the night before, we'd discovered that none of the electrical outlets in the room had covers. The little plastic prong units Terry had brought to seal the outlets couldn't stop D.J. from sticking his entire hand into the wall, grabbing ancient exposed wires, and electrocuting himself. When we explained this problem to the clerk, she moved us to a much nicer room at the other end of the hotel. Here the outlets had covers, but the ancient floor-to-ceiling windows couldn't be closed. We had to move furniture in front of them to prevent D.J. from crawling out onto the balcony and into other people's rooms.

At a quarter to ten, I went downstairs, leaving Terry in bed with D.J. On a large leather couch in the lobby, I sat under a gilt mirror and read the paper while I waited for Bacchus. At ten after, a well-dressed young guy in slacks, a button-down shirt, and a black overcoat walked into the lobby. He had D.J.'s hair, the same color blond, but this couldn't be Bacchus, not the way he was dressed. Melissa had told us back in Portland that Bacchus had a mohawk and dressed the way she did. The man stood in the doorway for a second before he saw me looking at him.

"Are you Dan or Terry?"

I got up and introduced myself, and we shook hands, looking each other up and down. He smiled and laughed nervously, and I asked him if he wanted to go upstairs and meet D.J. I had planned on sitting him down in the lobby for a few minutes, so we could talk face to face first, but that suddenly seemed cruel.

D.J. was standing at a dresser, pulling open drawers and laughing. Bacchus sat down on the edge of the bed; Terry scooped D.J. up, walked him over, and set him on Bacchus's lap. Melissa was right: the resemblance was remarkable.

"This is too much," Bacchus said, smiling at D.J. as Terry took their picture together.

Just as we had at the hospital with Melissa, Terry and I hung back. We sat in chairs by the window at the other end of our room, and let D.J. crawl all over his birth father.

Bacchus told us he stopped dressing like a punk after a run-in with New Orleans's famously corrupt police department, as we walked down Bourbon Street with the baby. Bacchus ran into a few friends he hadn't seen since being arrested. He introduced D.J. to everyone, and us, too, and the fears we had about meeting him melted away. He was nice in that affable, unflappable way only straight guys ever are. It helped that he was just as blown away by D.J. as we were. Bacchus's broad smile, open face, and easy laugh made him seem like the temperamental opposite of sullen and introverted Melissa. Bacchus was also clean, his mohawk grown out so that you couldn't tell he'd ever had one, and dressed like a student, not a punk. A little bit of street showed around his edges, though.

"PUNK" was tattooed on the knuckles of his right hand, and "ROCK" on his left. Sitting in a park on the grass, watching D.J. crawl around, Terry noticed that the "K" in "PUNK" was backward. Was that intentional?

Bacchus looked down at his tattooed hand and laughed.

"It was an accident. I did it myself and, like, I messed it up. It's kinda punk rock though, don't you think?"

Back in Portland

On D.J.'s first birthday, we packed the car and drove to Portland. The day before, we'd had a party and D.J. tore into his first birthday cake like a pro. Both of his grandmothers snapped pictures, and our friends brought him books and clothes and toys. D.J. performed his latest trick for his guests—pulling himself to a standing position and taking a couple of unassisted steps before plopping down on his big diapered butt. We had his party the day before his birthday because we wanted to be back in Portland, at the Mallory, as on the day we brought him home from the hospital.

We didn't have to argue about the music on the drive down. We hardly ever argue about music anymore, because now we listen to stuff we both hate. Terry saw something on TV about Mozart and Bach making babies smarter. With D.J. strapped into his new, larger front-facing car seat, we listened to Bach for three hours down I-5 to Portland. It wasn't a rental car this time, but our car; Terry finally convinced me to buy one by coming up with a car-related Worst Case Scenario: How would I feel if D.J. died while we waited for an ambulance to take him to the emergency room because we didn't have a car of our own? Two weeks later, we owned a Honda.

On D.J.'s first birthday, Melissa was still traveling with Ten Spot, though they had lost the van. They were stopped by cops in California, and since the van wasn't registered to them, and since Ten Spot didn't have a license, and since they didn't have any insurance, the police impounded the van they both had worked so hard to get running. Most of their stuff was impounded along with the van, though Melissa was able to get her dog and cat out before the police towed the van away. But Melissa didn't seem upset. They'd find another way to get around, she told me, and were planning on being in Seattle by June. Bacchus was still living in New Orleans. We sent him pictures; he called us once in a while to check on D.J.

My mother and Terry's mother continued to overwhelm us. Terry's mom came to town to see her grandchild, always with gifts, and loved to get down on all fours and chase D.J. around the house. My mother, who didn't live as close, didn't see D.J. as much as she'd like—she'd like to see him hourly—but that will change this summer when she retires. We spent D.J.'s first Christmas at my father's house, and my dad couldn't get enough of his new grandson. We had something in common now, me and my father, something we could talk about. We were both dads.

Carol and Jack adopted a beautiful baby girl three months after we brought D.J. home. They wanted another child right away, a little sister or brother for their daughter, so they went right back into the pool. Bob and Kate were always there for us, offering advice, and baby-sitting—so Terry and I still manage to play a little pinball in leather bars every once in a while. Bob and Kate's kids—Lucy, Gus, and Isobel—loved to play with D.J., and one day Lucy and Gus and D.J. will all share stories about their birth moms with each other.

So many very bad things could happen that I fear ending this with any happily-ever-after uplift. My Irish Catholic God, as pointed out earlier, is a murderous and psychotic God, the O. J. Simpson of Higher Powers. I don't want to tempt Him by predicting that any of the five of us—Terry, D.J., Melissa, Bacchus, me—is going to live happily ever after.

No, there's too much to worry about. We worry about D.J. falling in with the wrong crowd and becoming a fundamentalist Christian in an act of adolescent rebellion. We worry about anti–gay adoption laws, George W. Bush, *E. coli* in hamburger, and the clumps of dirt D.J. stuffs in his mouth when we're not looking. We worry about earthquakes, fires, floods, and storms. We worry about D.J.'s birthparents, especially Melissa. Without a van, she and Ten Spot will be jumping trains together. We worry that we're making mistakes, that we're not feeding D.J. enough, that we're feeding him too much, that he'll fall in the tub, that he'll choke on something.

We want D.J. to have a little brother or sister, but we worry that D.J. has spoiled us. He's just so mellow. He's curious about everything, and as long as he has something in front of him to examine, bang, break, or play with, he's happy. However much Melissa drank while she was pregnant, however much acid she took, it was precisely the right amount. D.J. is smart, good-natured and friendly. He cries only when we come at him with the big blue snot sucker.

When we arrived at the Mallory for D.J.'s first birthday, the same clerks who had been working last year when we brought him home from OHSU were at the front desk. They recognized us, and they remembered D.J. We took his picture with the clerks, and they took our picture sitting with D.J. on one of the lobby's overstuffed green sofas. We'd requested the same room we had last year, and when we opened the door, nothing had changed. D.J. crawled over to the desk to pull the phone off by its cord, I plopped down on the bed, and Terry walked over to the window and looked up at OHSU.

D.J. crawled around and smashed up the room for a couple of hours. After watching a little cable, we slipped him into his baby backpack and headed out. We walked past Melissa's apartment, Outside In, the steakhouse, and the Eagle. On impulse, we jumped in a cab and headed over to Lloyd Center. We walked through the toy store where we had bought his car seat with Melissa, then past the ice rink and the jewelry store where we bought Melissa's bracelet. We walked over the sky ramp to Lloyd Center's conference rooms. The door to the room where we grieved our infertility with seven straight couples almost two years ago was unlocked, and the conference room was empty. The tables and chairs were arranged as they were at our seminar. We went in, took D.J. out of his backpack, and set him on the table.

He sat there, looking around, smiling. Terry pulled off one of D.J.'s shoes and gnawed on the bottom of his foot, which he loves even more than peekaboo. I did the same with his other foot, and D.J. laughed harder, a great crackling baby laugh. D.J. leaned forward and grabbed us both by our heads. He pulled us toward his face, laughing and laughing and laughing.

About the Author

Dan Savage's column, "Savage Love," is a nationally syndicated sex-advice column read by more than four million people each week. He has written the column for eight years, and it runs in twenty-six newspapers in the United States and Canada. He also writes "Dear Dan," an on-line advice column for ABCNEWS.com Savage is the associate editor of *The Stranger* in Seattle and a regular contributor to *This American Life* on public radio and is the author of *Savage Love* (Plume), a collection of his advice columns. He lives in Seattle, Washington.